D1614521

Time, Duration and Eternity in Spinoza

Spinoza Studies
Series editor: Filippo Del Lucchese, Alma Mater Studiorum – Università di Bologna

Seminal works devoted to Spinoza that challenge mainstream scholarship
This series aims to broaden the understanding of Spinoza in the Anglophone world by making some of the most important work by continental scholars available in English translation for the first time. Some of Spinoza's most important themes – that right is coextensive with power, that every political order is based on the power of the multitude, the critique of superstition and the rejection of the idea of providence – are explored by these philosophers in detail and in ways that will open up new possibilities for reading and interpreting Spinoza.

Editorial Advisory board
Saverio Ansaldi, Etienne Balibar, Chiara Bottici, Laurent Bove, Mariana de Gainza, Moira Gatens, Thomas Hippler, Susan James, Chantal Jaquet, Mogens Laerke, Beth Lord, Pierre Macherey, Nicola Marcucci, Alexandre Matheron (1926–2020), Dave Mesing, Warren Montag, Pierre-François Moreau, Vittorio Morfino, Antonio Negri, Susan Ruddick, Martin Saar, Pascal Sévérac, Hasana Sharp, Diego Tatián, Francesco Toto, Dimitris Vardoulakis, Lorenzo Vinciguerra, Stefano Visentin, Manfred Walther, Caroline Williams.

Books available
Affects, Actions and Passions in Spinoza: The Unity of Body and Mind, Chantal Jaquet, translated by Tatiana Reznichenko
The Spinoza-Machiavelli Encounter: Time and Occasion, Vittorio Morfino, translated by Dave Mesing
Politics, Ontology and Knowledge in Spinoza, Alexandre Matheron, translated and edited by Filippo Del Lucchese, David Maruzzella and Gil Morejón
Spinoza, the Epicurean: Authority and Utility in Materialism, Dimitris Vardoulakis
Experience and Eternity in Spinoza, Pierre-François Moreau, edited and translated by Robert Boncardo
Spinoza and the Politics of Freedom, Dan Taylor
Spinoza's Political Philosophy: The Factory of Imperium, Riccardo Caporali, translated by Fabio Gironi
Spinoza's Paradoxical Conservatism, François Zourabichvili, translated by Gil Morejón
Marx with Spinoza: Production, Alienation, History, Franck Fischbach, translated by Jason Read
Time, Duration and Eternity in Spinoza, Chantal Jaquet, translated by Eric Aldieri
Affirmation and Resistance in Spinoza: The Strategy of the Conatus, Laurent Bove, translated and edited by Émilie Filion-Donato and Hasana Sharp

Forthcoming
Spinoza and Contemporary Biology: Lectures on the Philosophy of Biology and Cognitivism, Henri Atlan, translated by Inja Stracenski
Spinoza's Critique of Hobbes: Law, Power and Freedom, Christian Lazzeri, translated by Nils F. Schott
Spinoza and the Sign: The Logic of Imagination, Lorenzo Vinciguerra, translated by Alexander Reynolds
New Perspectives on Spinoza's Theologico-Political Treatise: *Politics, Power and the Imagination*, edited by Dan Taylor and Marie Wuth

Visit our website at www.edinburghuniversitypress.com/series/SPIN

Time, Duration and Eternity in Spinoza

Chantal Jaquet

Translated by Eric Aldieri

EDINBURGH
University Press

To the eternity of my father, his thirteen trades, his fourteen miseries.

Edinburgh University Press is one of the leading university presses in the UK. We publish academic books and journals in our selected subject areas across the humanities and social sciences, combining cutting-edge scholarship with high editorial and production values to produce academic works of lasting importance. For more information visit our website: edinburghuniversitypress.com

Sub specie æternitatis Étude des concepts de temps, durée et éternité chez Spinoza, Chantal Jaquet
© 2015. Classiques Garnier, Paris
English translation © Eric Aldieri, 2023

Edinburgh University Press Ltd
The Tun – Holyrood Road
12(2f) Jackson's Entry
Edinburgh EH8 8PJ

Typeset in 10/12 Goudy Old Style
by Cheshire Typesetting Ltd, Cuddington, Cheshire, and
printed and bound in Great Britain

A CIP record for this book is available from the British Library

ISBN 978 1 4744 8378 0 (hardback)
ISBN 978 1 4744 8380 3 (webready PDF)
ISBN 978 1 4744 8381 0 (epub)

The right of Chantal Jaquet to be identified as the author of this work has been asserted in accordance with the Copyright, Designs and Patents Act 1988, and the Copyright and Related Rights Regulations 2003 (SI No. 2498).

Published with the support of the University of Edinburgh Scholarly Publishing Initiatives Fund.

Contents

Preface

This work is the revised edition of a thesis published for the first time in 1997 with Éditions Kimé – a thesis that Jean-Marie Beyssade directed with a kindness, attention and dedication for which I am deeply grateful. I want to once more warmly thank both Alexandre Matheron, who was kind enough to review this work and generously enlightened me with his remarks, as well as Pierre-François Moreau, whose precious advice, trust and friendship constantly sustained me throughout the course of this research.

Apart from updating the bibliography on the subject and adding some notes and corrections, this new edition reproduces the previous text in its entirety.

Foreword

This book – being very concise and at the same time quite clear and quite dense, where nothing is missing, and nothing is overdone – is a good example of the type of scientific rigour appropriate for the history of philosophy. Chantal Jaquet, trained under the excellent instruction of André Lécrivain, then that of Jean-Marie Beyssade, had every means of carrying out this type of work effectively, and she completely succeeded at doing so. Its aim, precise and well defined, is, at root, to completely *explain* the possible definitions of both eternity and duration that we are given in the *Ethics*: What are their histories in Spinoza's first writings? What exactly do they mean? To what sort of beings does Spinoza apply the one or the other? What relations does Spinoza establish between the two forms of existence so defined? As for the accompanying method, it could be summarised in a single phrase: the texts, nothing but the texts, every text, with as little extrapolation as possible. Of course, such a method does not exclude philosophical reflection, much to the contrary: the author has a very sure knowledge of Spinozism, and the pertinence with which she uses it serves as its own evidence; but for this very reason, she only uses, at each step of her argument, what is absolutely indispensable for her aim. Without presupposing a comprehensive interpretation of the system in advance, without imposing anything in particular of it on us at the outset, she simply draws, with regard to the object of her work, a line of demarcation between plausible and implausible interpretations. This methodological asceticism, together with a modesty of intention, is precisely what guarantees the approach's effectiveness: the line is drawn in indelible writing. And its implications are enormous.

Just one example. The author's interpretation of the very subtle Spinozist definition of eternity – an interpretation that she opposes to mine, but no matter, since the consequences of it are the same – leads her to the conclusion that it is not improperly (as one often believes and as Gueroult himself seems sometimes to believe) but *strictly and literally speaking* that Spinoza attributes the property so defined not only to substance but also to infinite modes and, to a certain extent, finite modes, including the human intellect. Similarly, the author establishes that duration, if we take its definition literally, is strictly speaking attributable only to finite modes (to the exclusion of infinite modes). Similarly, and finally, the comparison of these two concepts allows her to show that they are mutually exclusive of one another, even when they apply to the same beings: what is eternal in us, taken as such, is certainly *indestructible*, but does not endure; and what is subject to duration in us, taken as such, is not eternal. All of this is simple, clear and perfectly explained. But the stakes of it all are crucial, for it is precisely these points that incite considerable resistances.

Which resistances? I have long believed that hardly anyone confused the eternity of our intellect, such as Spinoza conceives of it, with an immortality subject to duration; but it seems such is not the case: I recently came across a very surprising example of this confusion. To this extent, the author is probably right to reproach me for having formerly used the word 'immortality' to underscore, not without some provocation, that one had to take what Spinoza says of the indestructability of the eternal part of our mind literally. But I was thinking of another sort of resistance. There are good reasons for this one: we love Spinoza; we are reluctant to attribute to him claims that we today deem indefensible, and we seek to excuse him of these claims. Now, it is indeed certain, as our author reminds us, that the theory of the partial eternity of our mind is intimately tied to that according to which our intellect, an immediate finite mode of thought, is a part of God's infinite intellect. And it is no less certain that this last claim is hardly modern. We thus attempt to reinterpret the Spinozist conception of infinite intellect: when we do not reduce it to the mere sum (however necessarily finite) of all human intellects, we consider it to metaphorically designate something else: the propositional universe, or the set of all true theories, both real and possible, or the entirety of 'thought' in Frege's sense, etc. Eternity, then, becoming purely epistemological, no longer belongs to the truths conceived by our intellect and no longer belongs to our intellect itself, which must, as it were, be destroyed with our body and with the imaginative part of our mind. Unless we make our own eternity a metaphor, again, in order to designate the conformity of our existence to our essence (which, of course, it also is) during a present life at the end of which, nevertheless, we will be entirely annihilated. All of this is occasionally quite beautiful and interesting, perhaps even true in and for itself, but it should not be confused with Spinoza's thought. Against these persistent confusions, the present book, to the very extent that the validity of its claims does not depend on a comprehensive interpretation that we could always reject, constitutes an excellent safeguard.

The above is only one example. The list goes on. One will admire, for instance, the very illuminating way in which widening the field of application of the concept of eternity is connected to the development that, from the *Short Treatise* to the *Ethics*, brings it from the status of 'extrinsic denomination' to that of a common notion. One will appreciate the very convincing, even if too brief, explanation of the use of temporal expressions (*remanet, semper*, etc.) in relation to eternity, while perhaps wondering if it does not justify Bernard Rousset's formulations which the author nonetheless critiques. One will praise the insistent affirmation of the positive character of duration – neither an illusion nor a degradation – and the correlative affirmation according to which eternal salvation should be analysed *also* in terms of loss. One will love, without perhaps adhering entirely to them, the very original analyses contained in the remarks dedicated to the *TTP*. And one will grant without reservation that the problem of the 'passage' from eternity to duration is, in reality, a false one, despite its being tirelessly posed in order to accuse Spinoza of incoherence. On each of these points, equally, the safeguard holds strong.

'With Spinoza, I feel good', Chantal Jaquet once said to me. Reading her book, this can indeed be seen, and it makes the reading enjoyable. So, let's read it.

Alexandre Matheron

Notes on Translation and Acknowledgements

While one must always make choices as a translator, the consistency, clarity and technicality of Chantal Jaquet's prose is a joy to read and to translate. I must therefore thank her, first and foremost, for offering such a direct and illuminating engagement with Spinoza's concepts of time, duration and eternity, as well as the interplay among them.

The reader will find a few translator's notes throughout this text. Most of these notes highlight moments when I have modified the standard English translations, either those of Spinoza's works or those of other authors, such as Aristotle and Maimonides, so as to better cohere with either the original Latin or, more often, the French translations that Jaquet uses and cites. A few of these notes provide clarificatory explanations, offer English translations of the originally cited Latin, or point to discrepancies in the original citations and the corrected ones presented here.

Due to the technicality of Jaquet's study, there are only a few translation choices that merit attention in advance, and this because they carry deep philosophical significance for her interpretations and interventions.

One of the most essential contributions this study makes to research in Spinozist philosophy is its novel translation, from Latin to French, of the infamous phrase *sub specie aeternitatis*. Any attentive reader of Spinoza knows that much philosophical weight hangs on how one chooses to render this phrase, particularly its middle term. Jaquet highlights both the benefits and drawbacks of previous translations of the phrase, eventually opting to add her own well-defended thesis into the mix. As her analysis makes clear, the translation of the Latin *specie* into French is already riddled with issues. Given that its translation matters greatly for how we understand both the third kind of knowledge and the partial eternity of the mind, a secondary translation of each of these possible renderings into English only risks muddying the waters further and must be approached with care. For this reason,

I have included the French whenever a translation of this phrase is provided, whether it be someone else's translation to which Jaquet is referring or Jaquet's own proposal.

While Jaquet argues for the comparative salience of certain possibilities over others – seemingly favouring, for example, Geneviève Rodis-Lewis's form (*forme*) or Émile Saisset's character (*caractère*) over and against Charles Appuhn's sort (*sorte*), Henri de Boulainvilliers's way (*façon*) or Martial Gueroult's aspect (*aspect*) – she ultimately proposes *regard*. In English, *regard* can take the sense of look, gaze, viewpoint or, figuratively, eye, among other possibilities. I opt for gaze for a few reasons. First, to the extent that one of Jaquet's primary philosophical commitments in the translation of this phrase is to avoid terms that could convey a sense of illusion or falsity, the English term 'look', and related figurative options, must be avoided at all costs. There is nothing fictitious, deceptive or illusory about this knowledge or the eternity it entails. Second, while terms like 'perspective' or 'point of view' may have served as serious candidates (despite possibly continuing to imply some illusory quality), there are direct French correlates of these terms that Jaquet obviously did not choose. The standard 'gaze' therefore seems the best option in terms of both its conceptual accuracy and textual fidelity. Knowledge *sub specie aeternitatis* thereby becomes knowledge under the *gaze* of eternity, or knowledge gleaned from an eternal gaze.

Second, much of Jaquet's analysis concerns not only the respective natures of duration and eternity considered in isolation, but also the relation between these two natures as they are operative in the same individual while nevertheless remaining irreducible to one another. She therefore frequently refers to *l'articulation* between duration and eternity. This term typically designates something like a link, hinge or point of connection. But just because duration and eternity can coexist in the same individual does not mean that their natures can overlap. Further, the nature of their relation in the same individual can change over time or, when comparing multiple individuals, take on a different sense from one mode to the next in accordance with one's degree of virtue and the historical circumstances in which it is embedded. Following a suggestion from my friend and colleague, Michael Peterson, I therefore use the term 'interplay' to translate '*articulation*' in order to emphasise these shifting dynamics between the irreducible natures of duration and eternity. To the extent, then, that my durational existence can conform to or diverge from my eternal perfection in various degrees, there is an interplay between duration and eternity as they coexist in me without melding into one.

Third, and finally, one of the frameworks that Jaquet uses to help explain this shifting relationship is that of *l'écart convergent*. The notion of *l'écart convergent* refers to a position wherein one's durational existence is separated or distanced from one's eternal essence, but in a way that proves beneficial over the long term by drawing the former back toward the latter. While something more literal, like 'convergent distance' would work fine for this phrase, I opt for the slightly stronger and less literal 'corrective gap' due to the specific examples that Jaquet uses to flesh out this position. Within this position, Jaquet includes instances wherein sad affects are ultimately beneficial for one's joy, activity, understanding and virtue. For example, one stands in this corrective gap, or experiences it, when one undergoes a pain that serves to correct an excessive pleasure, or, alternatively, when a sadness like fear determines one to obey a just law. Here, sadness, which is nothing other than a passage from a greater to a lesser perfection, serves to improve our behaviour and encourages us to better conform to our eternal character down the road.

I am lucky to have several friends and colleagues whose input proved indispensable throughout this project. On this score, I am incredibly grateful for Gil Morejón, Michael Peterson, Maïté Marciano and David Maruzzella. Thank you also to Rick Lee for help with many of the Latin passages and to Elizabeth Rottenberg and Pascale-Anne Brault for teaching me everything I know about French. Finally, I would like to sincerely thank the amazing team at Edinburgh University Press and the Spinoza Series. This project would not exist without the effort and support of Filippo Del Lucchese, Carol Macdonald and many others. My sincerest gratitude to each one of you.

Eternity: A Problem 'that Remains'

Eric Aldieri

Studying a systematic philosopher like Spinoza, while resulting in enormous payoffs for those readers with the requisite honesty and patience, can be quite frustrating for those who seek to pick and choose certain elements while wanting to discard the rest. The idea of a rationalist philosophy, for example, that takes the persistence of the passions seriously while nonetheless affirming the possibility of attaining adequate knowledge has captivated scholars of many stripes. Few, however, care to admit that the condition of possibility for such knowledge is the eternity of the human intellect. It's a simple rule: no eternity, no adequate knowledge. No matter how great our attempts to dodge this thesis may be, then, it remains the case that Spinoza's conception of eternity forms the linchpin for much of what we otherwise know and love about the system. If the question of eternity and its role in the Spinozist system cannot simply be waved away by our all too modern sensibilities, or still less be assimilated to a more traditional, all too Christian theory of the soul's immortality, then we are forced to reckon with its specificity and significance for the system. What is eternity, according to Spinoza? What is its role in Spinoza's philosophy and how does it develop over time? In what way do finite modes possess or enjoy eternity? And why is this property so crucial for Spinoza's theory of knowledge, system of ethics and doctrine of salvation? With a certain reverence for the text and playful frustration with (often paired with admiration for) much of the secondary literature, such are the questions that Jaquet's study takes up so carefully.

Spinozists do not get to pick and choose. Instead, we must explain – rigorously and, therefore, often painstakingly – how one element of the system fits in with or stands out from the others. It is in this spirit, therefore, that Jaquet covers nearly the entirety of the Spinozist system – beginning in the early treatises and moving through *Metaphysical Thoughts* and Spinoza's treatment of Descartes before finally landing at the *Ethics* and *Theologico-Political*

xiv   ETERNITY: A PROBLEM 'THAT REMAINS'

Treatise – in an ambitious effort not only to analyse the meaning and function of eternity in Spinoza's thought, but also to trace, in detail, its precise transformation throughout it, as well as to analyse its relation (or, sometimes, lack thereof) to time and duration. Simply put, we cannot ignore or reject Spinoza's concept of eternity without ignoring or rejecting the system in its entirety. But neither can we pretend we already know what he means by the term, as if he were uncritically adopting previous conceptions, whether they be those of the ancients or the scholastics.

Eternity is a problem – and the care with which Jaquet navigates it across Spinoza's corpus and its inscription within the history of philosophy is startlingly impressive. As a scholar, she takes nothing for granted, often guiding the reader through several possibilities, and considering every plausible objection or alternative before landing on the interpretive prize – among which is her novel translation of the phrase *sub specie aeternitatis*.

In 2018, Matthew J. Kisner and Michael Silverthorne published a new English translation of Spinoza's *Ethics*. While their translation departs from that of Edwin Curley (whose *Collected Works* has served as the standard in anglophone scholarship for some time and is indeed the edition invoked throughout this present translation) on a few important scores,[1] one that stands out is the pair's rendering of the infamous phrase *sub specie aeternitatis* as 'from the vantage of eternity'.[2] They do so for good reason. First, while the Latin *specie* could reasonably refer to 'the Aristotelian notion of species', such a reading seems unlikely in the context of the *Ethics* for the simple reason that Spinoza 'does not distinguish between kinds of eternity'.[3] Second, something like character or aspect risks misleading the reader into believing that eternity is being attributed to the *object* of knowledge, as a quality, character or aspect is attributed to a thing, as opposed to the *kind* of knowledge in question. While the third kind of knowledge is more adequate than the others, it does not change the ontological status of the things it apprehends – rather, it refers to a new way of understanding them.[4] Finally, to use something like appearance risks a potentially greater

---

[1] See Steve Barbone's review of Kisner and Silverthorne's translation for a more complete analysis of these changes. Barbone, 'Review of *Ethics: Proved in Geometrical Order*', *Notre Dame Philosophical Reviews*, October 2018.

[2] Benedict de Spinoza, *Ethics*, trans. Matthew J. Kisner and Michael Silverthorne (Cambridge: Cambridge University Press, 2018), 82.

[3] Ibid., 'Notes on the Text and Translation', xlix.

[4] Julie Klein has made this case as well. See Klein, '"By Eternity I Understand": Eternity According to Spinoza," *Iyyun: The Jerusalem Philosophical Quarterly* 51 (2002): 295–324.

misunderstanding – namely, that this eternal appearance of things in the third kind of knowledge is somehow separated from its actual reality, rendering it somehow fictitious or unreal. As such, vantage becomes the best candidate for describing this type of knowledge without reducing it to something subjective or detached from reality.

Over twenty years prior to this new English translation, Chantal Jaquet first published *Sub Specie Aeternitatis* – the original title given to her 1994 doctoral thesis, the revised version of which is here translated into English for the first time. The fact that Spinoza's famous phrase serves as the main title for Jaquet's study should tell us something about its importance for her interpretation of the Spinozist system. Indeed, one of the central tasks of her study is to assess the competing French translations of the phrase and determine which, if any, should be preserved. After weighing the candidates put forth by Alquié, Appuhn, Caillois, Boulainvilliers, Gueroult, Rodis-Lewis and Saisset, among others, Jaquet remains unsatisfied. She therefore puts forth her own proposal: *sous un regard d'éternité*, under a gaze of eternity, or under an eternal gaze. Stressing the consistent ocular imagery that accompanies this phrase in Spinoza's text, Jaquet makes a strong case for *regard* over and against the alternatives. Her rationale is nearly identical to that of Kisner and Silverthorne above, pre-dating it by twenty-four years. Knowledge *sub specie aeternitatis* is knowledge seen from an eternal eye. It relates to the one and only eternity presented in the *Ethics*, has absolutely nothing illusory about it, and pertains to the vision itself as opposed to the thing seen. It should go without saying that Jaquet's translation is not only innovative, but deeply significant for the study of Spinoza's theory of knowledge, time, salvation and virtue.

What is perhaps most impressive about it is that she arrives at it by way of none other than the 'methodological asceticism' which Alexandre Matheron attributes to her scholarship in his Foreword to the text. When one pays attention to the text – really pays attention, without seeking out a predetermined answer, without attempting to confirm one's own biases – it is as if an adequate idea begins to impose itself on the reader. Jaquet's patience and attention, on this note, to the ubiquity of terms like *oculi mentis* (eyes of the mind), or phrases implying a *tota simul* or synoptic vision, leads her, in fact, to being somewhat surprised that no one had put forward this translation suggestion before! Whether one interprets this surprise in terms of philosophical humility, a gentle prod at previous interpretations, or some combination of the two, the fact remains that methodological asceticism is indeed the major principle of discernment in Jaquet's work, operating as a sieve that will only allow the finest and best-tested theses through its selective screen. Besides the translation of such a crucial phrase, what else will this principle allow us?

If one surveys the literature concerning Part V of the *Ethics*, its doctrine of salvation and the enigmatic eternity that secures it, one finds that perhaps more often than not, Spinoza's text serves as a repository for all of the hopes, fears and projections of his readers, devout traditionalists and staunch atheists alike. The first payoff of Jaquet's study is therefore negative: the sieve clears away, refuses and rejects anything that comes into direct, and even indirect, conflict with the text. In this operation, there are clear favourites among the propositions and their scholia, reference to which is often enough to expose the fragility of the often tempting but ultimately dubious theses of various well-respected scholars. To take perhaps my favourite example: Jaquet wields the scholium to VP23 like a weapon against unjustified extrapolations concerning the (non)relation between eternity and time. Spinoza's direct but oft-forgotten claim that 'eternity can neither be defined by time nor have any relation to time'[5] strikes against various interpretations with very few surviving the blow. As such, its invocation subdues Pierre-François Moreau's heralding of finitude as a constitutive condition for the feeling of eternity, Bernard Rousset's attempted temporalisation of eternity, and Harry Austryn Wolfson's use of the term 'immortality' to characterise the intellect, among others. All of these are fair and sympathetic critiques that proceed by way of a gentle reminder: we cannot pick and choose which propositions we take up and which ones we throw away. Everything must be taken into account. And when there is an apparent contradiction, it must be resolved rather than dismissed.

On this score, Jaquet's attention to Spinoza's place in the history of philosophy – who he was reading, what terms he picks up from earlier thinkers, how he modifies them, etc. – proves equally indispensable for this task of discernment. Comparisons to Plato, Plotinus, Aquinas, Suarez and Heereboord abound, but never gratuitously. Every reference serves a purpose and contributes to a point that could not have been made otherwise. To take only a few examples, it is with such patient treatment of Spinoza's philosophical precursors that Jaquet resolves an apparent tension between the term *perseverare* and the scholium recalled above (via a non-temporal reading of the term in Suarez), demonstrates how Spinoza's doctrine of common notions picks up where communicable attributes leave off in the scholastics, and refuses the reductive inscription of Spinoza's doctrine of eternity in the historical polemic between Uriel da Costa and Samuel da Silva. Again, these

---

[5] Spinoza, *Ethics* V, 23, Schol; CWS I, 607.

are just a few examples that attest to the clarity and specificity provided by Jaquet's endeavours in the history of philosophy throughout this study. This is all to say that when the original text alone cannot serve as an adequate referee, the solution is not to charge Spinoza with ambiguity or inconsistency, and still less to give in to the temptations of speculative haste. Instead, one turns to the texts behind the text in search of inspiration. In this respect, Jaquet's scholarship should be of inspiration to us all.

Of course, the principle of methodological asceticism does not prevent everything from getting through the interpretive sieve. In the wake of such discernment is a clearing, and it is here that some of the most interesting claims of this book are put forward. These victories are scattered throughout the text, but a few merit particular attention.

First, Jaquet demonstrates that eternity is not a property particular to only human minds, but to every mind. She does so, however, without admitting a strict qualitative equality between all minds. Instead, Jaquet argues that while every mind possesses its own eternity, one's awareness of that eternity has varying degrees. In this respect, even the rejected thesis of the soul's immortality is incorporated into and explained by the system, insofar as belief in an infinite durational afterlife ultimately signifies one of the lowest levels of awareness of the mind's eternity among humans. People feel and experience that they are eternal, but relate this feeling and experience to the imagination, which cannot conceive things *sub specie aeternitatis*. They therefore confuse eternity with duration, with the resulting chimera of infinite duration in and as immortality.

Second, and relatedly, Jaquet sketches four ethical and epistemological figures detailing the relationship between our durational existence and eternal existence. While provisional models, these figures provide a framework from which to view and make sense of an incredibly tricky metaphysical and existential dynamic. While the eternity of one's mind is absolutely perfect, indeed, necessarily more perfect than the imagination and memory, we know that our durational existence undergoes passages to and from various degrees of perfection. We fluctuate, sometimes in a sad and sometimes in a joyous manner. If this is the case – that our durational self changes while our eternal essence remains in pure perfection – then one has to conceive of their simultaneous relation in every finite mode without collapsing or confusing their natures. It bears repeating that neither term can be defined by the other.

So, how does Jaquet navigate this dynamic? In an intriguing comparison between the relationship between duration and eternity in the *Ethics* and that between the eternal doctrine of Scripture and its historically specific modifications in the *TTP* – a comparison that probably marks the most adventurous suggestion of the text, as justified as it may be – Jaquet shows that in its various states and passages, our durational existence can actually inch closer to or grow further away from the perfection proper to our eternal one. First, like Christ, or the Spinozist sage, one's durational existence can perfectly coincide with the perfection of one's eternal essence. Second, like Moses and his followers, one can also conform to this eternity without for all that perfectly coinciding with it. Here, we are directed by just laws and wise leadership without necessarily determining ourselves by reason. Still, this obedience brings us closer to the perfection of the eternal order, but by providing us with rules and habits that direct us toward our proper activity. On the other side of the ethical divide, one can, by contrast, diverge in one's durational life from one's eternal perfection. Thus, third, sadness and evil can gain the upper hand, leading us further and further away from our own beatitude. Fourth and finally, one can be paradoxically spared greater future suffering by heeding the wisdom entailed in a lesser present one – for example, when the pain of a hangover teaches one to drink less alcohol, correcting the excesses of a limited, immediate pleasure. This last figure is what Jaquet calls *l'écart convergent*, what we have here translated as 'corrective gap', in line with the considerations in the above note on translation.

The four models that Jaquet puts forth at such a late stage in her text stand out because they demonstrate that while much of the study remains in the textual, historical and metaphysical weeds of Spinozism and its philosophical context, the payoff is not limited to merely exegetical or academic concerns. We have all heard the by now commonplace remark that Spinoza named his crowning text the *Ethics* for a reason, but it is, indeed, true. Jaquet's study demonstrates this point quite well when, putting together the details of the text thus far, it provides the reader with what amounts to four ways of living, or four modes of existence,[6] to borrow one of Deleuze's phrases, resultant from the *Ethics*. Our virtue and power vary in accordance with our understanding. Thus, the more we understand, the closer we approach the perfection of eternal existence here and now, without our duration ever merging *in nature* with that which it approaches. Such are the ethical consequences of this study, consequences that drive toward a novel concept of salvation in Spinoza's work.

---

[6] See Gilles Deleuze's final essay on Spinoza, 'Spinoza and the Three Ethics', in *Essays Critical and Clinical*, trans. Daniel W. Smith and Michael A. Greco (Minneapolis: University of Minnesota Press, 1997), 138–51. Because Deleuze uses a different point of departure, his count is, of course, different than that of Jaquet.

Perhaps the most exciting moment of this text, then, comes in the very last paragraph before its conclusion. If eternity is communicable even to finite modes on account of its status as a universal common notion, but duration, because it is an effect of the infinite chain of finite causes, cannot, strictly speaking, belong to substance, then *only* finite modes can enjoy duration – for they are the only modes that answer to both the common order of nature and God's absolute essence. Given Jaquet's rigorous textual fidelity, however, we must also remind ourselves – as Jaquet herself does expertly in an article from around the same era as the publication of this book[7] – that memory and imagination, indeed all that belongs to duration including duration itself, are perfect and carry their own perfection. This degree of perfection is, of course, unstable and fluctuating, but it can never become or imply *imperfection*. There are, to be sure, better and worse uses of these durational capacities, but they remain perfect in their own right throughout this range. As such, the attribution of duration to finite modes alone is no reason to lament their 'fall' in relation to substance or infinite modes, but, in fact, reason to celebrate a power and a capacity that is theirs alone.

By reading duration, memory and imagination in light of their proper ontological perfection, Jaquet consequently leads the reader to a profound reformulation of the doctrine of salvation. While the eternal part of the mind, the intellect, is more perfect than the parts that perish with the body, we cannot and should not view death as some deliverance from a realm of suffering to a realm of sheer bliss – at least not crudely or unequivocally. Because we lose duration when we die, because we lose the capacity to remember and imagine, that is, the very capacity to conceive things as located in time and place, Jaquet urges that 'eternal salvation should not be systematically analysed in terms of gain, but also in terms of loss'.[8] The mind's eternity is a partial one. What we lose, we lose unconditionally, without recovery or reclamation. This final provocation should incite multiple programmes for further study. What happens if, instead of frustratingly trying to situate Spinoza's theory of the mind's eternity in terms of the traditional and tired terms of immortality or personality, instead of trying to flesh out what an experience of eternity beyond the grave might feel like, we were to investigate the notion of salvation from the perspective of loss, that is, as a subtractive affair? How could a committed exploration of the concept of salvation as loss affect our understanding of Spinoza's notions of

---

[7] See Chantal Jaquet, 'The Perfection of Duration', trans. Eric Aldieri, *Parrhesia* 35 (2022): 1–12.
[8] Below, **p. XXX**.

life and death, respectively? And refusing to cater to the various strands of misanthropy popular among Satirists, Theologians and Melancholics alike, can this loss be affirmed without diminishing its gravity? There are ample tools in this present text for getting started on such questions. And for this, much gratitude must be extended to its author.

Abbreviations

App.	Appendix
Ax.	Axiom
Cor.	Corollary
DA#	Definition of the Affects
Def.	Definition
Dem.	Demonstration
Exp.	Explanation
Lem.	Lemma
Post.	Postulate
Praef.	Preface
Schol.	Scholium
CM	Metaphysical Thoughts
CWS	Collected Works of Spinoza (Curley translation)
Ep.#	Letters
KV	Short Treatise
PP	Descartes' Principles of Philosophy
TdIE	Treatise on the Emendation of the Intellect
TP	Political Treatise
TTP	Theological-Political Treatise

Introduction

For a long time, the thesis of the eternity of the intellect – a thesis that crowns Part V of the *Ethics* – was subject to controversies, reviving the perennial quarrel concerning Spinoza's atheism. It disturbed believers as much as unbelievers, who strived either to drive the unholy man out from under the protective cloak of honest people's faith, or else to ultimately lead the mystic back to the flock of the religious tradition. Lerminier, a professor of law at the Collège de France, echoes this suspicion in his *Philosophie du droit*, published in 1831. Concerning Spinoza's record, he feels that

> we must still hold this inflexible pantheist accountable for the destiny of the soul. What is it that he has to offer man to satiate this thirst for another life that Christianity has not known how to both excite and satisfy? Alas! Timidity and silence here replace the arrogance and dogmatism of philosophy. He indeed says to us: 'Mens humana non potest cum corpore absolute destrui; sed ejus aliquid remanet, quod aeternum est.'[1] But what then becomes of this something that remains and vexes us with its eternity?[2]

Lerminier concludes his diatribe by denouncing the impotence of a pantheism that 'can only deliver to man one of two things: a series of terrestrial existences and transformations or an irrevocable void (*néant*)'.[3]

---

[1] TN: 'The human mind cannot be absolutely destroyed with the body, but something of it remains which is eternal.' *Ethics* V, 23; *CWS* I, 607.

[2] Jean Louis Eugène Lerminier, *Philosophie du droit*, as cited by Father Frédéric-Édouard Chassay in his *Conclusion des démonstrations évangéliques* (Chassay 1850: 462).

[3] Ibid.

For diametrically opposed reasons, certain Marxist thinkers also wonder what to make of this 'something that remains and vexes us with its eternity'. Helmut Seidel, for example, after having recognised in Spinoza a precursor of dialectical materialism,[4] finds the introduction of a metaphysical conception *sub specie aeternitatis* regrettable and critiques this as a hangover of ancient origin. This discomfort and its proceeding incomprehension sometimes take the form of pure and simple obfuscation. In this way, Marianne Schaub, in her general presentation of Spinoza, does not mention the presence of this theory of the intellect's eternity and makes absolutely no reference to it.[5] Does such an omission constitute a cautious effort to steer clear of a rather thorny issue, or, instead, an underestimation of the importance of the mind's eternity?

By insisting on the coherence of this theory of eternity and on its essential role in the general economy of the system, Bernard Rousset[6] has greatly contributed to curbing this desire to expunge from the *Ethics* its cumbersome Part V and consider its final propositions to be a minor and irrational appendix. He has thus paved the way for numerous investigations, to which the multiplicity of studies and publications centring on the theme of eternity attest.[7]

However, a crucial blind spot remains and finds itself strangely glossed over, as if the vexation were now displaced. Human finite modes are, due to their intellect, partially eternal and, since the imagination and memory disappear with the death of the body, partially perishable. In other words, they are eternal and durational – something that anyone will acknowledge upon reading propositions 21 to 23 of *Ethics* V. The existence of a 'double temporality' is thus commonly admitted and considered to be obvious. It is nevertheless curious to note that some commentators[8] have dedicated entire studies to separately examining the concepts of time, duration and eternity without ever approaching, in a central manner, the question of their conjunction and relation in the Spinozist system, sometimes even while making such a relation disappear altogether. What are we to do with this problem that remains and vexes us with its longevity (*pérennité*), as one might say following Lerminier?

---

[4] Cf. on this subject the article by Clemens Kammler and Rolf Löper published in *Cahiers Spinoza* 3.
[5] Schaub 1972.
[6] Rousset 1968.
[7] Cf. Rodis-Lewis 1986; Matheron 1972, 1994; Chalier 1993; Moureau 1994b.
[8] See Hallett 1930; Alexander 1992.

To be sure, Spinoza, unlike Plato and Plotinus, is hardly verbose when it comes to the origin of duration or the nature of the causality that presides over its genesis. He does, however, refer to the way in which duration 'follows from eternal things' in Letter XII.[9] But how can duration, strictly speaking, stem (*découler*) from eternal things? Its appearance remains a mystery insofar as it is true that, due to the heterogeneous character of the two properties, we cannot conceive of a passage between the eternal and the temporal. Is this not a tall order, drawing duration out from under the hat of eternity? Indeed, as great a challenge as seeking to compose a number by adding zeros! We can examine the problem from every angle, stepping back from the twists and turns of the path leading from eternity to duration in order to instead direct ourselves toward the one that goes, inversely, from duration to eternity – still, we would only be leaving the Charybdis of the beginning for the Scylla of the end. How is it actually possible for a finite mode beset by the fatal pressure of external causes to be, strictly speaking, eternal? If the eternity of substance is conceivable, that of a mode is hardly so. The invocation of a *credo quia absurdum* cannot stand in for an explanation, for it is as little compatible with a philosophy that proceeds *more geometrico* as is recourse to a theory of some mysterious alchemy by which the mode would be transformed into substance.

The temptation to minimise the problem, or to bury it under a heightened muteness, is thus quite strong. Nevertheless, a flood of difficulties suddenly arises out of this conjunction of an actual present existence and an actual eternal existence, a flood that hardly has any chance of being dammed up or restrained absent an investigation into the nature of their relations. Can we truly be aware of the eternity of our mind – and not confuse it with a *post mortem* survival – without distinguishing it from duration and elucidating the respective causes of the two? If our salvation depends on intuitively grasping the idea of the essence of our body *sub specie aeternitatis*, we can neither attain it nor enjoy beatitude or freedom without understanding the nature of this infamous conception *sub specie aeternitatis*. Now, we must acknowledge that it in large part remains an enigma to the extent that this Latin expression often constitutes a stumbling block

---

[9] *Ep.* XII [to Lodewijk Meyer]; CWS I, 203. Translation modified. [TN: The French translation of the *Ethics* that Jaquet uses here reads '*suit de choses éternelles*'. By contrast, Curley's translation uses the term 'flows'. Later in this book, Jaquet will want to draw a minor distinction between three terms: *suivre, découler* and *couler*. For these reasons, I have modified Curley's translation to reflect the slight terminological difference at play later in the text.]

for translators. The phrase is all the more mysterious insofar as it seems unprecedented before Spinoza and will gain later popularity under the pen of writers like Klima, in his work *Némésis la glorieuse*, and philosophers like Wittgenstein. To date, no commentator has found the origin of this expression in either the Latin, Jewish or Arab tradition, and all evidence suggests that it was created by Spinoza himself. The phrase *sub specie* is frequently used to specify that we do or say something under the cover or pretext of something else, but this observation does not allow us to make sense of the meaning of the whole phrase. The word *species* in Latin is ambiguous insofar as it designates both the more or less deceptive external appearance of a thing as well as the signature trait that allows someone to recognise it without fail. In its common use, it can mean view, gaze/look (*regard*), aspect, or character depending on the context. In its philosophical meaning, it remains equally ambiguous and indeterminate: it is used as an equivalent of the Greek *eidos* and expresses the Platonic concept of an idea and a form; it refers to species in opposition to genus, to aspect, to the point of view under whose angle an analysis is conducted. Finally, it designates 'intentional species (*les espèces intentionnelles*)' which are appearances or apparitions of a thing.

Aren't the difficulties and disagreements that accompany the translation of this Latin expression in reality linked to an insufficient analysis of the ontological status of eternity and its relationship with duration? Indeed, each translation brings an implicit representation of the nature of both eternity and duration into play. They therefore do not cease to have repercussions on the interpretation of the theory. If we choose, as Appuhn does, to render the term *species* with the word 'sort (*sorte*)', then we are implying that man cannot truly conceive of things in an eternal manner, as God can, but only gains access to a knowledge that would resemble that of eternity. Appuhn would then be in the company of Boulainvilliers, who decides to translate the term *species* either as 'way (*façon*)' or 'species (*espèce*)', here understood as a synonym for 'sort (*sorte*)', in order to show that while intuitive knowledge approaches a genuinely eternal grasping, it nonetheless imitates without fully attaining it.[10] This type of translation inevitably spills over onto the conception of the nature of the mind's eternity in Spinoza,

---

[10] Cf. *Ethics* II, 44 Cor. 2: 'Il est de la nature de la raison de percevoir les choses en quelque façon comme éternelles.' [TN: the Curley translation in English reads: 'It is of the nature of Reason to regard things under a certain species of eternity.' *CWS* I, 481. The original Latin is 'De natura rationis est res sub quadam aeternitatis specie percipere.']

for it tends to point the finger at the difference between finite and infinite modes, and can therefore lead one to think that the human intellect is, despite its development of adequate knowledge, not genuinely and strictly speaking eternal, as is that of God. Spinozism then seems like a variation of emanationist doctrines, since man would have to be content with an ersatz eternity, a pale copy comparable to what some call permanence (*pérennité*) or perpetuity. In this case, a conception *sub specie aeternitatis* seems like the means by which a being subjected to duration approximates eternity. The translation proposed by Appuhn presupposes the existence of intermediary categories serving as bridges between the eternity of substance and duration. In order to assess its validity, it is thus absolutely necessary to know whether duration follows directly from eternal things or if it entails the mediation of other temporal categories that insert themselves between them.

By contrast, if we give *species* the sense of 'form (*forme*)', pushing it closer to the Platonic Idea, as Geneviève Rodis-Lewis suggests, then we affirm the actually eternal character of the third type of knowledge. Émile Saisset, followed later by Ferdinand Alquié, has for that matter paved the way for this view by opting in favour of a translation of *sub specie aeternitatis* with the expression 'under the character of eternity (*sous le caractère de l'éternité*)'. This position implicitly leads one to grant credence to the theory which espouses a similarity in nature between the eternity to which the mind accedes and the eternity of substance. By conferring the same character to substance and modes, it seems to deny their ontological difference, whereas they cannot be said to be eternal in a strictly identical sense. This translation choice rests on a representation of eternity as a property equally applicable to beings exempt from duration and to finite modes subjected to it. It implicitly accepts the compatibility between the two concepts and thus the uselessness of mediations.

In a completely different valence, if we translate *species*, as do Roland Caillois, Bernard Pautrat and Robert Misrahi, with 'species (*espèce*)', we thereby resolve the problem of the distinction between the eternity of substance, that of immediate and mediate infinite modes, and that of finite modes by proposing that there are several species of eternity. In doing so, however, we assume that eternity is a genus and that Spinoza subscribes to Peripatetic custom. This translation bias presents a completely different field of investigation of and angle of approach for the relations between duration and eternity than does the preceding. If eternity is a genus divisible into multiple species, we can ask ourselves if duration, given its indefinite character, is part of or falls under its jurisdiction. The problems opened up by this lexical choice will turn around two questions: whether there is a difference in nature or a difference of degree between the two concepts, and whether or not the multiplicity of species should be thought of under the model of a gradation that would range from the duration of finite modes to the eternity of substance.

Finally, if we subscribe to Martial Gueroult's[11] analyses by preferring the word aspect (*aspect*) to all others, we risk stumbling over a double danger, for we must take care to strip this term of 'every illusory connotation', according to Geneviève Rodis-Lewis's expression,[12] and to steer clear of the abusive conversion of the *Ethics* into a monadology *avant la lettre* by insisting too much upon the notion of a point of view. In such a case, it becomes necessary to distinguish that eternal aspect from the one that is temporary and fleeting, and to determine precisely the nature of their relations.

We can therefore allow ourselves the hope that the translation will become less of a challenge when eternity becomes clearly defined. That is why it is important to analyse its ontological status and to confirm whether that status is one and the same for the whole of *natura naturans* and *natura naturata* or if, on the contrary, it is multiple and different for substance, infinite modes and finite modes. It is only at the price of an investigation into its essence that it will become possible to better discern the meaning of a conception *sub specie aeternitatis* and to clarify the origin of duration, its properties and its sphere of extension.

The analysis will not be centred around the *more geometrico* study of *Ethics* V, which has already been the object of abundant commentaries. Rather, it will attempt to grasp, from a historical and genetic perspective, the manner in which Spinoza, implicitly or explicitly and throughout his entire corpus, formulates the problem of the relationship between duration and eternity by constantly modifying its details in accordance with the state of his thought, the difficulties that it raises, and his interlocutors' questions. While rejecting the idea that a thought mechanically follows from a previous source and is limited to either reproducing or distorting it, we must accept the impossibility of perceiving its specificity, its stakes and its meanderings without comparing it to the previous doctrines that constitute its horizon. From this point of view, nothing seems vainer than the opposition between the internal analysis of a work and research into external sources. Even Gueroult, who is presented as the defender of a strictly internal reading, does not shy away, when necessary, from looking to Adriaan Heereboord's *Hermeneia*

---

[11] Gueroult 1974: appendix no. 17, 609–15.
[12] Rodis-Lewis 1986: 212, note 16.

logica for a principle of classification capable of clarifying the distinctions put forth by Spinoza between different types of causality.[13]

The method of investigation will therefore be based both on the internal examination of the doctrine by retracing its development as well as a confrontation with the earlier philosophical tradition. The choice of this method, which combines two approaches we traditionally tend to separate, seems particularly well-suited for Spinozist thought for several reasons:

1. It is clear that a philosophy is not a kingdom within a kingdom. It obeys laws that preside over the formation of ideas. It undeniably contains an internal dynamic of its own, but it is at the same time constituted against a backdrop of external causes and previous ideas that it either approves as common notions or reproves by virtue of their inadequate character.

2. Beyond this banal observation, we must recall that the only two books published together during Spinoza's lifetime and under his name are works on the history of philosophy. *Descartes' Principles of Philosophy* and *Metaphysical Thoughts* were written and published for the same purpose: laying the ground for Spinozist philosophy and preparing minds to receive that philosophy. Spinoza thus considers the history of philosophy as a necessary propaedeutic for his doctrine. He emphasises this in both the letter to Oldenburg from 17–27 July 1663 and the letter from 3 August 1663 to Louis Meyer where he reminds him that the goal of the publication of his two works is to 'generously and with good will invite men to study the true philosophy'.[14] Consequently, if we want to understand Spinoza, we must positively take into account his invitation to study Cartesianism and prior metaphysical doctrines. In this respect, *Metaphysical Thoughts* provides an interesting angle of approach, for Spinoza there discusses and refutes certain scholastic conceptions in light of Cartesian philosophy. Even if he does not always express his views directly, he at least presupposes the existence of a true philosophy, one serving as the measure of both itself and of the false, as a backdrop. The choice of authors summoned for comparison has therefore been essentially dictated by *Metaphysical Thoughts*. Aside from Plato, Aristotle and Descartes, who are explicitly mentioned, Spinoza refers to authors and philosophers in general, building upon a common culture strongly influenced, no doubt, by the manuals

---

[13] Gueroult 1968: 245.
[14] *Ep.* XV [to Louis Meyer]; CWS I, 216.

in use at the time in the academies, particularly Franco Burgersdijk's *Institutiones Metaphysicae*, a reference book for scholasticism. Whether Spinoza had himself read this author, who was a professor at Leyde until 1635, or had a second-hand familiarity with him from reading Heereboord's *Meletemata*, it is evident that he perfectly understood the subtleties of scholastic thought and its sources.

3. Finally, the confrontation with earlier doctrines isn't just a mere prelude for Spinoza; rather, it remains a constant preoccupation. In fact, Spinoza's method and style of writing in the *Ethics* seem to demand an approach that combines the internal analysis of a work with the study of external sources. To the geometric order of propositions and demonstrations that display the system according to an internal dynamic responds the more polemical tone of the scholia where Spinoza discusses and refutes earlier conceptions.

As for the method of internal analysis, it is based on two principles:

1. Due to the problematic character of the status of the *Short Treatise* and *Metaphysical Thoughts*, only those elements corroborated later, whether by the correspondences or other works, will be held as certain and expressive of Spinozist thought. Other elements will be accepted until proven otherwise – that is, until Spinoza explicitly renounces them.

2. Additionally, the analysis does not aim to review each work in order to successively and chronologically study the concepts of time, duration and eternity; it instead prioritises the examination of problems and endeavours to determine why and how Spinoza reformulates a question and modifies its details and solutions throughout the course of his work.

Based on this method, the task will be to study the origin and nature of the concepts of time, duration and eternity by identifying the meaning and impact that they assume and evaluating the internal development of the Spinozist doctrine, all while situating it in relation to the philosophical context and tradition in which it is inscribed.

Part I
Eternity or Eternities?

1

The Ontological Status of Eternity from the *Short Treatise* to the *Ethics*

To translate without betrayal, it is necessary to first determine whether eternity is a category, a genus divisible into species, a form capable of assuming several appearances (*aspects*), or that '*je ne sais quoi*' which differentiates between the finite and the infinite. An elucidation of its nature must serve as a prolegomenon to any interpretation of the phrase *sub specie aeternitatis* and entails, above all, the definition of its place in Spinozist ontology – an ontology that allows for only three well-known divisions between substance, attributes and modes. Should we then consider eternity at the level of a substance, an attribute or a mode? A slightly informed reader will immediately rule out the first hypothesis since there is only one unique substance, called God; such a reader will be equally tempted to immediately push back on the second by arguing that we are only familiar with, by Spinoza's own admission, two attributes – namely, thought and extension. If eternity figured among the infinity of attributes, Spinoza would have in all likelihood taken care to emphasise such a point. The author of the *Ethics* mentions nothing of the sort and limits himself to alluding to other attributes without providing any further details.[1] *Metaphysical Thoughts*, however, causes such an immediate certainty to waver, for the first chapter of Part II opens with a disconcerting claim according to which 'the chief attribute, which deserves consideration before all others, is God's *Eternity* . . .'.[2] Is this an ambiguity in vocabulary? A terminological mutation? A development in Spinoza's thought? Such are among many questions that only a careful examination can permit us to resolve.

---

[1] Cf. for example *Ethics* II, 7 Schol: 'Therefore, whether we conceive nature under the attribute of Extension, or under the attribute of Thought, or under any other attribute, we shall find one and the same order.' CWS I, 451.

[2] CM II; CWS I, 316.

The third hypothesis seems to better accommodate us in the lodge of evidence, but when it comes down to it, its accommodations are hardly comfortable. If eternity is a mode, is it so in the same way as singular finite things, as the divine intellect or the *facies totius universi*? As real as eternity is, it is obvious that it does not express substance in the same way as does Peter, Paul or Simon. In what sense can eternity be a mode? Eternity, like duration, cannot be reduced to a mere mode of thought, and is thereby distinguished from time, to which Spinoza confers this ontological status. The nature of eternity remains problematic, which is why it is important to analyse the stages in the formation of Spinozist doctrine on this subject by identifying the meaning and significance of the modifications carried out across the entirety of the system.

The Ontological Status of Eternity in the *Short Treatise*

It is undeniably risky to base an examination of the Spinozist conception of eternity on the *Short Treatise*. As Gilbert Boss[3] stresses, nothing allows us to say with certainty whether the differences between the *Short Treatise* and the later works are due to the intervention of students scarcely faithful in their note-taking, from Spinoza's own intellectual development, or from certain requirements which go along with adapting a teaching to a particular public. With a view to avoiding dubious interpretations, we must consider as authentic only those theoretical elements corroborated by the other works in the system and, when uncertainty remains, approach uncorroborated elements with necessary caution.

Attributes and Propria

Straightaway in the *Short Treatise*, Spinoza exhibits his desire to break with the metaphysical tradition and to assign a new status to the concepts of divine causality, providence, simplicity, eternity, etc. Generally, eternity is regarded as an attribute of God. Of course, God's infinity prevents us from drawing up an exhaustive list of his attributes – but on the whole, short of a few exceptions, theologians agree in acknowledging that eternity figures among a number of attributes analytically deducible from divine perfection. For example, some Jewish philosophers in the Middle Ages, like Bahya Ibn Pakuda or Abraham Ibn Daud, mention eternity in their lists. The first, in

---

[3] Boss 1982a: 6.

his *Hobot Ha Lebabot*,[4] accords existence, unity and eternity to God. The second forms a list of eight attributes: unity, truth, existence, eternity, life, knowledge, will and power. In the same manner, in Latin philosophers like Thomas Aquinas or Suarez, eternity is presented as an attribute of God just like oneness, immensity, immutability and omnipotence.

Spinoza joins his predecessors by affirming that God possesses an infinity of attributes but departs from them when it comes to including eternity among those attributes. This break with the tradition is, however, less radical than it may appear insofar as it had already been largely carried out, particularly by Duns Scotus who refused to call 'certain divine properties like sempiternity and eternity' attributes.[5] The concept of attribute takes on many meanings and has a scope that varies from philosopher to philosopher, so it is not necessarily original to contest this designation of eternity.

It is particularly important to understand why eternity is not an attribute and to determine its nature. Attributes in the *Short Treatise* are presented as substances that are infinite in their kind which express the essence of God and make God known as he is. The definitions of previous philosophers who accord God existence through himself, omniscience, omnipotence, eternity, infinity, etc. do not disclose God's essence, for they do not give us 'any Attributes through which it is known what the thing (God) is'.[6] A real definition of God must include the entirety of substances infinite in their kind of which God is formed, but because only two attributes are known to us, such a definition is limited to the inventory of attributes of extension and thought.

Even so, despite the fact that Spinoza never goes back on his claim according to which we can only know two attributes, it is not sufficient to prove that eternity is not one. The limitation of our knowledge is not a decisive argument, for it does not prevent us from imagining that eternity could well constitute one of these infinite attributes that we do not know. Spinoza himself leaves the possibility of an extension of our cognitive field open when he observes that 'so far, however, only two of all these infinite attributes are known to us through their essence: Thought and Extension'.[7]

---

[4] Cf. Harry Austryn Wolfson's analyses in *The Philosophy of Spinoza*, Vol. 1 (Wolfson 1962).

[5] John Duns Scotus, *Sur la connaissance de Dieu et l'univocité de l'étant*, Ordinatio I, distinction 8, 262. [TN: The Latin reads 'quaedam proprietates divinae, ut sempiternitas et aeternitas.' See Johns Duns Scotus, *Tomus 12, Ordinatio I*, Distinction 8, Question IV, 637. For the English translation, see Duns Scotus 1305: 349.]

[6] *KV* I, 7, 6; *CWS* I, 89.

[7] *KV* I, 7, note A; *CWS* I, 88. [TN: Emphasis Jaquet's.]

Supposing that the text is authentic, this formulation will not turn up again in later works. Everything thus happens as if the later author of the *Ethics* curbed his imagination and withdrew every last hope for research into such matters by transforming a limitation by fact into a limitation by right.

In order to leave any and all ambiguity behind, it is necessary to analyse the reasons why eternity cannot be reduced to an attribute. Because each attribute is unique and infinite in its kind, it cannot be related to another attribute. Thought cannot be said to be extended, nor extension said to be thinking. Eternity, by contrast, can apply to any attribute, to thought as well as extension. Additionally, each attribute is conceived through itself. Taken in isolation, however, eternity is inconceivable. It is always the eternity of an essence, of an existence, of thought, of extension ... It thus does not reveal to us anything substantial, even if it belongs to God. For these reasons, Spinoza does not put eternity in the category of *attributa*, but in that of *propria*.

Propria are, by definition, properties characteristic of a thing or a being, but they do not express its essence. 'Without them God would indeed not be God; but still, he is not God through them, for they do not make known anything substantial, and it is only through what is substantial that God exists.'[8] In the *Short Treatise*, propria constitute an intermediary category between what Spinoza calls 'essential attributes' and 'attributes that do not belong to God'. While essential attributes allow us to know and explain the thing, propria qualify it as an adjective added to a substantive, but do not reveal its essence to us. Propria, however, do indeed belong to God and are related to all of God's attributes, unlike other properties that only relate to a single one and that, consequently, do not belong to God 'in consideration of all that he is, or all his attributes'.[9] So, for example, omniscience, wisdom and mercy are neither essential attributes nor propria, for they do not relate to God in his totality, but only to the attribute of thought. Ubiquity and omnipresence, too, figure in the category of attributes that do not belong to God, for they specifically characterise extension. By contrast, eternity, immutability, infinity and existence through himself 'belong in their own right to God' and apply to the totality of God's attributes. Notwithstanding the introduction of the category of attributes that do not belong to God, Spinoza here picks up on the scholastic distinction between essential attributes and propria. The presence of the Latin term *propria* in the Dutch manuscript would suffice to attest, for that matter, to this filiation. As usual,

8 *KV* I, 3, note A; *CWS* I, 80.
9 *KV* I, 7, note B; *CWS* I, 89.

Spinoza does not limit himself to using terminology that he would divert from its initial meaning; he also rediscovers the spirit of the term. If his definition of propria does not have the same extension as the Aristotelian *idiom*, it nevertheless proves close enough to the general sense that the author of the *Topics* gives to that term. In fact, with the name propria, Aristotle designates that which without expressing the essence of a thing nevertheless belongs to it and is predicated convertibly of it (*se réciproque avec elle*).[10] The analyses of the *Short Treatise* constitute a faithful enough echo of Peripatetic thought even though Spinoza does not explicitly mention the reciprocity of the relationship between the proprium and the thing to which it belongs. He does, however, implicitly admit it, for he underscores the dependency of propria in relation to both attributes and substance and reciprocally maintains that 'God is, indeed, not God without them.'[11]

Spinoza does not draw up an exhaustive list of propria, but he does place eternity in this category alongside existence through itself, infinity and immutability. From this point of view, he remains relatively close to Stagirite analyses. To be sure, he does not himself take up the distinction put forth in the *Topics*[12] between different species of propria:[13] propria absolute in their own right, relative propria, permanent propria and temporary propria. Rather, it would seem that he retains only absolute and permanent propria. Nevertheless, this does not mean that he eliminates the other two species. The peculiar nature of his project, namely the determination of divine propria, very well explains the absence of a study of either relative or temporary propria and therefore does not allow us to jump to conclusions

---

[10] Aristotle, *Topics* I, 5, 102a. [TN: Jaquet's text here simply reads 'Les analyses du *Court Traité* constituent un écho assez fidèle de la pensée péripatéticienne bien que Spinoza ne mentionne pas explicitement la réciprocité de la relation.' I have chosen to translate the last bit with 'predicated convertibly of it' insofar as it more directly refers to the Aristotelian passage cited here. The relevant passage from the *Topics* reads: 'A "property" is a predicate which does not indicate the essence of a thing, but yet belongs to that thing alone, and is predicated convertibly of it. Thus, it is a property of man to-be-capable of learning grammar: for if A be a man, then he is capable of learning grammar, and if he be capable of learning grammar, he is a man.' We know that where the English translation reads 'property', Jaquet is using the term 'propria'.]

[11] *KV* I, 1, note E; *CWS* I, 64.

[12] Aristotle, *Topics* V, 1, 128b15–22.

[13] [TN: The English translations of these texts in Barnes's *Complete Works of Aristotle* translate the term with 'property'. We have here used 'propria' to maintain consistency with Jaquet's text. Similarly, the types of propria in that edition are rendered in the following manner: properties in themselves, relative properties, properties that always hold, and properties that hold for a time. See Aristotle 1984: 63.]

concerning his position on this subject. In any case, he at least joins the author of the *Topics* in holding that eternity belongs to the category of God's propria. It is, for that matter, striking to note that Aristotle chooses precisely God's immortality[14] to illustrate what he understands by permanent propria. The fact of being an immortal living thing is thus not, for Aristotle, an essential predicate expressing the essence of God, but it is well and truly a proprium.

It is important, then, to grasp why eternity fulfils the necessary criteria for fitting into the category of propria. First of all, it presents itself as a characteristic quality, necessary but insufficient for understanding the essence of substance. It belongs to God as a distinctive and constant property since it is impossible to conceive of God as mortal or perishable. Thus, without eternity, God would not be God. In itself, however, it does not entirely reveal the divine nature. Just like an adjective does not explain the substantive, but is instead applied to it, eternity does not explain substance, but is applied to it. It thus cannot reveal the content of an essence that it presupposes in order to be able to qualify. In other words, it is not constitutive of substance, but results from the constitution of substance. Conversely, it cannot be conceived independently of its relation to substance and the attributes.

Despite his refusal to consider eternity an attribute and subscribe to the analyses of previous philosophers, Spinoza, curiously, does not always rigorously maintain his own distinction, and rather indifferently refers to attributes as essential properties at some points and propria at others, and this without always taking care to specify the category intended by his denomination.[15] Before accusing either the teacher or the students of confusion and incoherence, we must note that in the medieval philosophical tradition, the terminology on this point remained loose, and propria were often designated by the term 'attribute'. *Proprium* is typically the Latin equivalent of the Greek *idiom*, but there are cases where the Greek term is translated with the word attribute. Incidentally, Wolfson observes on this subject that in the medieval Hebraic literature, and particularly in a Hebrew translation of a passage of the *Topics*, the term *idiom* is translated with the word that usually means attribute.[16] The invariable use of the same term of course lends itself to ambiguity. But it seems all the bolder to assume confusion in either the teacher's thought or student's notes given that Spinoza reiterates

[14] Aristotle, *Topics* V, 1, 128b19–20.
[15] Cf. *KV* I, 2, 28–30; 3, 1; 5, 1; 6, 1; 7, 1; *CWS* I, 73, 80; 84; 85; 88.
[16] Wolfson 1962: I, 140.

his distinction between essential attributes and propria, specifying of God's attributes that 'those which are known to us consist of only two, viz. thought and extension',[17] and taking care to emphasise, when he studies causality, providence, etc., that he is there concerned with attributes called propria. It is thus impossible to confuse 'Eigenschappen' with 'Eigen' or propria and entertain a controversy over the status of eternity in the Short Treatise.

Spinoza does not disclose the way in which eternity characterises God; he does, however, provide some indirect indications in his redistribution of propria into two groups: extrinsic denominations and actions. Propria that belong to God must 'either be an extrinsic denomination, such as existing through himself, being eternal, one, immutable, etc., or be in respect to his actions, such as that he is a cause, a predeterminer, and ruler of all things'.[18] If the nature of the second category appears all the clearer insofar as Spinoza dedicates many chapters to an examination of divine action, causality, providence and predestination, that of the first is, by contrast, enigmatic. What is an extrinsic denomination and why does eternity appear under this heading?

Extrinsic Denominations

Typically, in Latin, the term denominatio has two meanings. First, it translates the Aristotelian notion of paronym. Second, it designates names created from the root of a word which, while being related to it, are nevertheless distinguished from it by their inflection or ending. It is thus that Aristotle defines paronymous things in the first chapter of the Categories after having treated homonymous and synonymous things. 'When things get their name from something, with a difference of ending, they are called paronymous. Thus, for example, the grammarian gets its name from grammar, the brave get theirs from bravery.'[19] It is immediately obvious that this is not the paronymy Spinoza intends with the term 'extrinsic denomination'. Denominatio also designates that mental operation which attributes to a thing the name most likely to convey its nature and use. This is, for that matter, why Thomas Aquinas claims that a denomination is extracted from a thing's form, or from the element that determines its essence and behaviour.

Still, these semantic clarifications do not shed much light on the exact nature of the term 'denomination' in Spinoza. Nor do they clarify the phrase

[17] KV I, 2, 28; CWS I, 73.
[18] KV I, 2, 29; CWS I, 73.
[19] Aristotle, Categories, I. 1a13–1a15 (Aristotle 1984: 2).

'extrinsic denomination', of which he provides no explanation. 'What he means here by an extrinsic denomination is not quite clear', writes Wolfson on this topic.[20] Faithful to his method, the American commentator, in order to understand this distinction, suggests establishing a parallelism between extrinsic denomination in Spinoza and the classification of affirmative attributes in the philosophy of Maimonides.

The author of *The Guide for the Perplexed* actually divides affirmative attributes into five classes. 'First. The object is described by its definition, as e.g., man is described as a being that lives and has reason; such a description, containing the true essence of the object, is, as we have already shown, nothing else but the explanation of a name.'[21] According to Wolfson,[22] propria called 'extrinsic denominations' would belong to the first class of attributes that, according to Maimonides, are meant to explain a name. Propria applying to actions would, for their part, correspond to the fifth class – those where the thing has its action for an attribute.

In truth, the American commentator's interpretation is not convincing. By failing to clarify the reasons that would have made Spinoza select only two classes of attributes at the expense of the other three, it turns him into an eclectic philosopher forging his doctrine out of arbitrarily chosen pieces. Most importantly, it fails in its approximative character, for it does not sufficiently take the specificity of propria into account.

Unlike the first class of attributes distinguished by Maimonides, Spinozist propria do not allow us to express the real being of a thing by means of the definition of its name. The predicates 'rational animal' and 'eternal' are not placed on the same level. If I explain the name 'man' by substituting for it the expression 'rational animal', I make an analytic judgement exhibiting the components of the essence of the human being. By contrast,

---

[20] Wolfson 1962: I, 228. [TN: Wolfson's text is reproduced in English in Jaquet's book. He uses the term 'extraneous' instead of 'extrinsic', but I have modified it to read 'extrinsic' for the sake of consistency.]

[21] Maimonides 2002: I, 52, 69. [TN: The French translation used by Jaquet reads the following: 'La première est celle où la chose a pour attribut sa définition comme par exemple lorsqu'on désigne l'homme "en disant" qu'il est un animal raisonnable. Un tel attribut indique l'être véritable d'une chose et nous avons déjà exposé qu'il est l'explication d'un nom et pas autre chose.' The difference between the English and the French is significant insofar as the French preserves '*attribut*', a term for which the English translation substitutes 'description'. See Moïse Maïmonide, *Le guide des Égarés* (Paris: Verdier, 1979).]

[22] Wolfson 1962: I, 229: 'And thus Spinoza's properties correspond to what Maimonides described as (1) explanation of a name, and (2) actions, both of which are distinguished by him from essential attributes.'

when instead of saying 'God', I say 'the Eternal', I can still clearly identify the being intended under this denomination, but this characteristic at best allows me to recognise (*reconnaître*) God, not know (*connaître*) him. In all rigour, the predicates that might correspond to the first class of attributes would rather be those that, in Spinoza, serve to define substance. Thus, the expressions 'what is in itself and conceived through itself' much better explain the name 'God' than the terms 'eternity' and 'infinity', and could therefore more rightly be considered attributes of the first class. Wolfson's analogy is thus hardly illuminating on this point.

To shed light on the meaning of extrinsic denominations, it is actually necessary to resituate this concept in the context of the scholastic tradition from which it comes. According to Vicente Muñoz Delgado, the origin of the distinction between intrinsic and extrinsic denominations can be traced back to Durandus of Saint-Pourçain, who allegedly claimed that beings of reason would be extrinsic denominations derived from the activity of reason. At any rate, more generally and in the scholastic tradition, an intrinsic denomination comes from a form or quality internal to the subject. It concerns its essential prerogatives and its own unique qualities and can express a relation of identity and inherence. The term 'man', for example, will be applied to Socrates by virtue of his identity with the form humanity, or, to take another example, a wall will be called white due to the whiteness that is proper and inherent to it.

By contrast, although the term is rooted in the nature of things, an extrinsic denomination refers to a form external to and other than the designated object. So, when one says of a table that it is seen or recognised, one does not express a property inherent to the object, but rather utilises a denomination stemming from the fact that one relates it to something external by which it is seen or recognised. Extrinsic denominations thus concern the relations that a subject or object has with others. They imply the existence of a third element: a denominating form (the intellect or sight); something denominated (the object); and a denomination (the word that describes the object from the perspective of the apprehension of a perceiving or cognising subject). Suarez defines them in this manner in his *Disputationes Metaphysicae* when he claims that predicates can be reduced to two groups: negations or privations and extrinsic denominations.

> It seems that these predicates or attributes can be reduced to two groups. The first is formed by predicates that consist in a negation or privation: so, we say that a thing is indivisible, that a moral act is evil, that a man is old . . . The second is constituted by the predicates that consist in extrinsic

denominations taken from things themselves. It is in this manner that we say that God is a creator in time, that a wall is seen . . .²³

Suarez additionally specifies that these denominations are sometimes understood as actual (for example, when we say that a wall is seen) and sometimes as potential (when we say that a wall is visible). An extrinsic denomination thus does not express an essential property of the object. It characterises it in a relative as opposed to absolute manner, for it presupposes the setting up of a relation with an external subject or object. Thus, the fact of being seen or visible does not constitute an intrinsic property of a wall but implies a perceiving subject who applies this quality to the object. In the same way, it is only by reference to a relation between creator and creature that we can say that God is creator in time. Considered absolutely and in himself, God is outside of time, so the predicate 'creator in time' does not express an essential property of his nature. In a general manner, extrinsic denominations, for Suarez, are taken from relations. It now becomes possible, in light of these analyses, to solve the mystery concerning the meaning of extrinsic denominations in Spinoza, for the definition given by the author of the *Disputationes Metaphysicae* greatly overlaps with the one Spinoza gives for the second category of propria in the *Short Treatise*.

According to Suarez, extrinsic denominations do not express essential properties of objects; they are not, however, completely foreign to them, for 'they are extracted from things themselves'²⁴ and therefore do indeed belong to them in some manner. In this sense, their nature is close to the one that Spinoza assigns to propria.²⁵

Additionally, extrinsic denominations, for 'the pope of metaphysics', always concern the relations that an object maintains with another. Spinoza, too, associates extrinsic denominations with relations on multiple occasions.²⁶

---

²³ Suarez, *Disputationes Metaphysicae*, III, section I, paragraph 7. 'huius modi autem praedicata seu attributa videntur posse ad duo capita revocari. Unum est eorum, quae in negatione vel privatione consistent; sic euim dicimus rem esse indivisibilem, actum morale esse malum, hominem esse caecum, et simila. Aliud est eorum quae consistent in denominationibus extrinsecis sumptis ex rebus ipsis, quomodo dicitur Deus creator ex tempore, vel paries visis, etc.' Suarez 2009: 105. [TN: The in-text quotation is a translation from the French cited by Jaquet, not the original Latin.]

²⁴ Ibid. [TN: Translated from the French.]

²⁵ KV I, 7, 6; CWS I, 89.

²⁶ CM II, 2; *Ep.* LX [to Tschirnhaus]; *Ethics* II, Def. 4 and Exp.; CWS I, 318–19; II, 432–3; I, 447, respectively.

The comparison with Suarez may nevertheless seem forced insofar as we cannot prove that Spinoza read the *Disputationes Metaphysicae*. This metaphysical tome is not found in his library and Spinoza makes absolutely no mention of a debt to Suarez. He nonetheless could have had second-hand familiarity with Suarez's analyses insofar as they inspired numerous works including, in particular, a manual of scholastic logic, published in 1645 under the title of the *Synopsis Burgersdiciana (Institutionum Logicorum Synopsis, in usum scholarum hollandicarum)*, that was written by Franco Bügersdijck and used by students in Holland and West-Friesland.[27] This manual was edited in 1650, enriched with commentaries and explanations by his student, Adrian Heereboord, who did not hide his admiration for and debt to Suarez, a thinker he names, in his *Meletemata*, 'the pope and prince of all metaphysics'. Now, Spinoza knew Heereboord's work well, for he cites him in his *Metaphysical Thoughts*.[28] Even if it would be impossible to say with certainty whether he had read the *Synopsis Bürgersdiciana* in the teacher's original version or the student's enriched and commented version, it is undeniable that he had at least read the *Meletemata philosophica* in which Heereboord takes up and comments on broad excerpts of the scholastic manual. Trendelenburg, who sought to identify the sources of the *Short Treatise*, has made clear that the table from Part I, chapter 3 which displays the eight aspects of efficient causality is taken directly from Heereboord's *Philosophiae Naturalis, Meletemata*.[29] Not only does Heereboord, for his part, take up the distinction between essence and propria, he also makes a distinction within the second category. 'Proprium est vel internum, vel externum (Propria are either internal or external).'[30] Internal propria come from the essence of a subject,[31] can be separated from it neither by a real distinction nor even by thought,[32] and are incommunicable to subjects of differing species.[33] External propria, by contrast, are attributed to a subject by virtue of an external cause and therefore entail a relation.[34] Of course, Heereboord does

---

[27] See Gueroult 1968: 245, note 7.

[28] CM II, 12; CWS I, 340–6.

[29] See *Historische Beiträge Iller Band* (Berlin, 1867), 8th *Abhandlung*, 316, cited by Gueroult 1968: 245, note 7.

[30] Heereboord, *Meletemata Positionum logicorum, Disputatio septima, De praedicabilibus*, 10–11, paragraph 30.

[31] Ibid., paragraph 31: 'Internum emanat ab essentia subjecti.'

[32] Ibid., paragraph 33: 'Internum ab subjecto in quo est separiri nequit nec separatione reali, nec mentali.'

[33] Ibid., paragraph 34: 'Nec potest subjecto alteri specie diverso communicari.'

[34] Ibid., paragraph 32: 'Externum ponitur in subjecto posita causa extra subjectum.'

not use the term 'extrinsic denomination' to describe the second category of propria; he is clear, however, that his categories overlap with those of Suarez since external propria do not express the essence of a subject, but characteristics linked to an external cause. It is also interesting to note that the second type of propria falls under the category of attributes communicable to subjects of other species. Thus, if eternity is an external proprium rather than an internal one, it means that it is not the exclusive privilege of substance and can, in fact, be communicated to modes. Consequently, the fact that Spinoza presents it as an extrinsic denomination suggests that substance shares its enjoyment (*jouissance*) [TN: of eternity] with modes, as the second part of the *Short Treatise* will confirm.[35] Ultimately, it matters little whether Spinoza inherits the above distinctions straight from the pope of metaphysics himself or takes note of his thought through the medium of one of his zealous students. In either case, there is no doubt that the distinctions made before his readership constitute an extension of a certain Suarezian current.

The comparison with the author of the *Disputationes Metaphysicae* can be illuminating on another level, too, for it is curious to note that in the *Short Treatise* the division within the propria appears to take the form of an alternative – but this is not really the case, for Spinoza does not distinguish propria that are extrinsic denominations, on the one hand, from those that are intrinsic denominations, on the other. Contrary to all expectations, propria pertaining to the actions of God are what constitute the counterpart to the first category. Does this mean that Spinoza considers these propria to be intrinsic denominations? Nothing in the *Short Treatise* allows us to confirm this with any certainty. Still, if we accept the hypothesis of a connection to Suarez, the enigmatic character of this division within propria can be explained. For the author of the *Disputationes Metaphysicae*, actions indeed constitute intrinsic denominations, whereas relations constitute extrinsic ones.

In all rigour, however, Spinoza might take cues from some of Suarez's conceptions concerning extrinsic denominations without for all that entirely aligning himself with them. The discrepancy is obvious when we compare the examples that the two authors respectively choose to illustrate the category of extrinsic denominations. The Suarezian predicate 'creator in time (*creator ex tempore*)' and the Spinozist predicate 'eternal' are not exactly situated on the same plane. The first is an altogether inappropriate designation if we claim to rigorously apply it to God. The second, by contrast, expresses one of God's true propria.

[35] *KV* I, 16, 8; *CWS* I, 148–9.

It is, then, important to clarify the specific sense that Spinoza gives to the concept of extrinsic denomination in order to better discern the essence of eternity. In the *Short Treatise*, our author is on this subject hardly generous with explanations – in all likelihood because he is addressing a well-informed audience. In the *Treatise on the Emendation of the Intellect*,[36] he also refers to the distinction between intrinsic and extrinsic denominations but remains quite allusive. In the *Ethics*, by contrast, the meaning of these concepts shines through clearly on two occasions: in the definition of an adequate idea, on the one hand,[37] and the explanation concerning the various names of the affects, on the other.[38]

In the *Ethics*, the distinction between intrinsic and extrinsic denominations comes up in the definition of adequate ideas. By an adequate idea, Spinoza means 'an idea which, insofar as it is considered in itself, without relation to an object, has all the properties, *or* intrinsic denominations of a true idea'.[39] Denominations, in general, are distinguishing features that allow one to recognise and identify the nature or properties of a thing or idea. An intrinsic denomination, as its name indicates, designates the internal criterion by which the thing or the idea is recognised without needing the aid of an external sign. It suffices that the thing appear (*se montre*) for its identity to be disclosed. It is *index sui*, in such a way that its presence is the same as its presentation. An extrinsic denomination, by contrast, is an external sign by means of which it becomes possible to differentiate ideas or things that do not in themselves possess this distinguishing mark. It involves the assistance of an external mediation, of a third party, which draws attention to that which had not yet stood out in an internal examination. So, when two ideas or two things are not distinguished by an intrinsic denomination, they must be put in relation to a third term that will differentiate them in an extrinsic manner. The example of the criterion of the true clearly illustrates this distinction between two types of denominations. The true idea is distinguished from the false idea by an extrinsic denomination when the criterion that allows us to decide between them is conformity with the given object. In this case, it is the relation to the object that determines, from the outside, the respective value of each idea. The *adequatio rei et intellectus* is not, however, a satisfying criterion, for 'how can someone know certainly

---

[36] *TdIE*, 69; CWS I, 31.
[37] *Ethics* II, Def. 4; 43 Schol.; CWS I, 447; 479.
[38] *Ethics* III, Exp. DA 48; 56 Schol.; CWS I, 541; 527.
[39] *Ethics* II, Def. 4; CWS I, 447.

that he has ideas which agree with their objects?'[40] To be sure that my idea conforms to the object, I must already know the object, or have an exact idea of it. I am thus caught in a never-ending circle, for I have to assume as already acquired precisely that which I want to acquire. For this reason, Spinoza considers that 'a true thought is distinguished from a false one not only by an extrinsic, but chiefly by an intrinsic denomination'.[41] The true idea is distinguished from the false one by an intrinsic denomination when the standard that decides between them is internal. It is then that we have the mark of an adequate idea which 'considered in itself, without relation to an object, has all the properties, *or* intrinsic denominations of a true idea'.[42] In that sense, for Spinoza, true and false fall under the category of extrinsic denominations, and adequate and inadequate under the category of intrinsic denominations – but there is no real difference between these two designations. Spinoza clearly highlights the above in his response to Tschirnhaus: 'I don't recognise any difference between a true idea and an adequate one, except that the term "true" concerns only the agreement of the idea with its object, whereas the term "adequate" concerns the nature of the idea in itself. So really there's no difference between a true idea and an adequate one except for the extrinsic relation.'[43]

In the same manner, emotions (*sentiments*) are only distinguished from one another by an extrinsic denomination according to their objects and the multiplicity of circumstances. Taken in themselves, they are all reducible to desire, joy or sadness. This is what Spinoza means in his explanation of the nature of sexual appetite. 'Furthermore, from the definitions of the affects which we have explained it is clear that they all arise from Desire, Joy, or Sadness – *or* rather, that they are nothing but these three, each one generally being called by a different name on account of its varying relations and extrinsic denominations.'[44] Thus, 'Gluttony, Drunkenness, Lust, Greed, and Ambition . . . are only notions of Love or Desire which explain the nature of each of these affects through the objects to which they are related. For by Gluttony, Drunkenness, Lust, Greed, and Ambition we understand nothing but an immoderate Love or Desire for eating, drinking, sexual union, wealth, and esteem.'[45] These terms are thus only extrinsic denominations, designa-

---

[40] *Ethics* II, 43 Schol.; CWS I, 480.
[41] *TdIE*, 69; CWS I, 31.
[42] *Ethics* II, Def. 4; CWS I, 447.
[43] *Ep.* LX [to Ehrenfried Walther von Tschirnhaus]; CWS II, 432.
[44] *Ethics* III, DA 48; CWS I, 542.
[45] *Ethics* III, 56 Schol.; CWS I, 526.

tions that constitute variations of a single and same emotion according to its relation to different objects.

Basing ourselves on two occasions where Spinoza brings the distinction between the two types of denominations into play, we can clarify both the nature of eternity and any proprium that falls under the same category in the *Short Treatise*. A predicate is an extrinsic denomination when it expresses the nature of the object considered relatively and not absolutely. An extrinsic denomination qualifies a modality of relation and turns out to be a distinguishing characteristic determined on the basis of a comparison with a standard, namely, an external object. Thus, the qualities *one, eternal, immutable* and *infinite* indeed belong to God, but in a relative sense – for they are attributed to God in order to distinguish God from numerous, mortal, changing and finite beings. Considered absolutely, these adjectives designate nothing other than God's necessary existence and coincide with that designation. They explain God's nature in accordance with an object to which it is related. Oneness, eternity, immutability and infinity are only various denominations of divine existence according to which that existence is envisaged in relation to number, time, movement and scale.

A confirmation of these analyses is partially given in chapter 3 of Part II of *Metaphysical Thoughts* where Spinoza explains how God can be said to be immense and infinite. Infinity is presented as an intrinsic denomination, contrary to what was maintained in the *Short Treatise*, and immensity as an extrinsic denomination.

> God's *Infinity*, in spite of what the term suggests, is something most positive. For we call him infinite insofar as we are attending to his essence, *or* supreme perfection. But *Immensity* is only ascribed to God in a certain respect. For it does not pertain to God insofar as he is considered as the first cause, which, even if it were only most perfect in respect to secondary beings, would still be no less immense. For there would be no being, and consequently, no being could be conceived, more perfect than him, by which he could be limited or measured.[46]

The infinite, then, even though it serves as a counterpart to the finite, expresses the nature of God in an absolute sense. Immensity involves a relation between the first cause and its derived effects, as well as a comparison between the limited nature of secondary beings and the unlimited character of the primary being. One cannot conceive of immensity without tininess.

[46] CM II, 3; CWS I, 319.

It is thus following this relation with an external element that the subject receives one denomination rather than another. Eternity would then be a term that we apply to God in order to distinguish him from mere mortals. Strictly speaking, eternity would not be proper to God in an intrinsic manner but fitting only by virtue of an extrinsic relation. For this reason, the term expresses a distinctive characteristic of substance, not its absolute essence.

If eternity is a mere extrinsic denomination and can be boiled down to a relative quality that allows us to emphasise differences, then its ontological reality becomes extremely problematic. On several occasions, Spinoza insists on the fact that an extrinsic denomination would not be sufficient to establish a real distinction.[47] A real distinction must always be based on an intrinsic denomination, like we saw in the *Ethics* concerning true ideas. But in the *Short Treatise*, Spinoza makes no reference to an intrinsic denomination that would provide a foundation for extrinsic denominations. If eternity amounts to a mere extrinsic denomination, it seems to be deprived of real content. We can here apply the very reasoning that Spinoza develops in the *Ethics* to show that a real distinction between the true and the false must be based on an internal standard.

> If a true idea is distinguished from a false one, [NS: not insofar as it is said to be a mode of thinking, but] only insofar as it is said to agree with its object, then a true idea has no more reality or perfection than a false one (since they are distinguished only through the extrinsic denomination [NS: and not through the intrinsic denomination]) – and so, does the man who has true ideas [NS: have any more reality or perfection] than him who has only false ideas?[48]

If eternity is only distinguished from its opposite by means of an extrinsic denomination, it greatly risks having no more reality than that opposite.

---

[47] *TdIE* 69, CWS I, 31.

[48] *Ethics* II, 43 Schol.; *CWS* I, 479–80. [TN: The French translation that Jaquet quotes here does not include the [NS] and is not framed in terms of a question. It reads: 'Si une idée vraie se distingue d'une fausse (puisqu'elles se ditinguent par la seule dénomination extrinsèque) et par conséquent un homme qui a des idées vraies ne l'emporte pas non plus sur celui qui n'en a que de fausses.' See Spinoza, *Opera* II, ed. Carl Gebhardt, 124. The original Latin text reads: 'si idea vera, quatenus tantum dicitur cum suo ideato convenire, a falsa distinguitur, nihil ergo realitatis, aut perfectionis idea vera habet prae falsa (quandoquidem per solam denominationem extrinsecam distinguuntur), et consequenter neque etiam homo, qui veras, prae illo, qui falsas tantum ideas habet? Deinde unde fit, ut homines falsas habeant ideas?']

Under these circumstances, the ontological status of eternity remains fragile and uncertain, for the propria constituted by extrinsic denominations strongly resemble beings of reason. Spinoza does not just compare them to 'adjectives ... because they contain nothing substantive',[49] but ends up completely reducing them to adjectives. 'The following are called *Propria* because they are nothing but *Adjectives* which cannot be understood without their *Substantives*.'[50] In other words, extrinsic denominations would express manners of thinking and be thereby reduced to manners of speaking. This is, incidentally, what Spinoza implies in chapter 6 of Part I of *Metaphysical Thoughts* when he examines the origin of the meaning of the terms 'true' and 'false' and shows that they are not properties of a thing, but 'extrinsic denominations' that we can only 'attribute to things rhetorically'. When we speak of true or false gold,[51] for example, we do so only in a metaphorical manner, for truth and falsity are not properties of a thing. Extrinsic denominations are only designations, manners of speaking, and it is only by a rhetorical effect that we join the word to the thing. For these reasons, it is necessary to escape the trap of words and avoid the reification of language. Should we, then, consider extrinsic denominations as beings of reason or as actual beings?

One could dodge the question by claiming that the above constitutes a false problem insofar as Spinoza will reject these distinctions and deny any basis for the distinction between reason and beings of reason. Nevertheless, the fact remains that, in the *Short Treatise*, Spinoza makes use of this distinction, notably in relation to the division of extension. At that point, he claims that 'part and whole are not true or actual beings, but only beings of reason; consequently, in Nature there are neither whole nor parts'.[52] He will also mention this distinction in chapter 10 of the first part where he reflects on the nature of good and evil. Beings of reason are distinguished from actual beings, for they are the work of our intellect and not of nature. They help express relations between things, but not their real properties. Thus 'good' and 'evil' do not constitute properties of things but are applied to them following a comparison with better or worse things.

In comparing the Spinozist definition of beings of reason in the *Short Treatise* with that of propria, we must recognise that extrinsic denominations

---

[49] *KV* I, 1, note E; *CWS* I, 64.
[50] *KV* I, 3, note A; *CWS* I, 80.
[51] [TN: More idiomatically, we would say real or fake gold, but I preserve the terms true and false for consistency.]
[52] *KV* I, 2, 19; *CWS* I, 71.

could not be purely and simply reduced to beings of reason. Spinoza never mentions eternity and other extrinsic denominations, like oneness and immutability, when he attempts to illustrate what he means by a being of reason. He explicitly places notions like whole, part, good and bad in the list of 'entia rationis', but never makes eternity appear among them.

In any case, extrinsic denominations do fall into the category of modes of thought and, in this respect, contain a share of reality. This observation alone, however, does not prove much, for the notions of good and evil, insofar as they are produced by the intellect, are also modes of thinking and are not for that reason any less beings of reason. It turns out that extrinsic denominations are not quite reducible to modes of human thought, for they have a foundation not only in the intellect but also in the nature of God. Whereas good and evil do not pertain to things but instead characterise relations of comparison that we make between them, eternity indeed pertains to God and expresses something real about his nature, namely, the necessity of God's existence and essence. Spinoza is blunt on this point. 'For though *existing of itself, being the cause of all things, the greatest good, eternal,* and *immutable*, etc., are proper to God alone',[53] they do not allow us to determine God's essence or the nature of God's attributes.

All other things commonly attributed to God are not attributes, but only certain modes, which may be attributed to him either in consideration of everything (i.e., all his attributes) or in consideration of One attribute. For example, that God is one, eternal, existing through himself, infinite, the cause of everything, immutable – these things are attributed to God in consideration of all his attributes. That God is omniscient and wise, etc., are attributed to him in consideration of the attribute of thought.[54]

Spinoza thus considers propria as 'entia realia', not mere beings of reason. On this point, he agrees with Suarez who thought that extrinsic denominations were not entirely beings of reason.[55] We must nevertheless take care to distinguish purely rhetorical denominations from those that are based on things themselves. So, the predicate 'true' would be more akin to a being of reason when applied to gold than to an idea or a story. The difficulty, however, is not resolved, but merely displaced. Indeed, if eternity and extrinsic denominations in general are modes, are they modes in the same way as

---

[53] *KV* I, 7, 6; *CWS* I, 89.
[54] *KV* I, 7, note A; *CWS* I, 88.
[55] Suarez, *Disputationes Metaphysicae*, XXV, 1020b.

Peter, Paul or Jack? Piero Di Vona raises this issue in an article in *Studia Spinozana*. 'If propria are modes, in what sense are they so?'[56] They are modes insofar as they can neither exist nor be understood without the attributes to which they refer; but is the being of an adjective of the same kind as the being of Peter? It seems obvious that these two types of modes are not situated on the same plane and that extrinsic denominations present themselves sometimes as modes of substance, sometimes as modes of attributes, and other times as modes of modes, depending on whether we are speaking of an eternal God, eternal thought or eternal intellect. By the same stroke, the problem of the distinction between various modes also arises.

Whatever the case, the problem remains intact in the *Short Treatise*, for Spinoza does not specify in what sense propria are modes, and obviously does not mind putting them on the same level as those of which man is formed. It would nevertheless seem as though he later became aware of this ambiguity, for he will no longer use the term mode to qualify divine properties like eternity. The disappearance of this terminology is not fortuitous, but a result of an intentional decision. Spinoza clearly emphasises this point in Letter XII when he distinguishes between four terms: substance, mode, eternity and duration. A mode is clearly defined as an affection of substance. Eternity and duration are not presented as modes, but as properties which characterise the existence of substance and that of affections, respectively.

Ultimately, eternity belongs, in the *Short Treatise*, to the category of '*propria*', not that of '*attributa*'. And it is presented, more specifically, as an extrinsic denomination. It is thus important to set aside, for now, the teachings of this work and to find out what exactly is corroborated by the later writings.

Takeaways from the Short Treatise

The fact that eternity is not an attribute seems definitively accepted, for in both the *Ethics* and his correspondences, Spinoza reserves this term for extension and thought. However, we must note that in *Metaphysical Thoughts*, Spinoza defines eternity as 'an attribute under which we conceive the infinite existence of God'.[57] Must we conclude from this that he goes back on his analyses in the *Short Treatise*? Or that the latter remarks should be taken with a grain of salt? In truth, the hypothesis of a break or reversal

---

[56] Piero Di Vona, 'Il problema delle distinzioni nella filosofia di Spinoza', 154. [TN: Translation mine from the quoted French.]

[57] CM I, 4; CWS I, 310.

in his thought does not actually hold, for Spinoza, in *Metaphysical Thoughts*, uses the term attribute in its Cartesian sense. To be sure, disentangling the warp of Spinozist thought from the woof of scholastic and Cartesian thought in this complement to the *Principles* is a delicate business. It is none-theless clear that this word is used in conformity with the definition provided by Descartes in his *Principles*.[58] Several hints point in this direction. Not only does Spinoza adopt the distinction between principal and subordinate attributes, but he explicitly specifies that he draws his inspiration from the Cartesian definitions of substance and mode. 'This last is divided into Substance and Mode, whose definitions are given in the *Principles of Philosophy* I, 51, 52, and 56. So it is not necessary to repeat them here.'[59] Now, article 56 of the *Principles* establishes an equivalence between the terms 'mode', 'quality' and 'attribute'. 'The term "mode" as used here means exactly the same as "attribute" or "quality," but their usage differs.'[60] It is evident that for Descartes, the term mode is not really distinguished from the term attribute. The choice of one word over another concerns a distinction within thought in order to express certain nuances. So, for example, the term mode will be used to designate the introduction of variety within the unity of a substance, or to mark a modification, an alteration in its disposition. In short, the use of 'mode' corresponds to a desire to emphasise the presence of a change. The use of the term 'quality' is intended to highlight a change or a disposition so characteristic that it gives its name to the substance and unequivocally brings it to mind. By contrast, the word 'attribute' should preferably be reserved for expressing the immutable and constant relation between a substance and its properties. It serves to draw attention to identity and permanence.[61]

Since Spinoza openly declares his loyalty to the Cartesian definitions, it is obvious that, under his pen, the term 'attribute' used in relation to eternity in *Metaphysical Thoughts* is synonymous with 'mode' and is not really distinguished from it but only expresses a nuance within thought. The choice of the word attribute over that of mode in all likelihood aims to express the constant character of the possession of eternity and the permanence of this property in the divine existence. Lest we let ourselves get caught up in words, it is impossible to maintain that Spinoza here confers an identical status to eternity and the attributes of extension and thought.

---

[58] Descartes, *Principles of Philosophy*, I, 53–6.
[59] CM I, 1; CWS I, 302–3.
[60] Descartes, *Principles of Philosophy*, I, 56.
[61] Cf. Ibid.

If, as far back as the *Short Treatise*, eternity is irrefutably not an attribute, can we consider its assimilation to propria to be established once and for all? That is the commonly accepted view. Wolfson, for example reckons that the list of attributes enumerated in the second part of *Metaphysical Thoughts* – namely, eternity, unity, immensity, immutability, simplicity, life, intellect, will, power, status as creator, and concurrence – is nothing other than a list of propria.[62] He also maintains that in Letter XXXV addressed to Hudde, Spinoza lists four '*propria*' that 'any being existing through its own sufficiency and power must have'. Such a being must be eternal, simple, infinite and indivisible. Wolfson strengthens his analysis by referring, on the one hand, to a letter to Tschirnhaus[63] where Spinoza presents necessary existence, unity, immutability and infinity as properties, and, on the other, to the Appendix of *Ethics* I where an allusion is made to the properties of God.[64]

Nevertheless, this assimilation of propria to properties later enumerated by Spinoza seems hasty and dubious, for Spinoza, in the texts cited by Wolfson, never says that these are propria. According to Emilia Giancotti Boscherini's *Lexicon Spinozanum*, the term *proprium* only appears in the *Short Treatise*. In *Metaphysical Thoughts*, Spinoza uses the Cartesian term attribute, and in the letters to both Hudde and to Tschirnhaus as well as in the Appendix of *Ethics* I, he uses the word '*proprietates*'. According to Di Vona, the comparison between '*proprietates*' in the *Ethics* and '*propria*' in the *Short Treatise* seems plausible, bearing in mind the differences between the two works.[65] Still, nothing allows us to confirm the equivalence of the two terms with certainty. For that, it would be necessary to find a text of Spinoza's where the two words are presented as synonyms.

Such a text does in fact exist, for the inventory of the occurrences of the term *proprium* found in the *Lexicon* is not exhaustive. Spinoza also uses this word in the *Treatise on the Emendation of the Intellect* when he conveys the conditions that must be met for a definition to be perfect. 'To be called perfect, a definition will have to explain the inmost essence of the thing, and to take care not to use certain *propria* in its place.'[66] In order to illustrate the type of error to be avoided, Spinoza takes the example of the circle. 'If a circle, for example, is defined as a figure in which the lines drawn from the center to the circumference are equal, no one fails to see that such a

---

[62] Wolfson 1962: I, 230–1.
[63] *Ep.* LXXXIII [to Tschirnhaus]; CWS II, 487.
[64] *Ethics* I, App.; CWS I, 439.
[65] Di Vona, 'Il problema delle distinzioni . . .', 154.
[66] *TdIE*, 95; CWS I, 39.

definition does not at all explain the essence of the circle, but only a property (*proprietatem*) of it.'[67] The terms *proprium* and *proprietas* are here put on the same plane and designate characteristics that can be deduced from the definition of a thing, characteristics that allow one to identify it and differentiate it from others without for all that expressing its essence.

But have we not proven too much? If Filipo Mignini's[68] theory in favour of the anteriority of the *Treatise on the Emendation of the Intellect* in relation to the *Short Treatise* is right, it becomes difficult to use this synonymy between the two terms in the former as an argument that would, by treating the text as a solid link between the early works and the *Ethics*, guarantee the rough equivalence between the two terms throughout Spinoza's work. In that case, our lexical observations would at most prove that Spinoza initially uses the two terms indifferently only to subsequently abandon this loose vocabulary in favour of speaking solely of God's properties. In any case, if it is justified to note a similarity between the propria of the *Short Treatise* and the properties of the *Ethics*, it would be hasty to purely and simply equate them. For this reason, it will be necessary to re-examine the exact nature of properties in the *Ethics* and to determine their precise impact on the notion of eternity.

We must also note that we will find no trace of the division established between propria that constitute extrinsic denominations and those that relate to actions. If the second category remains, the first, by contrast, disappears, and eternity will no longer be presented as an extrinsic denomination. It then proves necessary to retrace the development or redefinition of its status in the later works, particularly in *Metaphysical Thoughts* where Spinoza will propose a new division internal to attributes.

The Ontological Status of Eternity in *Metaphysical Thoughts*

At first glance, an examination of the nature of eternity in *Descartes' Principles of Philosophy* and *Metaphysical Thoughts* presents less difficulties than in the *Short Treatise*, for the text, by Louis Meyer's own admission, had been written by Spinoza and was made public both in his lifetime and under his name. Still, because this work does not intend to demonstrate the philosopher's own teachings, but rather familiarise the young Casearius with the work of Descartes, it presents more details concerning the nature of Spinoza's teaching than his underling thought. To be sure, Spinoza does not limit himself

---

[67] Ibid.
[68] He is joined on this point by Edwin Curley, whose research confirms Mignini's theory. Cf. 'Le corps et l'esprit du *Court Traité* à l'*Éthique*'.

to the task of an historian of ideas; he provides an overview of Descartes'
philosophy and, in the appendix which follows the *Principles*, explicitly
proposes to straighten out some of the difficulties inherent to metaphysics. If
he reveals his concerns, however, he does not unveil his completed teaching
and, according to Louis Meyer, holds back the desire to correct Descartes
or 'depart a hair's breadth from Descartes's opinion'.[69] As we know that
Spinoza was wary of his young student and refused to communicate his ideas
to him 'until he had reached greater maturity', we are confident that the
Metaphysical Thoughts should be granted only a measured authority, and be
considered more as a propaedeutic to Spinoza's own philosophy.

The New Classification of the Attributes

Even so, there is absolutely no doubt concerning the status granted to eternity, for Spinoza openly claims authorship of his analyses through Cartesian
terminology. After having separately studied each one of God's attributes,
the author of *Metaphysical Thoughts* goes on to reject the standard division
of these attributes into communicable and incommunicable ones – a division which, to him, seems 'more verbal than real'. He will present his own
classification at the end of chapter 11 of Part II: 'But we give this division.
There are some attributes of God which explain his active essence, others
which explain nothing of his action, but only his manner of existing. Unity,
eternity, necessity, etc., are of the latter sort, but intellect, will, life, omnipotence, etc., of the former. This division is sufficiently clear and distinct, and
includes all of God's attributes.'[70]

Spinoza does not completely overhaul the distinction put forth in the
Short Treatise, but he does make significant changes to it. The first kind of
attribute roughly corresponds to the second category of propria in the *Short
Treatise*, for they are both tied to divine action. The second kind, in turn,
overlaps with the first category of propria, for it includes attributes like unity,
eternity and immutability, already mentioned in the *Short Treatise*. The
author of *Metaphysical Thoughts*, however, no longer reduces the second kind
of attributes to extrinsic denominations, but instead assigns it an explicative
function in relation to the divine mode of existence.

In order to determine the significance of this change, it is important
to first of all clarify the nature of this division that, according to Spinoza,

[69] Louis Meyer, PP, Pref.; CWS I, 229.
[70] CM II, 11; CWS I, 340. [TN: translation modified. Where I put 'distinct', Curley translates 'evident'.]

accounts for all of the attributes. Following that assessment, we must locate the reasons for the apparent departure from the analyses presented in the *Short Treatise*. What does this division between properties that explain active essence and those that explain existence mean? If God's existence and God's essence are one and the same thing, how is it possible to put forth a distinction between properties that pertain to one and those that pertain to the other? Must we thereby conclude that the division is more formal that real? If the author of *Metaphysical Thoughts* attempts to dispute the nominal character of the division put forth by the scholastics, it is not, in all likelihood, to then simply replace it with one that proves vulnerable to the same reproaches. To resolve the difficulty, it is necessary to make explicit in advance that Spinoza does not distinguish properties pertaining to existence from those pertaining to essence as such, but rather to *active* (*actuosa*) essence. What should we understand by this term? Spinoza is clearly alluding to divine power (*puissance*). The list of examples illustrating this category of attributes confirms this interpretation, for knowledge, will, life and omnipotence all characterise divine activity. In this sense, the division within properties corresponds to a distinction that Spinoza repeats on several occasions between existing and acting. To be is not only to exist but to act. God determines himself to exist and to act. Nevertheless, existence and action do not constitute separate or separable realities, for power (*puissance*), existence and essence designate one and the same thing. To exist, for Spinoza, is to act. Existence is this movement, this effort, which pushes being to produce effects. It is for this reason that inaction, in its stasis (*inertie*) is the lowest degree of existing. But if existence and action constitute a duo as opposed to a duality, then what can this Spinozist distinction mean?

As it turns out, attributes pertaining to existence characterise divine being insofar as it is grasped in its absolute nature, independently of either its effects or its productivity. Attributes pertaining to action express divine being insofar as it exerts its power (*puissance*) and produces an infinity of things in an infinity of modes. This distinction is actually a vestige of one that some scholastics had put forth between operative attributes and inoperative attributes.

Attributa operativa, as their name indicates, designate propria which explicate God's action and the manner in which God carries out his work. *Attributa non operativa*, by contrast, belong to the category of propria that reveal nothing of God's action, but that are meant to describe God's characteristics and mode of existence. Spinoza was not unfamiliar with this traditional classification which was in use in all the scholastic handbooks; without question, he had at least encountered it in his reading of Heereboord.

The Leyde professor, in his *Meletemata philosophica*, takes up the distinction between operative attributes, which form a pair with communicable attributes, and inoperative attributes, which roughly correspond to incommunicable attributes. Whether Spinoza was inspired by the analyses of Heereboord or Martini, as Caillois[71] claims in a note to *Metaphysical Thoughts*, it is clear that this famous 'division proper to the author'[72] does not constitute an innovation, but an inheritance. Further, the purpose of this later distinction is obviously not to overturn the earlier one, for Spinoza derives no later benefit from it. Paradoxically, he presents it after having exhausted all that he had to say concerning God's attributes before changing the subject to an examination of the human mind. 'These are the things I had decided to say about God's attributes. So far I have given no division of them.'[73] On the whole, this division was hardly necessary for understanding the analysis of divine attributes and likely responds to the pedagogic need to provide new points of reference after having quarrelled with the ancients and rejected the classical distribution of the attributes into communicable and incommunicable ones. Spinoza here plays one tradition against another, and his aim is first and foremost the elimination of a false distinction. Attributes, such as they are in God, are for Spinoza all incommunicable,[74] for 'God's knowledge agrees no more with human knowledge than the dog that is a heavenly constellation agrees with the dog that is a barking animal. And perhaps even much less.'[75]

Taking both the polemical and pedagogical purpose of the presentation of the Spinozist division of attributes into account, it is not yet safe to assume that the author of *Metaphysical Thoughts* goes back on or disavows his analyses in the *Short Treatise*, for his reflection here does not take place on the same level. Nevertheless, even though he explicitly claims that the true and the false 'are only extrinsic denominations of things',[76] he never again places eternity in that category.

---

[71] *Spinoza: Oeuvres complètes*, ed. Caillois, 293, note 3.
[72] Ibid.
[73] CM II, 11; CWS I, 340.
[74] He will later modify his analyses: Cf. *Ethics* II, 11 Cor.; CWS I, 456.
[75] CM II, 11; CWS I, 340.
[76] CM I, 6; CWS I, 312.

The Departure from the Status of Extrinsic Denomination

Must we conclude from the above that from Descartes' *Principles of Philosophy* on, Spinoza no longer considers eternity as an extrinsic denomination? His silence on this subject does not allow us to settle the question with full certainty; it does, however, highlight the insufficiency of such a designation, as it is true that eternity and the other properties cannot purely and simply be reduced to extrinsic denominations. It would be impossible to attribute them to God if he did not possess in himself internal characteristics justifying these qualifiers. For an extrinsic denomination to not be an outright being of reason or reducible to a mere rhetorical effect, it must be based on an intrinsic denomination.

It is true that the hypothesis according to which eternity would be reduced to an outright extrinsic denomination is plausible, for it does not seem contradictory to admit that nothing positive distinguishes an eternal existence from a non-eternal existence. Indeed, if eternity is not an intrinsic character, it means that there is no internal mark that would allow us to distinguish an eternal existence from a mortal existence. In other words, there is nothing real or positive in divine or human existence that allows us to draw conclusions concerning their duration or their eternity: existence in general is defined as the fact of persevering in being; it is self-affirmation, not negation. From this point of view, human existence is not distinguished from divine existence. It consists in affirming a power (*puissance*). Human existence does not in itself bear the causes of its own destruction; it thus does not involve a determined duration that could be measured with certainty which would differentiate it from an eternal existence. Duration is not an intrinsic character for it does not pertain to the essence of the body.[77] Thus, we can only have an inadequate knowledge of it.[78] Must we then admit that no internal mark can allow us to discern an eternal existence from a durational existence? Such an admission would amount to forgetting an essential, distinctive, intrinsic criterion: the nature of the cause that produces them. If a being is the cause of itself, its essence necessarily involves existence. In other words, it cannot be known otherwise than existing.[79] By contrast, if a being is not the cause of itself, its essence does not involve necessary existence. The latter thus depends on the common order of nature according to which 'it can happen equally that this or that man does exist, or that he

---

[77] *Ethics* II, 30; CWS I, 471.
[78] Ibid.
[79] *Ethics* I, Def. 1; CWS I, 408.

does not exist'.[80] Consequently, eternity is only attributed to God following a comparison between an infinite existence and a finite existence, leading to a distinction between what endures and what is unfamiliar with duration. Eternity is applied to God in accordance with an internal character, namely, the necessity of God's existence. The *causa sui* is thus an intrinsic denomination that corresponds to eternity.

It is thus absolutely possible that Spinoza abandons extrinsic denominations for the same reasons as those pronounced by Leibniz in the *New Essays on Human Understanding*.[81] Throughout the dialogue concerning the notion of relation, Theophilus observes to Philathetes that, in all metaphysical rigour, 'there is no entirely external denomination (*denominatio pure extrinseca*) because of the real connection of all things'.[82] For Leibniz, the distinction between beings cannot rest on mere extrinsic denominations; it must be based on internal characteristics. 'Every substantial thing, from the soul to the body, has its relation with every other thing, which is proper to it, and the one must differ from the others by intrinsic denominations.'[83] What matters here in the Leibnizian system can be very well applied to the Spinozist philosophy of immanence in which the idea of an entirely extrinsic denomination cannot be conceived in a perfectly adequate manner. There can be no absolute exteriority because of the necessary connection between things. Since eternity cannot be strictly reduced to an extrinsic denomination, we must either do away with this designation in its tendency to lead to confusion or find an analogous distinction to that which is established in the *Ethics* between the true and the adequate in order to express God's eternity considered absolutely in an intrinsic manner and God's eternity considered relatively in an extrinsic manner. Spinoza opts in favour of the first solution, for the second not only seems useless, but scarcely conforms to his later doctrine. Further, if eternity also applies to minds, then there is no reason to bring the distinction between intrinsic and extrinsic denominations into play, since eternity becomes a property common to the part and the whole, linked by an internal and immanent necessity.

---

[80] *Ethics* II, Ax. 1; *CWS* I, 447.
[81] Leibniz, *New Essays*, Book II, Chapter 25.
[82] Ibid.
[83] Leibniz, *New Essays*, Book II, Chapters 1 and 2.

The Ontological Status of Eternity in the *Ethics*

The Upshot

By no longer presenting eternity under the form of an extrinsic denomination, *Metaphysical Thoughts* undeniably marks a turning point. But it only
constitutes a preparatory step toward the Spinozist doctrine. For this reason,
it is necessary to identify both the main takeaways of and the later changes
made to the status of eternity. At first glance, the *Ethics* does outline a
change, for there is no longer any trace of the division of divine propria or
attributes in the Cartesian sense of the term. Should we consider this abandonment as a rupture or a readjustment in relation to the earlier analyses? In
truth, Spinoza does not undertake a radical reworking of the earlier theory.
We must first of all note that the division of the attributes in *Metaphysical
Thoughts* never took the form of a genuine dichotomy or a strict disjunction.
The second type of attributes, which include, for instance, unity, eternity
and necessity, not only serves to qualify the existence of God, but can also
be applied to God's active essence, even the whole set of the first type of
attributes, for causality, will, life and omnipotence, which belong to the
first type of attributes, can also be called necessary, eternal and infinite.
The spheres of extension of the two categories overlap, and such potential
overlap thwarts the attempt to devise a perfectly settled distinction. Spinoza
himself implicitly recognises this fact since he takes care to specify that his
'division is sufficiently clear and evident',[84] thereby suggesting that it is not
perfect, and can thus be improved.

In the *Ethics*, he does not reject this classification. Rather, he implicitly
takes it up without marking a clear and distinct separation between the
two types. When he analyses God's properties in Part I, he reproduces the
earlier division of the attributes faithfully enough, for he dedicates himself
to an examination of necessary existence, unity, indivisibility, infinity and
eternity one after the other and finishes his inventory by studying how God
predetermines and directs all things. It is thus possible to discern, within
this enumeration, attributes that pertain to existence, on the one hand, and
actions, on the other. The change in relation to *Metaphysical Thoughts* thus
turns out to be minimal, and the abandonment of a settled distinction can
be explained not only by the exigencies proper to a monist philosophy, but
also by the inadequacy of a distribution that would arrange attributes into
discrete groups. Is not every attempt to classify divine propria a confused

[84] CM II, 11; CWS I, 340.

product of a mind that imagines, for the sake of mere convenience, the existence of an order in things?

Not only is *Metaphysical Thoughts* not fundamentally called into question on this point, despite the absence of a marked division in the *Ethics*, it actually lays an essential foundation for the constitution of the Spinozist doctrine of eternity. The modification in the ordering of attributes in relation to the *Short Treatise* makes eternity appear as a property which explains God's mode of existence. Eternity can, of course, be applied to essence and power (*puissance*), since these terms designate one and the same thing, but its application to existence is something on which Spinoza will not go back. All his correspondences testify to this observation. In his response to Louis Meyer,[85] Spinoza claims that eternity is the prerogative of the existence of substance, and distinguishes it from duration, which is characteristic of the existence of modes. In order to demonstrate to Hudde that there is only a single being which persists by and through its own sufficiency, he lists properties that a being must have in order for that being to involve necessary existence: eternity, simplicity, infinity and indivisibility.[86] Finally, definition 8 of *Ethics* I clearly ties eternity to necessary existence: 'By eternity, I understand existence itself, insofar as it is conceived to follow necessarily from the definition alone of the eternal thing.'[87] But does this mean that Spinoza restricts the field of application of this concept of eternity? Does this mean he limits the term to describing necessary existence? Must we conclude that, unlike the *Short Treatise* – where eternity is a proprium that belongs to all substantial attributes – it becomes an inappropriate term from the moment it is limited to describing a modality of existence?

In order to avoid hasty conclusions, we must note that, paradoxically, it is the application of the concept of eternity to existence that is problematic, for we typically take it for granted that every essence is an eternal truth and that existence is inscribed in duration. The attribution of eternity to an existence is seen as an exception. If eternity is a property of the existence of substance, it is precisely because in substance, existence is not distinguished from essence. The crux of the demonstration of God's eternity in *Metaphysical Thoughts*[88] rests precisely on the principle of identity between essence and existence as well as showing the absurdity of attributing a duration to God, which would needlessly introduce a distinction where there is

[85] *Ep.* XII [to Louis Meyer]; CWS I, 200–6.
[86] *Ep.* XXXV [to Hudde]; CWS II, 26–8.
[87] *Ethics* I, Def. 8; CWS I, 409.
[88] CM II, 1; CWS I, 315–18.

none. 'Duration is an affection of existence, and not of the essence of things. But since God's existence is of his essence, we can attribute no duration to him.'[89] As a result, the affiliation of eternity with necessary existence must not be understood as a narrowing of this concept's field of application, but, on the contrary, as an extension of a property characteristic of divine essence to an existence that is not distinguished from it.

On this point, Spinoza agrees with Suarez who maintained that eternity without existence could neither be conceived nor imagined by the mind.[90] For the author of the *Disputationes Metaphysicae*, eternity expresses the necessity of God's existence and the identity of God's essence and existence.[91] We must nevertheless remind ourselves that Spinoza probably does not inherit this position directly from Suarez, for the idea according to which eternity is tied to a necessary existence is held widely enough among medieval thinkers.

From Proprium to Property

The significance of the terminological change mentioned above remains to be determined: in the *Ethics*, eternity is no longer defined as a proprium, but as a property of necessary existence. Does this constitute a mere change in vocabulary or a profound transformation of its status? To answer this question, we must examine the nature of what Spinoza calls *proprietas*. Properties are necessary consequences deduced from the essence of a thing and really contained in it. The demonstration of proposition 16 of *Ethics* I proves this beyond any reasonable doubt: 'the intellect infers from the given definition of any thing a number of properties (*proprietates*) that really do follow necessarily from it (i.e., from the very essence of the thing)'.[92] Properties should not be confused with the essence of the thing. In this regard, let us recall Spinoza's word of caution when he gives the criteria of a perfect definition.[93]

Properties are not for all that reducible to mere logical consequences; they should be conceived as real effects. In this same proposition, 16, Spinoza establishes a relation between the degree of reality of a thing and the number of its properties. '[The intellect] infers more properties the more the defini-

---

[89] CM II, 1; CWS I, 316.
[90] Suarez, *Disputationes Metaphysicae*, XVII, 431, 2. 'Aeternitas sine existentia nec mente concipi, nec fingi potest.'
[91] Suarez, *Disputationes Metaphysicae*, L, Section 3.
[92] *Ethics* I, 16 Dem.; CWS I, 425.
[93] *TdIE*, 95; CWS I, 39.

THE ONTOLOGICAL STATUS OF ETERNITY

tion of the thing expresses reality, i.e., the more reality the essence of the defined thing involves.' While the reality of propria in the *Short Treatise* remained problematic, insofar as they were presented as adjectives appended to a substantive, that of *proprietas* is undeniable. Properties are real beings and not mere predicates. If this were not the case, then the proportionality between the quantity of the reality of a thing and the number of its properties would become incomprehensible.

Ultimately, the substitution of the term *proprietas* for the term *proprium* becomes perfectly understandable. A *proprium*, even though it is not a being of reason, can still be suspected of being one, particularly when it is viewed as an extrinsic denomination. A property, by contrast, is never an extrinsic denomination; it expresses an intrinsic character. It belongs to an object not relatively, but absolutely. While a *proprium* is like an adjective, a property is like a substantive which can in turn receive qualifying terms itself. This analogy allows us to understand that eternity is a property capable of having many modalities depending on whether it is applied to substance, infinite modes or finite modes.

The Consequences of the Determination of the Ontological Status of Eternity

What conclusions and what lessons can be drawn from the discovery of eternity's essence? Determining its exact nature has crucial repercussions for the interpretation and translation of the mysterious phrase *sub specie aeternitatis*. If eternity is not a proprium, but a property endowed with an actual reality outside of the intellect, it cannot be reduced to a mere aspect or point of view. These considerations allow us to reject translations of the phrase *sub specie aeternitatis* that would reduce eternity to a pure appearance or subjective apprehension.

If eternity is a real property, it goes without saying that it is not a genus divisible into species because, for Spinoza, genera are mere modes of thinking by which we retain things. At least, this is how he characterises them in a passage in *Metaphysical Thoughts* where he demonstrates that what is called a being of reason is nothing other than 'a mode of thinking, which helps us to more easily *retain, explain, and imagine* the things we have understood'.[94] He distinguishes three types of modes of thinking, those that are related most particularly to memory, those that allow us to explain things like time, number and measure, and those that depend on the imagination like

[94] CM I, 1; CWS I, 300.

extremity, end, limit and obscurity. Spinoza explicitly includes genus and species in the first category[95] and renders them auxiliaries to memory:

> That there are certain modes of thinking which help us to *retain* things more firmly and easily, and when we wish, to recall them to mind or keep them present to the mind, is sufficiently established for those who use that well-known rule of Memory, by which to *retain* something very new and imprint it on the memory, we recall something else familiar to us, which agrees with it, either in name or in reality. Similarly, the Philosophers have reduced all natural things to certain classes, to which they recur when anything new presents itself to them. These they call *genus*, species, etc.[96]

These modes of thinking help lead the unknown back into the known and place a new natural thing in a determined class in order to be able to better retain and imprint it in memory. That does not imply that genus and species are mere mnemonic devices with no connection to reality. Spinoza indeed specifies that the way in which we memorise a new thing rests on a simultaneously nominal and real adequation with some other thing that is already familiar to us; he does not intend to disqualify these modes of thought which strengthen memory and introduce order into the confusion of sensible perceptions. Rather, he considers them to be just as useless as common logic and philosophy when it comes to exercising the intellect.[97]

Eternity is neither a genus nor a species, and this for two reasons. First, as a property, it cannot be reduced to a mere mode of thinking. Second, it cannot serve to strengthen memory, for the perception of the eternal character of a thing is in no way linked to duration and does not reinforce memory, but the intellect. From this point of view, if eternity were a logical category, it would not fulfil the mnemonic function attributed to common logic and philosophy. It would be in the service of a timeless logic of the intellect. With these observations, we can conclude that it is illegitimate to translate the term *species* with species (*espèce*) and that we must dismiss all interpretations that go along with such an opinion.

Nor can eternity be reduced to a category of the intellect. For this reason, we cannot fully subscribe to the translation of the expression *sub specie aeternitatis* by the phrase 'under the category of eternity (*sous la catégorie de l'éter-*

---

[95] Ibid.
[96] Ibid.
[97] CM, I, Prologue; CWS I, 299.

nité)'.[98] The term category does not appear in the Spinozist glossary and remains marred with connotations foreign to the thought of the author of the *Ethics*. Only one of the following things can be true: either categories are mere modes of thinking, or else they express a real division (*subdivision*) of Being. In the first case, they would refer to the operation of an intellect that apprehends Being by creating tools of thought. From this point of view, the term category would be better suited for time than eternity, the latter being irreducible as a property to a mere mode of thinking. In the second case, categories would be stripped of their instrumental function and stop being pure operational concepts in order to instead express real ontological distinctions. Still, eternity could not be placed in this grouping. Outside of substance and modes, Spinoza does not allow for any other division of Being; he rejects the division of being into real Being and Being of reason, substituting for such a division one that distinguishes Being whose essence necessarily includes existence and Being whose essence only includes possible existence.[99] The necessary and the possible could, if pushed, be assimilated to ontological categories, though the second concept expresses more of a deficiency (*défaut*) in our knowledge than a reality [TN: in some external thing]. Only substance and modes express a real division of Being and could be called categories. It is true that we could read the distinction put forth in *Metaphysical Thoughts* as a division between eternal and non-eternal Being and thereby consider eternity as an ontological category equivalent to that of necessary existence. The same classification in the *Ethics*, however, becomes extremely dubious, for eternity seems to concern all beings, and no longer fits the contours of ontological distinctions as closely. It is thus absolutely necessary to analyse the scope of the concept in order to better discern its underlying nature and its status as a property.

---

[98] Cf. Brunschvicg whose translation is taken up by Pierre-François Moreau.
[99] CM I, 1; CWS I, 299.

2

Eternity, Coeternity and Aeviternity: The Status of Infinite Beings

Eternity is undeniably a property of the existence of the absolutely infinite substance. Does this mean that it exclusively belongs to divinity? Whatever the case may be, if it belongs to God because its essence involves existence, it seems inappropriate to attribute this quality to a being whose essence only involves possible existence. It is for this reason, incidentally, that Spinoza puts forth a distinction between duration and eternity. 'From our earlier division of being into being whose essence involves existence and being whose essence involves only possible existence, there arises the distinction between eternity and duration.'[1] Strictly speaking, eternity is the prerogative of substance and is deduced from the necessary character of its existence. At the same time, 'created things', according to the terminology of *Metaphysical Thoughts*, are said to endure and not go on forever (*s'éterniser*). They cannot, strictly speaking, be called eternal. Spinoza is very clear on this point. 'Infinite actual existence pertains to God in the same way as infinite actual intellect pertains to him. And I call this infinite existence *Eternity*, which is to be attributed to God alone, and not to any created thing, even though its duration should be without beginning or end.'[2] How, then, can he affirm the eternity of the human mind in the *Ethics*? Does this constitute a shortcoming in the vocabulary, as an observation in *Metaphysical Thoughts* would suggest? 'We are accustomed, on account of a defect of words, to ascribe eternity also to things whose essence is distinguished from their existence, as when we say that it does not involve a contradiction for the world to have existed from eternity; also we attribute eternity to the essences of things so long as we conceive the things as not existing, for then we call

[1] CM I, 4; CWS I, 310.
[2] CM II, 1; CWS I, 318.

them eternal.'[3] Or is it rather a change in perspective, as the development in vocabulary would suggest? Keeping with his principles, Spinoza reserves the term eternity for God and attempts to demonstrate the mind's immortality.[4] Yet, in the *Ethics*, he will no longer speak of the mind's immortality, but rather of its eternity. Must we then interpret this change as a misuse of language or as the definition of a real eternity? To put it differently, and to put it in terms of a distinction that Spinoza rejects, is eternity a communicable or incommunicable attribute? Must we take God's eternity to have no more relation with human eternity 'than the dog that is a heavenly constellation' does with 'the dog that is a barking animal', or can we indeed say that it must be a property applicable to substance and modes in the same sense?

To be able to resolve this difficulty, it is necessary to analyse the very nature of eternity as well as the forms that it takes on in accordance with whether it is applied to substance, its attributes, infinite modes or finite modes.

The Eternity of Attributes

If substance is eternal by virtue of the necessity of its existence, it goes without saying that its attributes are also eternal since they must involve everything that pertains to it. This is what issues from proposition 19 of *Ethics* I where Spinoza establishes that 'God is eternal, or all God's attributes are eternal',[5] based on their respective definitions. The demonstrative form of the proposition, however, does not imply that the eternity of attributes is an eternity deduced and derived from substance. The equivalence posited in the proposition between God and all the attributes should be enough to ward off such an error. The eternity of substance neither precedes nor proceeds from that of the attributes. As each attribute is conceived in itself and through itself, it could not have been produced by something other; it thereby involves necessary existence. In this sense, substance and its attributes are coeternal.

Eternity and Coeternity

The idea of a coeternity, despite its apparently adequate character, is still met with reservations. It rightly stresses the simultaneity of the eternity

[3] CM II, 1; CWS I, 317.
[4] CM II, 2; CWS I, 318–19.
[5] *Ethics* I, 19; CWS I, 428.

of God and God's attributes by dismissing the possibility (*l'éventualité*) of some genesis or derivation, but it risks masking their unity and solidarity. Originally, the concept of coeternity was used to designate the mode of existence of the demiurge and the uncreated, chaotic matter to which the former gives form. It thus pertained to two separate realities, initially independent of one other, and implied a relative exteriority. Now, even if an attribute is conceived in itself and through itself, it is not for all that independent of substance. To be distinctly conceivable does not mean to exist separately. The idea of coeternity bears with it an inadequate component insofar as it obscures the necessary link between every attribute united in one and the same substance. It thereby fosters the belief that substance is a composite aggregate and that the attributes are simply juxtaposed in an absolute indifference and exteriority. For this reason, it is better to proscribe this inappropriate designation and instead follow the Spinozist prescriptions such as they implicitly appear in an excerpt from *Metaphysical Thoughts* where the idea of coeternity is explicitly connected to that of independence and seems consequently incompatible with a philosophy of immanence. Spinoza adamantly maintains that 'there is not something outside God, and coeternal with him'.[6] For this same reason, if everything that is is in God and needs God's support in order to exist, it becomes useless to 'waste time in refuting the opinion of those who have set up the world, or chaos, or matter devoid of all form, as coeternal with God, and therefore independent of him'.[7] To be sure, the formulation of this proposition does not categorically rule out the possibility that there are things that are themselves coeternal *in* God, but we must then take care to strip this concept of any and all separatist connotations. It is thus not surprising to note that this term does not appear under the pen of the author of the *Ethics*, for he refrains from resorting to expressions or phrases that would call into question the unity and simplicity of substance. In this respect, it is interesting to analyse how Spinoza demonstrates the eternity of the attributes in proposition 19 of *Ethics* I. He could have directly established this property by basing it on proposition 10, which claims that each attribute of a substance must be conceived through itself, but he instead opts to base it on definition 4, thereby showing that the eternity of an attribute stems (*découle*) from its vocation of expressing the nature of substance. In this way, he is able to avoid either feeding erroneous interpretations or jeopardising the theory of substance's unity by presenting the eternity of the attribute in an independent manner, for if attributes are

[6] CM II, 10; *CWS* I, 335.
[7] CM II, 10; *CWS* I, 336.

conceived as really distinct, it is tempting to thereby conclude that they constitute different beings, or, in other words, different substances. Spinoza needed an entire scholium[8] to refute this idea; he will thus not take the risk of reawakening this prejudice and instead chooses a formulation that reinforces the cohesion and solidarity between substance and its attributes. For this reason, he simultaneously posits that 'God, or all of God's attributes, are eternal'. Spinoza abandons the assimilation of attributes to substances,[9] which came up on several occasions in the *Short Treatise*, for similar reasons, and the decision can be explained by a desire to clear away any ambiguity. In the end, there is no need to mark a difference between the eternity of substance and that of its attributes, for they are of the same nature. The concept of coeternity cannot therefore be invoked to substantiate the thesis of the existence of difference species of eternity.

Absolute Eternity and Eternity in Its Kind

Still, this conclusion seems to be countered by the clarification that Spinoza makes in his letter to Hudde where he attempts to explain to his correspondent why 'there could not be many beings, existing through themselves, but differing in nature'.[10] Hudde calls into question the theory of a unique substance and asserts that thought and extension are different and yet can subsist through their own sufficiency. Spinoza then replies that if we grant necessary existence to a being that is indeterminate and perfect in its kind, then we must also attribute necessary existence to an absolutely indeterminate and perfect being. Consequently, if extension and thought exist in a self-sufficient manner, then there is even more reason for a being containing every perfection to exist through its own power. Now, complete perfection, by definition, leaves nothing to be accomplished outside of itself. It is not compatible with the autonomous existence of absolute realities but must instead include everything. To this end, extension and thought must belong to it and it becomes clear that there can only be one unique and necessary being.

To establish his theory, Spinoza puts forth a distinction between a being perfect in its kind, like an attribute, and an absolutely perfect being. Given this distinction, it must be admitted that extension, for example, is not

---

[8] *Ethics* I, 10 Schol.; CWS I, 416.

[9] *KV* I, 2, 17, note 6; 7, 1, note 1; CWS I, 60; 88: 'Regarding the attributes of which God consists, they are nothing but infinite substances . . .'.

[10] *Ep.* XXXVI [to Johannes Hudde]; CWS II, 30.

absolutely eternal and that this property is, strictly speaking, only appropriate for a necessary and perfect being. Extension is perfect in its kind, not
absolutely perfect; it acknowledges the existence of other perfections like
thought and thus does not express every perfection. It is consequently only
indeterminate and eternal from a certain perspective.

It cannot exist self-sufficiently, but must belong to God or be something
that in a certain way expresses God's nature; it does not have necessary existence absolutely, for it cannot strictly speaking exist in a distinct manner outside of God. If it did exist outside of God, 'one and the same Nature which
involves necessary existence would exist in two forms'.[11] Since God includes
every perfection, it also includes extension. For this reason, if extension
implies existence, it is not for all that absolutely eternal, for it could not exist
necessarily in and through itself outside of God. In the same manner, it can
no more be considered as absolutely indeterminate, for its nature consists in
a certain kind of being and not in being as a whole; it is only indeterminate
in relation to itself, for it could not tolerate internal limitation without
contradiction. Ultimately, extension is only eternal and indeterminate in
its kind – not absolutely. It is thus exclusively from the point of view of a
certain kind of being and not from the point of view of the infinite whole of
being that extension is eternal.

Must we conclude from this observation that there are several distinct
forms of eternity, one absolute and substantial, the others relative and
proper to each attribute? Should we infinitely multiply the forms of eternity,
recognising as many of these forms as there are kinds of beings and different
attributes? If that's the case, what relations do these diverse forms of eternity
have with that of substance, on the one hand, and with each other, on the
other? Lastly, should we understand eternity in its kind as a degenerated and
fallen eternity in relation to the absolute perfection of that of substance?
The stakes of these questions are huge, for if it proves possible to study distinct types of eternity, it would cast a new light on the interpretation and
translation of the infamous phrase *sub specie aeternitatis*.

To resolve this difficulty, we must first pay attention to elementary lexical
considerations. While Spinoza explicitly distinguishes two types of infinity
(infinity in its kind and absolute infinity), not once does he use the expression 'eternal in its kind' in his system. This does not necessarily imply that
such a designation be forbidden due to some fundamental incompatibility.
Still, we should be clear that we cannot make us of the *corpus* to justify it. No
more does Spinoza use the term *species* in relation to the eternity of attrib-

[11] *Ep.* XXXV [Johannes Hudde]; CWS II, 28.

utes, for the phrase *sub specie aeternitatis* is only used to characterise a type of knowledge or conception and not a kind of being or reality. Additionally, an eternity in its kind is not a fallen or lessened figure of absolute eternity. To think so would be to commit the same error as that which consists in believing that extension is imperfect and incomplete because it does not think, for it is only in relation to its nature that extension can know (*connaître*) privation. It is for this very reason that Spinoza takes care to specify that the evaluation of perfection and determination of a being can only be carried out from the point of view of that type of being. We thus cannot claim that extension is imperfect because it does not think; it cannot lack thought, for thought does not belong to its nature. The absence of thought does not constitute a privation or a lack that would sully its essence.[12] In the same manner, it is only in relation to the kind of being to which it is applied that the quality of eternity can be gauged. From this perspective, the eternity of extension is as perfect as it can be and there is therefore no essential difference in relation to that of substance, for it fulfils the same criteria. Just like substance, extension possesses an essence that involves its existence; it is the cause of itself and it is neither engendered nor determined by another attribute. Nothing limits it, just as nothing threatens its necessary existence. We must then recognise that there is no need to establish a real distinction between the eternity of substance and that of attributes. It is likely for this reason that Spinoza did not deem it necessary to apply the distinction he had developed for the concept of infinity – that is, the distinction between the absolute (*absolute*) and in its kind (*in suo genere*) – to the concept of eternity.

The Eternity of Infinite Modes

If the eternity of *natura naturans* is self-evident, that of *natura naturata* remains, by contrast, problematic – for it inescapably appears to be derived, whether immediately or mediately. The demonstrations of propositions 21 and 22 from *Ethics* I clearly articulate this point: the eternity of immediate infinite modes is a consequence of the eternity of the attributes to which

[12] Cf. the demonstration carried out by Spinoza in *Ep.* XXXVI: 'if the term extension involves necessary existence, it will be as impossible to conceive extension without existence as it is to conceive extension without extension. And if this is maintained, it will also be impossible to conceive a limited extension. For if it were conceived to be limited, it would have to be limited by its own nature, namely, by extension. And this extension by which it was limited would have to be conceived under the negation of existence. But by hypothesis, this is a manifest contradiction.' *Ep.* XXXVI [to Johannes Hudde]; *CWS* II, 29.

they necessarily belong and serves as a relay for ensuring the eternity of mediate infinite modes. Spinoza seems to be aware of the difficulty, for he takes time to establish the eternity of God and its attributes in proposition 19 even though it seemed to have already been proven by proposition 7, as he himself recalls during the demonstration. If 'it pertains to the nature of a substance to exist',[13] it follows that substance is eternal by definition. Why, then, deploy an arsenal of supplementary proofs if not to firmly establish the foundation for the eternity of infinite modes by making their eternity rest on the absolute or modified nature of the attribute?

That basis is not, however, as firm as it initially appears, for if eternity is, strictly speaking, the property of that which exists through itself, it cannot rigorously pertain to a mode that exists through something else. Eternity can only be attributed to it in a derived manner, that is, as an effect of a necessary cause. Martial Gueroult makes precisely this claim. Eternity is here no longer 'the absolute necessity of existing through itself, but only the necessity of existing through another'.[14] As such, Gueroult concludes that this borrowed eternity is not a genuine one. 'It is, at most, perpetuity or sempiternity'; 'it is *aevum* rather than *aeternum*'.[15] Can we still maintain that infinite modes are really eternal, or are we rather dealing with derived and degraded forms of eternity which involve the appearance of durational characteristics? Should we subscribe to Gueroult's claims, deeming it better to speak of *aevum* as opposed to *aeternum* and replacing the concept of eternity with that of aeviternity? If we want to determine whether or not such a denomination can be legitimately applied to modes, we must analyse the nature of the concept *aevum*, specifying its essential properties.

The Nature of Aevum

Historically, the term *aevum* was used as a synonym for the Greek *aiôn*, whose meaning is itself problematic. *Aiôn*, according to Homer, is synonymous with life. This is particularly emphasised in verse 453, Book XVI of the *Iliad*, when Hera tries to persuade Zeus to abandon his son Sarpedon to the murderous hands of Patroclus and 'as soon as the life has gone out of him, send Death and sweet Sleep to bear him off the field and take him to the broad lands of Lycia, where his brothers and his kinsmen will bury him

---

[13] *Ethics* I, 7; CWS I, 412.
[14] Gueroult 1968: 309.
[15] Ibid.

with mound and pillar, in due honour to the dead'.[16] In Herodotus, it more exactly designates the course of a life, or what delimits the time of each being's life.[17] Even so, the semantic contours of the term remain rather fuzzy, for the word also takes on the sense of eternity. For example, Plato uses the term *aiôn* in the *Timaeus* when he defines time as 'the moving image of eternity'. Plotinus will be even more explicit on this point, for he distinguishes the adjective *aiônios* from the adjective *aïdios*, equating the first with the eternal and the second with the perpetual (*perpétuel*), or sempiternal.[18] *Aïdios* is the qualifier generally applied to gods to designate the fact that they always exist (*sont toujours*) and to characterise their immortality. It is thus strange that *aevum* is historically associated with *aiôn*, for if translators had followed Plotinus' view logically, they would not have established an equivalence between *aiôn* and *aevum*, but rather between *aiôn* and *aeternum*, on one hand, and *aïdios* and *aevum* on the other. This apparent aberration can, in truth, be explained by the fact that the conceptual distinctions between the two Greek terms are not so clear cut. Aristotle, for example, generally applies the word *aiônios* to God and the intellect, reserving the word *aïdios* for the sky and other celestial bodies,[19] but he occasionally assimilates them, claiming that God's life is both eternal and everlasting (*perpétuelle*).[20]

In the Latin language, *aevum* takes on the same meanings as those that have been imputed to *aiôn* and shares with it the same ambiguities. The term designates life and the course of a life, notably in Lucretius[21] and Ovid.[22] When accompanied by the appropriate adjectives, it can also convey the idea of eternity. Lucretius, for example, uses the expression '*immortali aeuo*' in relation to gods who enjoy immortality. There too, the conceptual borders are not marked clearly and it is only with Boethius and Saint Thomas that *aevum* eventually takes on its own rigorous meaning, distinct from both time and eternity.

Philosophers generally agree in recognising *aevum* as an intermediary between eternity and time, but they diverge from one another when it comes to spelling out its distinguishing properties. If we follow Saint Thomas:

---

[16] Homer, *Iliad*, XVI, 453 [TN: The French translation of the text cited by Jaquet reads: 'd'envoyer la mort et le sommeil profond le porter jusqu'à la vaste Lycie, quand l'auront quitté l'âme et la vie'.]

[17] Herodotus, *History* I, 32.

[18] Plotinus, *Enneads* III, 7, 3.

[19] Cf. Aristotle, *Metaphysics*, 1075a10 and 1050b.

[20] Cf. Aristotle, *Metaphysics*, 1072b29.

[21] Lucretius, *De Natura Rerum*, II, 16.

[22] Ovid, *Metamorphoses*, XII, 208.

'Aeviternity differs from time, and from eternity, as the mean between them both.'[23] The nature of the differences between the three concepts nonetheless remains problematic, so much so that some thinkers end up assimilating *aevum* to time. This is, for that matter, the reason why the author of the *Summa Theologicae* dedicates an article to the examination of 'the difference of aeviternity and time'.[24] Aquinas proposes three major categories of possible distinctions before going on to reject two of them.

The first includes thinkers who maintain that 'eternity has neither beginning nor end; aevum has a beginning and no end; time has a beginning and an end'.[25] This definition cannot help clarify the nature of the temporality of Spinozist modes for two reasons. The difference between the three concepts is not sufficiently established, for it is not essential but rather accidental. As Saint Thomas observes, if time had neither beginning nor end, it would not be for all that eternal, but sempiternal; on this subject, Aquinas recalls the distinction put forth by Boethius in his *Consolation of Philosophy*:

> Some have founded this difference on the fact that eternity has neither beginning nor an end; whereas time has a beginning and an end. This, however, makes a merely accidental, and not an absolute difference because, granted that time always was and always will be, according to the idea of those who think the movement of the heavens goes on forever, there would yet remain a difference between eternity and time, as Boethius says (*De Consol.* V), arising from the fact that eternity is simultaneously whole; which cannot be applied to time: for eternity is the measure of a permanent being; while time is the measure of movement.[26]

Aquinas puts forth exactly the same argument in relation to *aevum* in article 5 of question 10. If *aevum* did not have a beginning or, on the contrary, if it did have an end, it would nonetheless still be differentiated from eternity and time insofar as it remains suitable neither for a permanent being nor for a being in motion.

Even if the distinguishing criteria at hand proved sufficient, it is obvious that such a conception of *aevum* is incompatible with a Spinozist perspective insofar as infinite modes do not begin to be; they are posited at the same time as substance and do not have the status of creatures.

---

[23] Aquinas, *Summa Theologicae* I, Quest. 10, art. 5.
[24] Ibid.
[25] Ibid.
[26] Ibid., art. 4.

More attentive to rigour, some philosophers refashion the definition by specifying that eternity allows for neither a before nor an after; time, a before and an after, inclusive of a beginning and an ageing process; and *aevum*, a before and after without beginning or aging. This position is hardly more satisfying, for it is contradictory. Aquinas denounces the incoherence of this delineation, for it is clear that the before and the after cannot be simultaneous and necessarily imply a chronological interval. If *aevum* contains a before and an after, then when one disappears, the other is on the horizon as something new and 'thus there would be a beginning in *aevum* as well as in time'.[27] It might be possible to bypass this difficulty by stressing the relative character of beginnings and by showing that they are just as well ends in accordance with the frame of reference in which one is placed. In the absolute sense, *aevum* would have neither beginning nor end and would pertain to a duration unlimited in both directions. This definition would better agree with the Spinozist conception than the preceding one, but it causes a new difficulty to arise. If *aevum* were the form of temporality proper to infinite modes, in what sense could they be called eternal? It is indeed out of the question for Spinoza to assimilate eternity to a duration unlimited in both directions. If one were to doubt this claim, it would be sufficient to refer to the explanation of definition 8 from *Ethics* I which formally rules out such an interpretation. One of two things must be the case: either Spinoza is incoherent in speaking of eternity in relation to modes, or else *aevum* thus understood cannot adequately be applied to modes. In any case, this second definition runs up against the same objections as the first, for it rests only on accidental characteristics and does not provide us with the essence of *aevum* itself.

The Thomist Model

To discern the very nature of *aevum*, we must comprehend the respective nature and causes of eternity and time and subsequently determine the status of this intermediary category. Aquinas attempts to do exactly this by showing, first, that the eternity of a being is the consequence of its immutability. In what is without motion, we cannot distinguish between a before and an after. Eternity thus proves to be the measure of permanence (*permanence*) and is applicable to God alone. Aquinas indeed specifies that the term measure does not imply the existence of a standard that we could apply to God, for infinite being is by nature incommensurable: 'Eternity is nothing else but God Himself. Hence God is not called eternal, as if He were in any

---

[27] Ibid., art. 5.

way measured; but the idea of measurement is here taken according to the apprehension of our mind alone.'[28] As soon as there is motion, by contrast, it becomes necessary to introduce a measure that assesses change. Time thus constitutes the measure of motion and allows for some beginning and some end, a before and an after. It is the property (*propre*) of changing and corruptible beings.

Aevum is a middle between the two that measures that by which a thing deviates from permanence in being without for all that changing. The difference between the three categories can be summarised in the following manner: time is the measure of motion in accordance with a before and an after; eternity is the measure of absolutely motionless beings and does not allow for a before and an after in any way whatsoever; *aevum* is the measure of beings that do not substantially change but are nonetheless subject to potential or actual motion and that therefore reconcile immutability with some sort of mobility. *Aevum* does not in itself contain a before and an after but neither is it incompatible with either of them. What kind of beings, then, stray from permanence without for all that becoming corruptible like corporeal things? Aquinas provides two series of examples of beings measured by *aevum*: celestial bodies and angels.

Celestial bodies fulfil the necessary conditions for being declared aeviternal insofar as their being remains shielded from any substantial change because their form actualises all of the matter's potentiality. Matter, in fact, is not in itself in act (*en acte*), but, according to the Thomist expression, in potentiality (*puissance*) to the substantial form with which it will constitute a being. Two scenarios can thus be produced.

The first concerns the inferior bodies whose matter can, following an alteration, tolerate the privation of the substantial form that had up to that point actualised it. Under the influence of the action of an external agent, a being is susceptible to changing accidentally,[29] little by little, to the point where it ends up losing the accidents without which the form cannot be. The latter disappears and cedes its place to another form in order to make a new being appear. Thus, the previous form had not actualised all the potentiality of the matter since the latter remained in potentiality (*en puissance*) to another form. Due to this fact, inferior bodies have a limited duration and are subjected to the devastating effects of time.

There are other cases, by contrast, where the form actualises the entire matter such that the latter can no longer be in potentiality to another

---

[28] Ibid., art. 2.
[29] [TN: As opposed to substantially.]

form. This is the case for celestial bodies, which cannot consent to a new form insofar as the one that constitutes them adopts and exhausts all of the matter's potentiality. They are thus exempt from substantial change and in this way more closely approach divine immutability and eternity. We must note, however, that they do change place and make revolutions. They are thus both substantially immutable and locally mobile. Due to this fact, they cannot be called eternal. If eternity is a consequence of immutability and measures permanence, then it is compatible neither with motion nor with rest which, due to its fickle and fleeting nature, implies a reference to change and time. Celestial bodies are no more temporal, however, for they know neither generation nor corruption and preserve their integrity throughout the course of their revolutions. Privation of place should not be confused with the privation of form. They are thus aeviternal, for they conserve themselves throughout change and combine immobility and motion.

As for angels, they are also aeviternal, but for different reasons, for they are not made up of form and matter. They are intermediary spiritual creatures between God and corporeal creatures. Aquinas accepts their existence and justifies it in the name of the exigencies of the perfection of creation. For this, he bases himself on the principle according to which the end of creation, which is the good, is realised when creatures are integrated with God. Now, an effect is perfectly similar to the cause only if it imitates the principal agent within it. Since God creates through his intelligence and will, there must be creatures which perfectly reflect his act. Only purely intellectual creatures are capable of divinely imitating an act of intellection. Such an act cannot be accomplished by a body. The perfection of the universe thus demands that angelic creatures exist.

Angels combine immutability and change. They are incorruptible by virtue of their immateriality. Indeed, all corruption stems from a separation between form and matter. Angels are pure subsisting forms. Besides this form, there is no other potentiality (*puissance*) in them that would be susceptible to change. Angelic creatures thus remain stable. To prove this fact, Aquinas draws a comparison between the pure geometric form of a circle and a bronze ring: 'Roundness can never be taken from the circle, because it belongs to it of itself; but a bronze circle can lose roundness, if the bronze be deprived of its circular shape.'[30] Still, angels are not eternal. Like all creatures, they are subject to change, even if they are free from degradation (*altération*). Aquinas even attributes a double mobility to them, one concerning [final] ends and the other place.

[30] Aquinas, *Summa Theologicae*, I, Quest. 50, art. 5.

Angels are free creatures that have the possibility of choosing between good and evil. They are in potentiality in respect to their end and consequently subject to the fall. Only the grace of God delivers them from this liability and imparts them with the enjoyment (*jouissance*) of the immutability of free choice. This grace does not detract from their freedom but allows them to freely choose the good without end.

Spiritual creatures also undergo local change. It should nevertheless be specified that angels do not occupy any place, for they are not corporeal. To say that an angel is in a place simply means that its power is applied in a certain manner to that place. Spiritual substances vary with respect to place, for their finite power (*pouvoir*) cannot be exercised everywhere at the same time, unlike that of God. An angel can thus move itself locally in order to extend its power (*pouvoir*) to a place that it had not before then reached. Naturally immutable when it comes to its being, supernaturally immutable in its free choice of the good as an effect of divine grace, an angel changes with respect to place. It thus fully meets the criteria for being aeviternal. But even if angels were immobile with respect to place, they would remain aeviternal as creatures, for according to Aquinas, creatures are in a general manner 'mutable by the power of the Creator, in Whose power is their existence and non-existence'.[31]

Thomist *Aevum* and *Spinozist Eternity*

It remains to be seen if this model can be applied to Spinozist philosophy and shed light on the type of temporality that pertains to infinite modes. The aim of this comparison is not to establish a direct connection between Aquinas and Spinoza. To do so would be to perform an abrupt chronological jump with little regard for the conceptual history of *aevum* and its transformations through the Middle Ages. The choice of this comparison is not merely random, however, but responds to legitimate concerns. It is called for, in large part, by commentators who import Thomist concepts into Spinoza's work, referring explicitly to the author of the *Summa* to explain the nature of the temporality of modes. Martial Gueroult, for example, refers directly to Aquinas and question 10 when he maintains that infinite modes experience '*aevum* rather than *aeternum*'.[32] He thus invites us to conduct this analysis and weigh its significance.

---

[31] Ibid., I, Quest. 9, art. 2.
[32] Gueroult 1968: 309, note 1.

The famous commentator's approach is not arbitrary, but completely justified, for Thomist analyses greatly marked scholastic philosophy and served
as a paradigm for philosophical thought from the Counter-Reformation up
through the seventeenth century. Heereboord, with whom Spinoza was
familiar, mentions question 10 of the first part of the *Summa Theologica* by
name in his chapter dedicated to God's eternity.[33] He, too, distinguishes
among three species of temporality, attributing *aevum* to angelic creatures
for the same reasons as Aquinas. While time is the property of creatures
subjected to change, *aevum* is the prerogative of beings invariable in their
substance but variable in their accidents and affections, which is to say the
prerogative of angels.[34] For Heereboord, eternity also follows from immutability; he bases his major proof of God's eternity on a syllogism whose
premises rely on a necessary connection between the two concepts. 'What is
immutable is eternal. Or, God is immutable.'[35]

Aquinas shares with Boethius the merit of having created and clarified
the concept of *aevum* and, in this respect, proves to be an obligatory source
and reference. Nothing allows us to confirm that Spinoza spent much time
with question 10 of the first part of the *Summa*. He could very well have
had a second-hand familiarity with it, however, thanks to his reading of
Heereboord. It is for these main reasons that a comparison between the two
authors seems pertinent despite the chronological gap.

To this end, we must first of all note that the Thomist distinction between
various forms of temporality rests on a principle according to which eternity is the measure of permanence and is deduced from immutability. For
Spinoza, however, eternity is absolutely not presented as a measure, but as
a property (*propre*) inseparable from divine existence. Still, the divergence
with Aquinas is not very sharp on this point. Aquinas had highlighted the
inadequate character of the use of the term 'measure', in a quantitative
sense, in relation to God and specified that 'eternity is nothing else but
God Himself'.[36] Spinoza, by contrast, does not conceive eternity as a consequence of immutability and actually disentangles the two properties (*pro-
priétés*). In *Metaphysical Thoughts*, not only does eternity not proceed from
immutability, but it actually precedes it insofar as it is considered 'the chief

[33] Heereboord, *Meletemata, Disputationem ex philosophia selectarum vigesima-quinta. De dei
aeternitate*, thesis I, section 1, 93.

[34] Ibid.

[35] Ibid., section 6, 195: 'Quid est immutabilis est aeternus: at Deus est immutabilis
Probatur major.'

[36] Aquinas, *Summa Theologica*, I, Quest. 10, art. 2, reply 3.

attribute, which deserves consideration before all others'.[37] Immutability is examined fourth, after unity and immensity. The Letter to Hudde from 10 April 1666 confirms these analyses, since eternity is named as the first of four fundamental properties that a necessary being must possess. It is here interesting to note that immutability does not appear in this list and that it is relegated behind simplicity, infinity and indivisibility.

Eternity is thus conceived independently of immutability. It is not a consequence of the permanence of existence, but of its necessity. This shift in perspective has crucial consequences, for if eternity does not result from immutability, but from the necessity of existence, then there is no longer anything to prohibit us from applying it to modes that involve change so long as these modes necessarily follow from the attribute they modify. By separating eternity from immutability, Spinoza allows for the extension of the former to all modes, particularly infinite immediate modes, like movement and rest, and infinite mediate modes.

Even supposing that Spinozist eternity did derive from immutability, infinite immediate modes would still be eternal, for God's infinite intellect is immutable. God does not change its ideas or its decrees. Infinite immediate modes of extension experience no more change than those of thought. We must not fall into the error of thinking that modes which express movement and rest are themselves in movement or rest. As early as the *Short Treatise*, it is clear that universal *natura naturata* is eternal and immutable. On this subject, Spinoza specifies that we only know two creatures that immediately depend on God: movement, when it comes to matter, and the intellect, when it comes to thinking things: 'We say, then, that these have been from all eternity, and will remain to all eternity, immutable.'[38]

The *Ethics*, while rejecting the concept of creation, establishes in a definitive manner[39] the eternity of infinite immediate modes by showing that everything that necessarily follows from the absolute nature of an attribute of God is eternal. Thus, the idea of God in thought must necessarily exist and be immutable. If that idea did not possess those properties, it would mean that thought would cease to either have or modify the idea of God and would thus not itself be eternal and immutable. Such a scenario would be incompatible with the nature of the attribute. Infinite immediate modes thus do not belong to the category of beings that deviate from permanence

---

[37] CM II, 1; CWS I, 316. [TN: This is mistakenly cited as CM II, 7 in Jaquet's original text.]

[38] KV I, 9, 1; CWS I, 91.

[39] *Ethics* I, 21; CWS I, 429.

in order to allow for a certain form of change. Consequently, they are not measurable by *aevum*.

That concept seems to instead more adequately apply to infinite mediate modes, which allow for change while remaining the same. Thus, the *facies totius universi*, a mediate mode of extension, would be, in contrast to infinite immediate modes, capable of being measured by *aevum*, for it reconciles permanence and change. If we take seriously the famous Letter LXIV to Schuller, which provides some clues as to the mysterious nature of infinite modes, the whole universe, 'however much it may vary in infinite ways, nevertheless always remains the same'.[40] Spinoza refers his correspondent to the scholium of lemma 7, which precedes proposition 14 of Part II of the *Ethics*, where it is specified that nature in its totality is a single individual whose parts, which is to say each and every body, vary in an infinity of ways without changing the whole individual. It would thus, thanks to *aevum*, be possible to measure that by which a thing deviates from permanence in being, moving away from eternity in order to approach duration.

Before coming to hasty conclusions, we must not forget that, in any case, eternity does not result from immutability, but is deduced from the necessity of existence. In this respect, infinite mediate modes possess eternity, for they necessarily derive from the nature of the modified attributed. To be sure, they do not directly pertain to the absolute nature of the attribute and their necessity, though undeniable, is not immediate.

Further, *aevum* proves to be an obsolete category, for it rests on contestable grounds. It assumes that the duration of mobile things is of another nature than that of immutable things. However, nothing really permits us to think that the duration of a thing in motion is of a radically different essence than that of a thing that is motionless or at rest. It is for this reason that Descartes, in a letter to Arnauld from 4 June 1648, objects to certain scholastic conceptions: 'What is proposed concerning duration and time is based on a school of thought from which I have departed greatly, namely, that the duration of motion would be of another nature than that of non-moving things like I have explained in article 57 of the first part of my *Principles*.' For Descartes, the existence of motion is not the cause of the existence of a duration specific to the body. The duration of minds and unmoved things is not of a different nature than that of the body and things in motion, for in both cases duration takes on a successive character. The true dividing line occurs between the duration of created things and that of the creator who is *tota simul*. This point arises clearly later in the letter:

[40] *Ep.* LXIV [to G. H. Schuller]; CWS II, 439.

'And even if there weren't a body of the whole, we would not be able to say that the duration of the human mind is all at once, like the duration of God, because we obviously have knowledge of succession in our thoughts, while no succession can be admitted in divine thought.' The duration of a thing is thus not a property linked to its mobility, but 'a mode under which we conceive this thing, insofar as it continues to exist'.[41] In article 57, to which he explicitly refers, Descartes indeed shows that the duration of a body is not a function of its movement. It does not become greater or lesser in accordance with its movement accelerating or decelerating; it is not superior for fast things and inferior for slow ones: 'We do not understand that the duration of things that are mobile is other than that of things that are not so, as it is clear that if two bodies moved during an hour, the one quickly and the other slowly, we would still suppose that there would be more movement in one of these two bodies.'[42] How then can we explain the error which consists in believing that the duration of moving things differs from that of things that do not move? Descartes succinctly hands us the key to this question at the end of article 57. Because we need, for theoretical and practical imperatives, to measure the duration of things, we choose convenient standards thanks to which we are able to assess, by comparison, their respective temporal length: 'But that we may comprehend the duration of all things under a common measure, we compare their duration with that of the greatest and most regular motions that give rise to years and days, and which we call time; hence what is so designated is nothing superadded to duration, taken in its generality, but a mode of thinking.'[43] For want of sufficient attention, we are inclined to attribute time to things whereas such an attribution depends only on our thought. We thus confuse time with duration. Still, since the unity of temporal measurement is furnished by regular astral motion, we end up believing that there is a duration proper to the body in motion and distinct from that of minds and other motionless things. The duration of created things is one and the same throughout. There is thus no need to make use of forms of measurement other than time. Descartes here renders obsolete any investigation into intermediary categories like *aevum*. We can now understand why this concept disappears for good from philosophical speculations after the Cartesian critique and does not appear in Spinoza despite the efforts of commentators to find it there.

[41] Descartes, *Principles of Philosophy*, I, 55.
[42] Descartes, *Principles of Philosophy*, I, 57
[43] Ibid.

Just as eternity is not the consequence of immutability, duration is not, for Spinoza, the consequence of mobility, but expresses, as it does for Descartes, existence in its indefinite continuity. Not only does the appearance of duration not result from the existence of motion, but their systematic association with one another actually leads to unfortunate consequences. In determining duration with the aid of some measure of motion, we become incapable of fixing our ideas and memories in the mind without spatio-temporal references and wind up obscuring and misrecognising the proper nature of the duration of our ideas. Memory thus plays tricks on us, for even if it can be strengthened by the intellect, it is not of a mental but of a corporeal origin. It therefore imports categories of motion and rest, illegitimately attributing them to the mind. A note from the *Treatise on the Emendation of the Intellect* makes this dynamic clear. Spinoza, thanks to a definition of memory and forgetting, there analyses the mechanism of memory.

> But if the duration is indeterminate, the memory of the thing is imperfect, as each of us also seems to have learned from nature. For often, to believe someone better in what he says, we ask when and where it happened. Although the ideas themselves also have their own duration in the mind, nevertheless, since we have been accustomed to determine duration with the aid of some measure of motion, which is also done with the aid of the imagination, we still observe no memory that belongs to the pure mind.[44]

Paradoxically, memory is all the more deceptive the better any individual memory is anchored in us, for the more we determine events by fixed temporal references, the less we perceive the continuity of the mind's duration and, insofar as we reduce it to that of motion and rest, the more mistaken we are concerning its nature. We invert the order and connection of things in an enticing succession of mutilated and confused ideas. Just because movement measures duration, it does not necessarily follow that duration measures movement. Still, we imagine this to be the case. And, in the attempt to find a middle category between duration and eternity that would measure the distance between what is permanent and what is changing, we only persist in our error. In short, the search for an aeviternal touchstone resembles the quest for a philosopher's stone in that it merely reveals the fantastical hold the imagination has on the intellect.

Anyone who adequately reflects on this question understands that the search for intermediaries between duration and eternity is necessarily

---

[44] *TdIE*, 85, note D; *CWS* I, 36.

destined for failure. For this reason, Spinoza limits himself to the use of two concepts. If *aevum* serves to measure that by which a thing strays from eternity, it winds up being an utterly useless category. We cannot apply this category to an infinite mediate mode considered in itself (as a whole) – for an infinite mediate mode is either really eternal (which would therefore make it inadequate to speak of it in terms of *aevum*) or else it deals with a mere permanence across change. In this case, it endures because, in accordance with Cartesian analyses, there is no need to believe that the duration of a thing in motion is of another nature than that of unmoving things. *Aevum* can be no better applied to individuals contained within another whole individual, as great as they may be, for as soon as an individual nearly as complex as the *facies totius universi* is produced, it begins to endure. Its existence is indeed indefinite, and no longer infinite, for the possibility of an external cause of destruction, unlikely as it may be, cannot be excluded. No matter how much we envision ever more complex individuals that would asymptotically tend toward the total individual, they will still be durational and, in this respect, measurable by time, not *aevum*. Ultimately, it is impossible to adhere to Martial Gueroult's assertions – for *aevum* is not a suitable category for Spinoza's conception of the temporality of infinite modes. Between duration and eternity, there is no middle. Should we then give up the search for intermediary categories, confessing the vanity of such an endeavour?

Spinoza, however, does seem to get behind the theory of the existence of different types of eternity. When he claims that 'all the things which follow from the absolute nature of any of God's attributes have always had to exist and be infinite (*semper et infinita existere*)',[45] does he not equate the eternity of infinite immediate modes with a form of sempiternity? Does he not make a distinction between infinite immediate modes and substance, on the one hand, and infinite mediate modes, on the other, when he specifically grants eternity to the former but only necessary existence and infinity to the latter? We must note that Spinoza does not explicitly say, in proposition 22 of *Ethics* I, that a mediate mode is eternal, but rather that it 'must also exist necessarily and be infinite'.

Still, the presence of the adverb *semper* is not on its own enough to prove that Spinoza actually modelled the temporality of modes after a duration with neither beginning nor end – particularly insofar as he presents the expression 'always exist' as synonymous with being eternal.

The comment concerning infinite immediate modes is no more convincing – for in the demonstration of the following proposition, necessary

[45] *Ethics* I, 21; CWS I, 429.

existence is explicitly equated with eternity: 'So if a mode is conceived to exist necessarily and be infinite, [its necessary existence and infinitude] must necessarily be inferred, *or* perceived through some attribute of God, insofar as that attribute is conceived to express infinity and necessity of existence, *or* (what is the same, by D8) eternity.'[46]

Then again, Spinoza seems to undeniably make use of intermediary categories when he distinguishes what is eternal, properly speaking, from what is from all eternity. If what is eternal cannot be reduced to a duration, even one unlimited in both directions, what is *ab aeterno*, by contrast, corresponds to a duration both without beginning and inexpressible with number, if by it we understand the meaning that is attributed to this expression in *Metaphysical Thoughts*.[47] We might consequently conclude from this point that in the *Short Treatise*, when Spinoza claims that infinite immediate modes, which constitute universal *natura naturata*, 'have been from all eternity, and will remain to all eternity, immutable',[48] he does not genuinely grant modes an eternity, but a sempiternity, or a duration with neither beginning nor end.

Such a conclusion would, however, be erroneous, for it is clear that the expression *van allen eeuwigheid*, in the *Short Treatise*, cannot refer to duration because Spinoza uses it in relation to the essence of things. In the same manner, it is obvious that this phrase does not express a sempiternity in the scholium of proposition 17 from *Ethics* I, for neither the essence of a triangle nor the power of God can be said to endure. We must thus admit that the definition given in *Metaphysical Thoughts* is, in accordance with Spinoza's intentions, valid in that context only. Does he not take care to specify that he speaks only of what the words 'from all eternity' mean *here*, implying by this adverb of place that elsewhere the term does not mean exactly the same thing?[49] Apart from this exceptional use of the expression *ab aeterno* to characterise an unlimited duration, we must acknowledge that the phrase is generally a synonym for eternity and cannot serve as proof

[46] *Ethics* I, 23 Dem.; CWS I, 430.
[47] CM II, 10: '*What is denoted here by the words: from eternity* – To understand the question rightly, we must attend to this manner of speaking: *from eternity*. For by this we wish to signify here something altogether different from what we explained previously when we spoke of God's eternity. Here we understand nothing but a duration without any beginning of duration, or a duration so great that, even if we wished to multiply it by many years, or tens of thousands of years, and this product in turn by tens of thousands, we could still never express it by any number, however large.' CWS I, 336.
[48] KV I, 9; CWS I, 91.
[49] Yannis Prélorentzos makes this observation in his doctoral thesis, *La durée chez Spinoza* (Prélorentzos 1992: 163–4).

for the theory according to which there would exist intermediary forms of temporality.

One could, however, object that Spinoza invites us to search for medial categories between duration and eternity, particularly when he alludes to the capacity of reason to conceive of things *sub quadam specie aeternitatis*.[50] Doesn't the adjective *quadam* serve to mark a distinction between knowledges of the second and third type? Does it not introduce a determination that would have the value of mediating between a conception *sub specie durationis* and a conception *sub specie aeternitatis*?

Whatever the exact meaning and significance of the famous *quadam* may be, it cannot serve to assure the theory which proposes the existence of different species of eternity and forms of transitional temporality between duration and eternity. Spinoza does not put forth a distinction in nature between the two perceptions, for he sometimes effectively assimilates, without further clarification, reason's conceiving things *sub quadam specie aeternitatis* with that of understanding them *sub specie aeternitatis*. The demonstration of proposition 29 of Part V leaves no room for doubt on this subject, for Spinoza explicitly writes that 'it is of the nature of reason to conceive things under a species of eternity' while omitting the word *quadam* and referring precisely to corollary 2 of proposition 44 of Part II where the adjective did appear. It is thus false to think that conception *sub quadam specie aeternitatis* would be characteristic of reason, thereby limited to knowledge of the second type, while conception *sub specie aeternitatis* would belong to intuitive knowledge. From this point of view, there is no need to distinguish two types of knowledge that can both be considered as perceptions *sub specie aeternitatis* insofar as they apprehend the necessity of things as they are contained in the eternal necessity of God. In the *Treatise on the Emendation of the Intellect*, Spinoza was already entirely of this opinion, for he attributed to the *intellectus* in general the property of conceiving things *sub quadam specie aeternitatis* and did not reserve such a characteristic only for reason.[51] In truth, as both paragraph 108 of the *Treatise on the Emendation of the Intellect* and the scholium of proposition 29 of *Ethics* V illustrate, there are only two ways of perceiving things: *sub duratione*, in relation to a certain time and a certain place, or *sub specie aeternitatis*. To conceive them *sub quadam specie aeternitatis* is not to consider them under a third angle according to some enigmatic temporality.

---

[50] *Ethics* II, 44 Cor. 2: 'It is of the nature of Reason to perceive things under a certain species of eternity.' *CWS* I, 481.

[51] *TdIE*, 108; *CWS* I, 43–4.

One cannot therefore use the presence of this adjective as an occasion for substantiating the idea of a plurality of forms of eternity that would pro-gressively degrade into duration. For this reason, there is no need to suspect Spinoza of subtly introducing intermediary categories under the cover of his demonstration of the eternity of infinite modes. In this regard, the problem of the eternity of finite modes will serve as a decisive test, for if it constitutes a real eternity, that of infinite modes would find itself secured *a fortiori*. For this reason, the question concerning the nature of the temporality of infinite modes naturally leads us to an examination of the status of finite modes.

3

Eternity and Immortality:
The Status of Finite Modes

If the *Ethics* were to end with the twentieth proposition of Part V, it would appear as the handbook for honest men desiring to attain the highest freedom and greatest happiness possible in this present life. Spinoza, however, does not close his reflections directly after the inventory of remedies for passional troubles and the means of affirming the power of the mind here and now. Having finished his examination of 'everything which concerns this present life', he 'passes to those things which pertain to the Mind's duration without relation to the body'.[1] The entire conclusion of the *Ethics* will thus be dedicated to demonstrating the eternity of the human mind or, more precisely, the intellect, since the imagination and memory perish with the body.[2] We must note, however, that Spinoza does not break with his preceding analyses insofar as he had already prepared the ground for this demonstration. So, as corollary 2 of proposition 44 from *Ethics* II points out, knowledge of the second kind allows us to perceive things *sub quadam aeternitatis specie*, thereby paving the way for a grasping of the mind's eternity.

Still, this doctrine of salvation and the mind's eternity does not fail to surprise, for we know that in *Metaphysical Thoughts* Spinoza had reserved this property exclusively for God: 'And I call this infinite existence Eternity, which is to be attributed to God alone, and not to any created thing, even though its duration should be without beginning or end.'[3] He did, by contrast, grant immortality to the human mind.[4] Should we then consider the eternity of which he speaks in the *Ethics* to be only a variant of immortality,

[1] *Ethics* V, 20 Schol.; CWS I, 606.
[2] *Ethics* V, 40 Cor.; CWS I, 615.
[3] CM II, 1; CWS I, 318. [TN: Jaquet incorrectly cites CM II, 2.]
[4] CM II, 12; CWS I, 342.

resembling a form of unlimited duration, as the wording of the scholium[5] announcing the intention to analyse the duration of the mind without relation to the body suggests? If this is the case, then Spinoza would have strangely relaxed the function of this concept, for he would have broken his own admonition against assimilating eternity to a duration, even one without beginning or end.[6] Or should we, on the contrary, take his reservations on this subject seriously and confer to finite modes the same eternity as substance? But to what extent can the finite share the lot of the infinite? How, in other words, could what had been impossible in *Metaphysical Thoughts* become possible in the *Ethics*? Are we dealing with a derived eternity, or a derivative of eternity? Such are the stakes of the question that raises anew the spectre of intermediary categories – this time under the cloak not of aeviternity, but of immortality.

Mortality, Immortality and Eternity

The Hypothesis of the Mortal Character of the Mind

Spinoza's theory of the mind's eternity was not widely accepted or acknowledged – far from it. Some have even claimed it to be a diversion intended to deceive readers and mask an underlying belief in the soul's mortality. The devout Willem van Blyenbergh initiated an era of suspicion by accusing the Spinozist doctrine of depriving men of hope for an eternal contemplation of divinity and condemning them to simply disappear after death. In his response to Letter XIX, Spinoza's correspondent is unequivocal on this point.

> When I consider this short and fleeting life, in which I see that my death may occur at any moment, if I had to believe that I would have an end, and be cut off from that holy and glorious contemplation, certainly I would be the most miserable of all creatures, who have no knowledge that they will end . . . And this is where your opinions seem to me to lead: that when I come to an end here, then I will come to an end for eternity.[7]

The theory according to which Spinoza would be deeply convinced of the mortal character of the soul is typically based on some remarks from

---

[5] *Ethics* V, 20 Schol.; CWS I, 606.
[6] *Ethics* I, Def. 8 Exp.; CWS I, 409.
[7] *Ep.* XX [from Blyenburgh]; CWS I; 373–4.

his youth conveyed to us by biographers. Spinoza would have profoundly shocked Amsterdam's Jewish community by declaring 'When Scripture speaks of the soul, the word is used simply to express the life of all living things. It would thus be useless to search for some or another passage supporting its immortality.'[8]

The young Spinoza would then be in the company of Dr Juan de Prado in his initial refusal of the soul's immortality. I. S. Revah maintains this position in his work *Spinoza et Juan Prado*. He relies on the testimony of Father Tomàs Solano, who claims, in a statement dated 8 August 1659 in Madrid, that the doctor Juan de Prado and the Dutch philosopher Spinoza thought that the soul died with the body. This Augustinian priest, who came to report a case to the inquisitor of Madrid, was also questioned about the Jews of Spanish origin that he had met in the course of his journey to Amsterdam between 18 August 1658 and 21 March 1659. He claims that Spinoza and Prado 'said themselves to the witness that they were circumcised and had observed Jewish law, and themselves had changed their opinion because it seemed to them that the law said it was not true and the soul died with the body and there was only a God philosophically speaking'.[9]

This hypothesis concerning a Spinoza deeply convinced in his youth of the mind's mortal character does not, in truth, withstand a serious examination. Even if the statements that Lucas attributes to him before the Jewish community are authentic, they only prove that Spinoza thought that Scripture is unable to provide proof of the soul's immortality. It in no way means that he was convinced of the mortal character of the soul. The later endeavour to demonstrate the eternity of the intellect, by contrast, forces us to understand his claim in relation to the meaning of the word 'soul' in Scripture as a recognition of both the speculative fables of the sacred text and the superiority of natural reason over revelation insofar as the former can establish a truth *more geometrico*. Revelation, indeed, as Chapter II of the *Theologico-Political Treatise* shows, grants prophecy a moral certainty, not a mathematical one. The character of moral certainty is its uncertainty, for it needs an external sign to confirm or validate it. For this reason, the prophets 'were not certain about God's revelation by the revelation itself, but by some sign. Genesis 15:8 – where Abraham asks for a sign after he had heard God's promise – makes this evident.'[10] Mathematical certainty, by contrast, is intrinsic and does not require the intervention of any external standard.

[8] Lucas 1927. [TN: No page number given.]
[9] Revah 1959: 31–2.
[10] *TTP* II; CWS II, 95.

Consequently, it is pointless to search through the false lights of etymology and sacred texts to once and for all prove the immortality of the soul. In this sense, it is not because he doubts the soul's eternal character but because he has mathematical certainty of it that Spinoza, armed with this model of truth, can critique the failures of Scripture.

As for Father Tomàs Solano's testimony, we should be wary of it not only because it constitutes a denunciation before the inquisitor, but also because it is not actually confirmed by Captain Miguel Pérez de Maltranilla's deposition from 9 August 1659. According to Revah,[11] de Maltranilla had stayed in Amsterdam at least from November 1658 to 14 January 1659 and had lived in the same house as Father Tomàs Solano. The information that he provides concerning Spinoza and Juan de Prado does not corroborate those of his compatriot on all points, for no mention is made of conversations in which Spinoza and Juan de Prado had supposedly voiced the opinion that the soul dies with the body.

No one today seriously considers the last section of the *Ethics* as a strategic appendix intended to appease ecclesiastic authorities. Of course, everyone knows the motto '*Caute*'; caution (*prudence*), however, does not lead Spinoza to disavow his own ideas, but rather to postpone their publication or disclosure, as was the case for the *Ethics* in 1675. Despite the accusations against him, Spinoza is not a clandestine Epicurean who believes that death is the painless end of a psycho-somatic combination of atoms. The demonstration of the intellect's eternity is not some sly accent to (*pièce rapportée*) but a centrepiece (*pièce maîtresse*) of the *Ethics*. The Spinozist ambition is not limited to the attainment of a sovereign good during this present life, for from as early as the *Treatise on the Emendation of the Intellect*, the objective is consistently to attain an eternal beatitude. After having noted the vanity and futility of life's ordinary events, the philosopher expresses his intention to 'try to find out whether there was anything which would be the true good, capable of communicating itself, and which alone would affect the mind, all others being rejected – whether there was something which, once found and acquired, would continuously give me the greatest joy, *to eternity*'.[12] It is thus not only a question of escaping perishable goods in order to dedicate oneself to the search for an eternal good, but also of reaching an eternal joy. Considered from a temporal point of view, the Spinozist enterprise is, according to Gabrielle Dufour-Kowalska's expression, one of 'eternalisation (*éternisation*)'. The *Ethics* does not prepare man to die, but to live for eternity

[11] Revah 1959: 32–3.
[12] *TdIE* 1; CWS I, 7. Emphasis Jaquet's.

thanks to adequate knowledge and union with God. For this reason, Spinoza claims that 'a free man thinks of nothing less than of death, and his wisdom is a meditation on life, not on death'.[13] In this sense, he presents himself as the heir of King Solomon for whom wisdom is the source of life and allows one to conquer death. Spinoza claims this filiation elsewhere and pays great homage to the presumed author of the Book of Proverbs in chapter IV of the *Theological-Political Treatise*. Solomon prevails over every sage, for he sees in the development of human understanding a fountain of true life and a source of beatitude. 'The teaching of the wise is a fountain of life, turning a person from the snares of death.'[14] Still, the Spinozist aim is not to fight time and death or to carry out their defeat. Far from hypostatising death and seeing in it a privileged adversary, Spinoza puts death to the side by refusing to make of it an object of meditation for the wise. He thereby avoids getting mixed up in the wrong fight, for it is less a question of conquering death than it is one of conquering the fear that death engenders. In this sense, we should be afraid of fearing, not dying. For this reason, the realisation of the mind's eternity is the only victory that strengthens the power of human freedom by replacing the fear of death with the death of fear. The effort to persevere in our being finds its crowning moment in the constant and eternal love of God. It is in this intellectual love that human salvation resides, for in it we escape total annihilation thanks to the eternal part of our mind.[15] Thus, to philosophise is not to learn how to die, but to understand one's eternity.

Immortality and Eternity

If Spinoza is not a secret disciple of Pomponazzi or Uriel da Costa, must we then place him in the camp of partisans of the soul's immortality? Wolfson, in particular, supports such a position when he claims that Spinoza's objective in *Ethics* V is to demonstrate the soul's immortality and refute those who deny it, in particular Uriel da Costa. He explicitly adds that Spinoza defends, alongside his teacher Menasseh ben Israël and Samuel da Silva, the colours of tradition against Uriel da Costa's heretical claims.[16] He even purports that Spinoza directly opposes the author of the *Exemplar vitae humanae* when he writes in proposition 23 of Part V that 'the human mind cannot

---

[13] *Ethics* IV, 67; CWS I, 584.
[14] Proverbs 13:14, New International Version. Cf. Sylvain Zac's analysis in *L'idée de vie dans la philosophie de Spinoza* (1963: 176).
[15] *Ethics* V, 38; CWS I, 613.
[16] Wolfson 1962: II, 323 and after.

be absolutely destroyed with the body, but something of it remains which is eternal'.[17] The author of the *Ethics* would thus be a champion of the soul's immortality and would support the theses of the *Tratado de immortalidade da Alma* in the controversy between Samuel da Silva and Uriel da Costa.

Such an interpretation is not only reductive, for it gives credence to the idea that Spinoza's final statements could be boiled down to negations of Uriel da Costa's propositions, but also false.[18] It inscribes the Spinozist doctrine in a polemical context that is not its own. Spinoza upholds neither the immortality nor the mortality of the soul. The *Ethics* demonstrates the eternity of the intellect, not its immortality. Still, some commentators, like Alexandre Matheron,[19] do not hesitate to use this latter term to describe the indestructability of a part of the mind. Does this mean that the two concepts are interchangeable with one another?

According to Emilia Giancotti-Boscherini's lexicon, the term *immortalitas* does not appear in the *Ethics* and is not once used to describe the nature of God's existence or that of the mind without relation to the duration of the body. Spinoza uses the adjective 'immortal' once in the scholium of proposition 41 in Part V, but as Geneviéve Rodis-Lewis also points out, he alludes there to common belief and not to his own conception. His aim is to denounce the absurd behaviour of one who refuses to live in accordance with reason 'because he sees that the mind is not eternal, or immortal (*aeternam, seu immortalem*)'.[20] How is the conjunction *seu* functioning here? Does Spinoza pose the issue as a strict alternative? Or does he understand the terms to be synonymous?

Everything leads us to believe that Spinoza recognises an equivalence between eternity and immortality insofar as he uses both concepts indiscriminately in the *Short Treatise* to characterise the immutable state of the human intellect joined to God. In the preface to the second part, he maintains that the soul can, 'uniting itself with these substances (which always remain the same), make itself eternal'.[21] At the same time, he demonstrates the indestructability of the human soul joined to God in a chapter titled 'Of the Immortality of the Soul'.[22] ('Van des Ziels Onsterselykheid'). It is, to be sure, always possible to attribute this fluctuation in vocabulary to a lack of

---

[17] *Ethics* V, 23; CWS I, 607.

[18] On this subject, see Osier 1983: 78 and subsequent pages.

[19] See 'Remarques sur l'immortalité de l'âme chez Spinoza', in Matheron 1986/2011.

[20] *Ethics* V, 41; CWS I, 616.

[21] KV II, Pref. 1 CWS I, 96.

[22] KV II, 23; CWS I, 140.

rigour in the notes' transcription. The slide from one term to the other is not, however, accidental, but repeated. Immediately after having clarified the nature of our union with God and announced his intention to show that an 'eternal and immutable constancy (*een eeuwige en onveranderlyke bestendigheid*)' follows from it,[23] he goes on to say that 'if we once consider attentively what the soul is, and where its change and duration arise from, we shall easily see whether it is mortal or immortal (*of zy sterfelyk of onsterfelyk zy*)'.[24] Three chapters later, he deduces the eternity of the intellect[25] by presenting it as a combined consequence of the impossibility of its being destroyed by either an internal or external cause and the immutability of the eternal God that has produced it.

The two concepts are of course closely intertwined, but before concluding that they are actually synonyms, we must note that in the works written by Spinoza himself, they are systematically differentiated. *Metaphysical Thoughts*, by reserving eternity for God, precludes in advance an eventual attribution of this property to the human mind; this text therefore limits itself to establishing the mind's immortality, basing it on the immutable laws of nature. The *Treatise on the Emendation of the Intellect*, by contrast, refers not once to the doctrine of immortality, but suggests searching for a good that 'would continuously give me the greatest joy, to eternity'.[26] An examination of the works earlier than the *Ethics* thus does not allow us to assign a definitive meaning to our notorious *seu* since Spinoza oscillates between both concepts. Only a rigorous comparison of their respective natures can provide a conclusive proof for either their identity or difference in the Spinozist system. Such a task is, however, made difficult by the absence of an explicit definition of immortality. For this reason, it becomes necessary to track the various forms of this term based on evidence provided by the tradition and confirmed by Spinoza.

At first, immortality may seem like the property of an existence endowed with a beginning but lacking an end. This form of immortality is inherent to the nature of most Greek gods who enjoy creation without degradation. It is not, however, the privilege of these gods alone; it can crown a human existence that is naturally mortal, but nonetheless capable of enjoying a posthumous destiny due to its exemplary behaviour. In this case, immortality

---

[23] *KV* II, 22; *CWS* I, 140.
[24] *KV* II, 23; *CWS* I, 140.
[25] *KV* II, 26; *CWS* I, 148–9.
[26] *TdIE* 1; *CWS* I, 7. [TN: The French translation of the *TdIE* that Jaquet quotes here reads 'pour l'éternité, la jouissance d'une joie suprême et incessante'.

presents itself either as a mere survival of the mind or one of its parts after the destruction of the body, or as a resurrection of the body and soul after death.

Whether the property of gods or deserving men, this form of immortality cannot be conceived without chronological points of reference or categories of before and after. It implies a duration preceding birth, before which the being did not exist and after which it begins to exist. It cannot, therefore, be applied to the Spinozist conception [TN: of eternity] which excludes all temporal references.[27] We must nevertheless note that the realisation of the eternal character of our mind is effectuated during present existence. Consequently, life *sub specie aeternitatis* would in this sense imply a beginning bound to an historical occasion: that of the discovery of our eternity through knowledge of the third kind. Everything happens as if we start being eternal after having completed our intellectual trek in duration. The adventure of the *Ethics* would thereby consist in the search for a passage from a precarious and indefinite duration to an infinite one.

We can, in truth, have the illusion that we pass from duration to eternity when we discover with time and patience that knowledge of the third kind paves the way for salvation. But the historical character of this discovery should not make us forget the distinction between the gnoseological order and the ontological order. It should not lead us to believe that we start being eternal simply because we start to know (*connaître*) ourselves as such. We are 'always already' eternal, even if we do not know (*savons*) it. Consequently, this eternity can have no beginning, neither after our death nor even after the historical moment of our temporal life wherein we would have accessed knowledge of the third kind and become aware of our eternity. Spinoza is very clear on this subject in the scholium of proposition 31 from *Ethics* V. Recourse to the notion of 'beginning' is justified only for pedagogical reasons and in that sense allows us to explain the passage to an understanding of things *sub specie aeternitatis*. However, it should not mislead us – for it does not substantiate the idea that eternity implies a point of departure. It is thus not cogent to assimilate Spinozist eternity to an immortality understood as the property of a being that does not die but lives on from the moment it begins to exist.

Still, immortality does not necessarily entail a beginning. It can belong to a sempiternal being, endowed with a boundless existence. In this case, the conception of immortality approaches the commonplace representation reducing eternity to an infinite life with neither birth nor death. So defined,

[27] See *Ethics* V, 23 Schol., CWS I, 607–8.

immortality more closely approaches Spinozist eternity, which excludes any beginning, any end, and any reference to a period prior to existence or after death.[28]

This conception of immortality, however, still cannot be confused with Spinozist eternity, for it more accurately corresponds to a form of perennity (*pérennité*) and always implies reference to a duration, even if unlimited in both directions. Spinozist eternity, however, is free from any temporal dimension and cannot be conceived either as an indefinite duration or even as an infinite duration. Spinoza is upfront on this point: eternity 'cannot be explained by duration or time, even if the duration is conceived to be without beginning or end'.[29] He was already of this opinion in the letter to Louis Meyer dated 20 April 1663. Eternity is not defined as an infinite duration, but as 'the infinite enjoyment of existing'. Of course, one could object that eternity, as it is defined here, concerns substance and not modes. Spinoza specifies elsewhere in this same letter that 'we conceive the existence of substance to be entirely different from the existence of modes . . . for it is only of modes that we can explain the existence by duration. But [we can explain the existence] of substance by eternity.'[30] So, because we cannot conceive the existence of modes without duration, it would not be false to consider that the mysterious species of eternity that the mind acquires through knowledge of the third kind would only be a variant of immortality understood as a duration having neither beginning nor end. Just as time is 'the moving image of eternity' for Plato, the immortality of the mind would be the image of the eternity of substance for Spinoza.

This interpretation, however, does not withstand close scrutiny, for Spinoza takes great care to distinguish two types of actuality:

> We conceive things as actual in two ways: either insofar as we conceive them to exist in relation to a certain time and place, or insofar as we conceive them to be contained in God and to follow from the necessity of the divine nature. But the things we conceive in this second way as true, or real, we conceive under a species of eternity, and to that extent they involve the eternal and infinite essence of God.[31]

[28] *Ethics* V, 23 Schol., CWS I, 607–8: 'It is impossible that we should recollect that we existed before the body – since there cannot be any traces of this in the body, and eternity can neither be defined by time nor have any relation to time.'
[29] *Ethics* I, Def. 8 Exp.; CWS I, 409.
[30] *Ep.* XII [to Louis Meyer]; CWS I, 202.
[31] *Ethics* V, 29 Schol.; CWS I, 610.

The eternity of the mind must thus be distinguished from its present existence here and now and cannot be conceived as the prolongation of duration. Every mode has a double actuality, temporal and eternal. These two
forms of actuality are irreducible to one another; we can therefore add
minutes, hours and years to the infinite – we will not reach eternity by
doing so.

Commentators who affirm the presence of a real immortality in Spinoza,
however, do not commit the error of believing that Spinozist eternity is of a
temporal essence. The immortality in question does not take on its ordinary
meaning and indeed excludes any and all reference to duration. It is conceived in the rigorous sense of the term as the property of a being that does
not die. It is in this sense that Alexandre Matheron understands it in his
article titled 'Remarques sur l'immortalité de l'âme chez Spinoza'.[32]

Stripped of all temporal connotation, the concept of immortality seems
more adequate and better adapted to the Spinozist conception insofar as
we take into consideration that the intellect, unlike memory, the imagination and the body, does not die. The term nonetheless remains imprecise
(*impropre*) for several reasons. For starters, it leads one to define Spinozist
eternity with reference to death by distinguishing what dies in us, on the
one hand, from what remains, on the other. Proposition 23 from *Ethics* V
indeed makes use of this distinction by claiming that 'the human mind
cannot be absolutely destroyed with the body, but something of it remains
which is eternal'.[33] Spinoza, however, avoids a distinction between a mortal
part and an immortal part, sticking to a demonstration of the eternity of the
intellect. In a philosophy where the sage thinks of nothing less than death,
there can be no question of defining eternity in relation to this event. The
concept of immortality is, however, always tainted by this reference, if only
to deny it. For this reason, it would be better to avoid the term altogether,
engaging instead in a meditation on life. Let us nevertheless note that it is
no more legitimate to conceive Spinozist eternity as an eternity of life, for
this expression does not appear in the *Ethics*; our author prefers the concept
of eternal existence, which is more in line with his thought. The idea of
eternal life remains distinctly marked by theological connotations, but that
alone cannot explain why Spinoza rejects it, for he is typically not reluctant
to use religious vocabulary and adapt it to his purposes. Does he not speak
of beatitude and glory by explicitly referring to Sacred Scripture?[34] The

[32] Matheron 1986/2011: 7.
[33] *Ethics* V, 23; CWS I, 607.
[34] *Ethics* V, 36 Schol.; CWS I, 612.

concept of eternal life is likely avoided on account of its unsuitability since it necessarily implies a form of bodily permanence. Compatible with a theology of resurrection, it does not fit into a philosophical framework where the body is destroyed.

Whatever one says of it, immortality remains confusedly tied to temporal considerations, for the distinction between a mortal part and immortal part leads one to make death the historical event whereupon this separation between the intellect and the perishable parts of our being is performed. It thus surreptitiously introduces the idea of a before where the body and mind are united and an after where only the intellect remains. By the same stroke, eternity appears as a *post mortem* survival distinguished from a pre-life in duration. Admittedly, immortality could be used for pedagogical ends intended to make people understand the distinction between the eternal part and perishable part on the condition that one avoids the errors tied to the introduction of a temporality or chronological order in eternity. However, while the preservation of the notion of beginning might be justified on the condition that one distinguishes the order of being from the order of knowledge, that of immortality remains questionable. The discovery of the distinction between an eternal part and a perishable part is not effectuated at the moment of death, but results from an examination of the nature of our body and mind. Death is thus not the necessary condition of this realisation and cannot serve as a point of illumination. It is likely for this reason that Spinoza has no need of resorting to the notion of immortality to present his conception.

At any rate, the use of the word immortal in the place of the word eternal constitutes, by the very admission of the author of the *Treatise on the Emendation of the Intellect*, a usurpation attesting to the hold of the imagination. It keeps us at the level of the first kind of knowledge and involves a degree of inadequacy. Paragraph 89 emphasises this fact. There, Spinoza recounts the formation of negative notions as part of his analysis of language:

Moreover, [words] are established according to the pleasure and power of understanding of ordinary people, so that they are only signs of things as they are in the imagination, but not as they are in the intellect. This is clear from the fact that the names given to things that are only in the intellect, and not in the imagination, are often negative (for example, infinite, incorporeal, etc.), and also from the fact that they express negatively many things that are really affirmative, and conversely (for example, uncreated, independent, infinite, immortal). Because the contraries of these are much more easily imagined, they occurred first to the earliest men, and they used positive names.[35]

Eternity can thus only be understood by the intellect, but the imagination, in its incapacity to conceive it positively, represents it as the negation of 'mortal'. It thereby forges, from its opposite that is more familiar to it, the notion of immortality that then supplants that of eternity and ends up illegitimately taking its place. Immortality is thus the negative and imaginative version of a positive reality comprehensible only to the intellect. Strictly speaking, we must prefer the term eternity to immortality to avoid a common cause of confusion and error. In the following paragraph, Spinoza warns us of the risk we run:

> We avoid, moreover, another great cause of confusion which prevents the intellect from reflecting on itself – viz. when we do not distinguish between imagination and intellection, we think that the things we more easily imagine are clearer to us, and think we understand what we imagine. Hence, what should be put later we put first, and so the true order of making progress is overturned, and no conclusion is arrived at legitimately.[36]

It would therefore be best to proscribe the concept of immortality altogether or, if it is unavoidable, use it with caution by calling explicit attention to its imaginative origin, its inadequacy and the limits to its validity. More generally, it is completely illegitimate to situate the author of the *Ethics* alongside proponents of immortality, even if one were to insist upon the particular and atemporal nature of this concept in Spinoza.

This being the case, one could rightly ask why the two concepts are apparently used interchangeably in the *Short Treatise*. Does Spinoza not become the target of his own critique, succumbing to the temptations of the imagination and entertaining confusion with recourse to negative notions like immortality? A more attentive examination of the occurrences of the two terms actually reveals that they are not entirely used as synonyms. They

---

[35] *TdIE*, 89; *CWS* I, 38. [TN: The French translation of the *TdIE* from which Jaquet quotes uses the term '*usurpèrent*' in the last line where Curley translates 'use'. This is relevant insofar as Jaquet uses the French term '*usurpation*' above to describe the supposed interchangeability between eternity and immortality in the *Treatise on the Emendation of the Intellect*. The Latin term used by Spinoza is '*usupurant*'.]

[36] *TdIE*, 90; *CWS* I, 38.

are neither equivalent nor interchangeable. Although the title of chapter 23 can lead to confusion, Spinoza's aim throughout Part II of the *Short Treatise* is to establish the eternity of the intellect. Both the intentions stated in the preface and the clear-eyed conclusions in the last chapter attest to this fact.[37] The immortality of the soul is only a step in the demonstration of the eternity of the intellect and cannot be confused with it. Chapter 23, as a matter of fact, simply limits itself to showing that the duration of the soul depends on the object with which it is united. It is perishable if it is united to the body alone, imperishable if it is united to an unchanging object like God. Immortality is here synonymous with indestructability and character-ises the state of a being that depends on an imperishable cause. This nature of this inalterability remains, however, obscure and will only be revealed in the final chapter. It depends on the essence of the cause that produces it and communicates its properties to its effect. For this reason, the demonstration of the intellect's eternity involves something more than an illustration of its immortality. It demands three conditions: first, the absence of an internal cause of destruction; second, the absence of an external cause of destruction; and third, the presence of an eternal generative internal cause (*une cause intérieure productrice éternelle*). If the third condition were not met, the intel-lect would enjoy a sempiternity, an aeviternity, or some other form of tem-porality that its cause would communicate to it, but could not be declared eternal. Consequently, the two concepts do not fully coincide: if every eternal being is immortal, not every immortal being is eternal. Immortality is indeed a negative and incomplete notion, for it only indicates the absence of a cause of destruction without specifying the nature of the inalterability in question. The use of this concept in the *Short Treatise* should not, however, be denounced as an incoherence; it is perfectly justified, for at that stage of his demonstration, Spinoza has only established the indestructability of the soul and has not yet analysed the character of its inalterability, even though it may be obvious considering the essence of God. As a result, it is not by speaking of the soul's immortality, but rather its eternity that Spinoza would have betrayed rigor insofar as he would have skipped a step in his reasoning.

Based on the above, it becomes possible to understand why *Metaphysical Thoughts* restricts itself to a doctrine of the soul's immortality without once mentioning the eternity of the intellect. While eternity is an extrinsic denomination in the *Short Treatise* and in this respect proves communica-ble to types of beings other than substance, it is, in *Descartes' Principles of Philosophy*, an incommunicable attribute jealously possessed by God. The

---

[37] *KV* II, Pref. and 23; *CWS* I, 93–6 and 140–1.

human mind must content itself with enjoying an indestructibility based on the immutability of the decrees of God who has, to be sure, the power of changing his laws but who nonetheless has created a nature regulated in a fixed and constant manner. 'Moreover, since it clearly follows from these laws that a substance can be destroyed neither through itself nor through another created substance . . . we are compelled, from the laws of nature, to maintain that the mind is immortal.'[38] The crux of the demonstration resembles that of the *Short Treatise*, for immortality is there too based on the absence of internal and external causes of destruction. The result, however, does not take on the same degree of certainty, for in *Metaphysical Thoughts*, Spinoza admits that the one who has 'the power of creating a thing, has also the power of destroying it' and that God can change his laws.[39] It is for this reason, moreover, that he takes care to say that here he judges the nature of things based on their laws and not on the power of God.[40] The conception of divine omnipotence and the doctrine of eternity's incommunicability incidentally provide evidence for the anteriority of *Metaphysical Thoughts* in relation to the *Short Treatise*, whose theses strongly resemble those of the *Ethics*. They are not limited to a demonstration of the mind's immortality, and indeed abolish the divine monopoly on eternity.

One difficulty remains to be resolved, however: why does Spinoza entirely abandon the concept of immortality in the *Ethics*? Why doesn't he preserve it as a necessary step in the demonstration of the eternity of the intellect? To resolve this problem, it is necessary to retrace the development of Spinozist thought in respect to *Metaphysical Thoughts*, on the one hand, and the *Short Treatise*, on the other. Abandoning the concept of immortality for that of eternity is no mere accident, but the result of replacing the idea of creation with that of necessary immanent causality. In *Metaphysical Thoughts*, Spinoza deliberately reserves the term eternity for God and that of immortality for the human mind. Indeed, he places himself as a direct inheritor of the Cartesian concept of continuous creation and draws every logical consequence from it. Eternity is the privilege of God, for only God exists by virtue of the necessity of its nature. Creatures, by contrast, have only a possible existence insofar as their essence does not include existence. Created things depend on God for their essence as well as their existence. It is therefore necessary that the former preserve them or continuously create them at each moment. For this reason, they are said to endure. They have

---

[38] CM II, 12; CWS I, 342.
[39] CM II, 12; CWS I, 341.
[40] CM II, 12; CWS I, 342.

a beginning and indefinitely continue to be so long as God preserves them. They thus do not possess eternity insofar as eternity excludes the idea of beginning. A contingent being and a necessary being cannot receive the same attributes. Spinoza is therefore perfectly consistent when he claims that 'it is quite false that God can communicate his eternity to creatures'.[41] Creation introduces a distance and a separation between the creator and its creatures. Spinoza explicitly carries out this rupture by refusing eternity to God's effects, granting them no more than immortality. In *Metaphysical Thoughts*, the human mind is immortal by virtue of natural laws established by God. Since the decrees of a perfect being must be immutable, no created thing can be destroyed by God. The mind therefore does not die but lives on (*demeure*) by means of divine support.

In the *Ethics*, by contrast, where Spinoza rejects the idea of creation, modes are not separate from substance, but constitute its ways of being. As such, the eternal necessity of substance can be communicated to them. Of course, the essence of man does not include existence, but 'must be conceived through the very essence of God, by a certain eternal necessity'.[42] The relation that unites man to God is no longer a relation of creature to creator, but of cause to effect. The human intellect is a part of the divine intellect and thus enjoys the same eternity as the latter when it adequately understands. The necessity of the bond that ties the effects to the cause thus makes possible the eternity of modes. The scholium of proposition 40 of *Ethics* V emphasises this point: 'our mind, insofar as it understands, is an eternal mode of thinking, which is determined by another eternal mode of thinking, and this again by another, and so on, to infinity; so that together, they all constitute God's eternal and infinite intellect'.[43] As a result, Spinoza intentionally speaks of the mind's eternity as opposed to its immortality by virtue of the necessary bond that unites the human intellect with the divine intellect. God thus does not have a monopoly on eternity, and we can indeed subscribe to Bernard Rousset's formula: 'for Spinoza eternity is a proprium of God; but it is immediately necessary to add that every singular thing is nothing other than a mode of God: in the end, no substantial distinction keeps them from eternity'.[44]

We must now clarify the reason why, in the *Ethics*, Spinoza, unlike his approach in the *Short Treatise*, completely forgoes the notion of immortality

---

[41] CM II, 10; CWS I, 337.
[42] *Ethics* V, 22 Dem.; CWS I, 607.
[43] *Ethics* V, 40 Schol,; CWS I, 615.
[44] Rousset 1968: 48.

in order to prove the eternity of the intellect. The reservations developed in the *Treatise on the Emendation of the Intellect* concerning the confused character of negative notions do not themselves provide enough of a justification for the removal of this concept. Imaginative ideas are not systematically prohibited, for they can sometimes serve as valuable aids to thought. The main reason for the change is the fact that a real certainty concerning the mind's immortality is actually conditional upon the demonstration of its eternity. For a being to be called immortal, it must be indestructible and, for that, meet three conditions: have no internal cause of destruction, no external cause of destruction, and be produced by an inalterable agent. But how can we know for sure that the intellect escapes both death and the threatening pressure of external causes when the most quotidian experience shows that the body perishes, memory fades away and the imagination is fleeting? In short, what guarantees that these three criteria for immortality are met? While we admit that suicide is always an effect of unfavourable external causes and that a mode can no more destroy itself than it can produce itself insofar as it is not self-caused, the fact remains that a human is always at the mercy of external factors of corruption. Consequently, in the best case scenario, it is clear that the first condition is met, but doubt remains in relation to the second: how could I know that no external cause is going to destroy me considering the infinity of causes and events that my finitude prevents me from foreseeing in spite of their necessity? Spinoza counters this objection by asserting that whatever is not produced by external causes has nothing in common with them and thus cannot be destroyed by their action.[45] All destruction presupposes a causal efficacy and consequently a link or connection. To assure ourselves of the soul's immortality, we must therefore prove that it escapes the clutches of external causes and has nothing in common with them. The only means of attaining such assurance is to reveal its productive cause and prove that this cause communicates its invulnerability to the soul. In other words, the only possible way to establish the mind's immortality beyond a shadow of a doubt is to demonstrate its eternity by basing the latter on the immanent connection that unites the mind to its cause. Thus, it is not the soul's immortality that is the necessary condition for its eternity; rather, it is eternity that is the condition of possibility for immortality. Pointing out the immortality of the soul is thus not an obligatory step in the argument, but instead constitutes a superfluous and onerous detour, for it is simpler and more direct to prove the eternity of the intellect while basing it on the presence in God of an idea that expresses the

---

[45] *KV* II, 26, 7, note 3; *CWS* I, 147.

essence of the body *sub specie aeternitatis*.[46] Confused, useless and vague, we now see why in the *Ethics* the concept of immortality fades away in exchange for that of eternity. Ultimately, Spinoza is the champion of neither the soul's mortality nor its immortality, for the ultimate perspective of the *Ethics* does not cater to the terms of the traditional problematic and is in fact located distinctly outside the sphere of theological conflicts which led to the black-listing of the *Exemplar vitae* and the flogging of Uriel da Costa.

The Conditions of Possibility for the Eternity of Finite Modes

The Definition of Eternity in the Ethics

Still, the extension of eternity to modes remains problematic, for it assumes a redefinition of this property formerly reserved exclusively for substance. Putting aside the disappearance of the concept of creation in favour of that of immanent causality, what precisely makes this extension more possible in the *Ethics* than it had been in *Metaphysical Thoughts*? Has the meaning and nature of eternity changed? To answer this question, we must examine the infamous definition 8 in an attempt to identify any traces of a possible mutation. At first glance, it seems both unsettling and sophistic insofar as it apparently transgresses the logical prohibition against using the term to be defined in the definition. Indeed, by eternity Spinoza understands 'existence itself, insofar as it is conceived to follow necessarily from the definition alone of the eternal thing'.[47] Unless we suspect the author of the *Ethics* of being inadvertently trapped in the vicious circle of defining a thing by itself, we must resolve this paradox and get to the bottom of this phrase.

Commentators often tend to interpret this definition by falling back on that of *Metaphysical Thoughts*. Martial Gueroult, for example, resolves the difficulty in two steps.[48] First, he reduces eternity to existence through itself and considers it to be based on the property of a thing to include necessary existence. He thus brings the definition of the *Ethics* closer to that of *Metaphysical Thoughts* while nevertheless noting an irregularity:

> If the definition of eternity, as a property of existence, is not based on the eternal essence of the thing, if it is only based on its property of necessarily including existence, could we not simply do without the word eternal

---

[46] See *Ethics* V, 22; CWS I, 607.
[47] *Ethics* I, Def. 8; CWS I, 409.
[48] Gueroult 1968: 78–9.

altogether and speak only of the thing? In *Metaphysical Thoughts*, was
eternity not precisely defined as the property (*propre*) of a being – and not
of an eternal being – whose essence includes existence?[49]

The commentator is thus led to ponder the reasons why Spinoza does not
give up on this term and shows, basing himself on the explanation that
follows definition 8, that 'the reference to the eternity of essence or truth is
meant to guard against a confusion between the eternity of existence and its
duration with neither beginning nor end'.[50]

This interpretation, however, allows some doubts to linger. If we stick
to the text, Spinoza does not explicitly tie eternity to existence through
itself, but to 'existence itself (*ipsam existentiam*) insofar as it is conceived to
follow necessarily from the definition alone of the eternal thing'.[51] Unlike
Metaphysical Thoughts, where he reserved eternity for substance and presented it as 'an attribute under which we conceive the infinite existence
of God', he never openly specifies that he exclusively means the existence
of divine substance.[52] By using this term, he allows for the possibility of
an extension of this property to every existence that fulfils the conditions
provided.

It would be tempting, then, to strengthen this reading by relying on the
ambiguity of the Latin text, for the absence of an article allows one to translate definition 8 in two ways. Eternity can designate 'existence conceived
to follow necessarily from the definition of *the* eternal thing' or '*an* eternal thing'. Martial Gueroult opts for the first translation by equating eternity with 'the existence necessarily implicated by the concept alone of *the*
thing'.[53] But if we choose to translate the Latin phrase with the indefinite
article, the Spinozist definition lends itself to a double reading, as Alexandre
Matheron has shown. The existence of a thing is eternal insofar as it is conceived to follow necessarily from the definition alone of *another* thing. In the
first case, the thing gets its eternity from itself. In the second, it owes it to
something else that is itself eternal. The definition would thus split into two,
encompassing both an immediate and a mediate eternity. The choice, therefore, of the indefinite over the definite article by the French translator is not
neutral, for it makes the extension of eternity to modes possible. We must

[49] Ibid., 79.
[50] Ibid., 79–80.
[51] *Ethics* I, Def. 8; CWS I, 409.
[52] CM I, 4; CWS I, 310.
[53] Gueroult 1968: 78.

recognise, however, that these considerations do not constitute decisive arguments and instead have to do with a translation bias, arbitrary insofar as it is not the text which determines the reading, but the reading which determines the text. The first line of the definition's explanation, which uses the word *rei*, would, incidentally, lend further credence to Gueroult's reading.[54]

Then again, we should draw attention to a crucial change in relation to *Metaphysical Thoughts*: Spinoza no longer ties the eternity of existence to essence, but to the *definition* of an eternal thing. He therefore does not reduce, as he did earlier, eternity to the property of an essence to include existence. If he did, it would in a way exclude the attribution of eternity to modes whose essence do not include existence. The presence of the word 'definition' in place of that of 'essence' is not insignificant, for it makes possible the extension of eternity to modes. At first glance, there is no difference between the adequate definition of a thing and its essence; there is, however, a crucial distinction for our purposes. A perfect definition must reveal the inner essence of a thing by revealing its cause. In the case of modes, the definition must encompass their proximate cause,[55] namely, God. An essence, by contrast, designates 'what the thing can neither be nor be conceived without, and vice versa, what can neither be nor be conceived without the thing'.[56] Spinoza declares this reversible condition in order to avoid the error underlying traditional definitions which, by limiting themselves to the first part of the statement, suggest that God pertains to the essence of things. The essence of a mode of course depends on God, but does not contain God as a property. On this basis, the reason why Spinoza substitutes the word 'definition' for that of 'essence' throughout his analysis of the concept of eternity becomes clear. The proximate cause is not included in 'essence', while it is included in 'definition' – and this makes all the difference in the world. If eternity cannot be deduced from the essence of a mode, since it does not include existence, it can, by contrast, follow from its definition. Seeing that the definition of a mode encompasses its proximate cause, it can, through the essence of God, indeed include existence and thereby be eternal. Consequently, by substituting the word 'eternal thing' for that of 'substance' and the term 'definition' for that of 'essence', Spinoza allows for a broadening of this property formerly reserved for God to beings that do not through themselves possess necessary existence.

---

[54] Thank you to Jean-Marie Beyssade for drawing my attention to this point.

[55] *TdIE* 96; *CWS* I, 39: 'If the thing is created, the definition, as we have said, will have to include the proximate cause.'

[56] *Ethics* II, 10 Schol. to Cor.; *CWS* I, 455–6.

Terminological considerations aside, it is certain that the hypothesis of a real extension of eternity to modes better respects the Spinozist conception. If we restrict the meaning of the definition of eternity to necessary existence through itself, then we are unable to grasp why Spinoza then applies this term to infinite and finite modes and are subsequently led to deplore the extension of the term as illegitimate or else concede that 'there is there a sin against terminological rigour'.[57] By contrast, if we expand the scope of this concept, the Spinozist approach is perfectly coherent and the difficulty tied to the apparently tautological character of the definition disappears. Indeed, if eternity also designates a mediate and derivative eternity, it becomes crucial to clarify that it stems from the definition of a thing that is itself eternal; the presence of this adjective is thus completely justified.

Some could, however, object that this reading confers to the existence of a mode a necessity that it does not have and instead assert that eternity is the privilege of a being whose essence includes existence. It is true that modes do not enjoy such a privilege. Nevertheless, their existence is in a certain sense necessary insofar as it is involved in the essence of God. If I conceive my existence as implicated in God's essence, then I will conceive it as necessary and eternal. To conceive existence in this way is nothing other than conceiving things *sub specie aeternitatis*. The demonstration of proposition 30 from *Ethics* V clearly highlights this fact. Spinoza claims that eternity is the property of an essence implying necessary existence, but he does not conclude from this that it applies exclusively to substance. On the contrary, he concludes that 'to conceive things *sub specie aeternitatis*, therefore, is to conceive things insofar as they are conceived through God's essence, as real beings, or *insofar as through God's essence they involve existence*'.[58] Consequently, the interpretation according to which in definition 8 eternity could also be applied to a modal existence, conceived as following from the definition alone of substance, is not only possible but necessary, since it is simply a literal transcription of what Spinoza calls conception *sub specie aeternitatis*. Eternity thus turns out to be a 'communicable attribute' according to the expression sanctioned by the tradition.

Eternity, a Common Notion

It remains to be seen how a property of substance can pertain to modes. Does this not imply a negation of divine specificity, or else a contradiction,

[57] Gueroult 1968: 81.
[58] *Ethics* V, 30 Dem.; CWS I, 610. Emphasis Jaquet's.

insofar as what is specific (*propre*) becomes common? In reality, the property of a thing is not necessarily specific (*propre*) to that thing, not necessarily possessed in an exclusive manner. It can be extendible and shareable. Common notions, the foundation of our reasoning, testify to this fact because they express properties equally present in the part and the whole. In short, for eternity to be at the same time specific to God and communicable to humans, it is necessary and sufficient that it be a common notion. This hypothesis is not out of place, for eternity well meets the criteria required for being a common notion. Under this designation, Spinoza indeed gathers notions expressing the set of properties common to all or to certain things and present equally in the part and the whole. Now, eternity is a property common to substance, attributes, infinite modes and the human intellect. It is found equally in the part and the whole. It is easy to confirm this at the level of both the divine intellect and the human intellect, envisaged each in their turn as wholes or totalities. In the first case, the eternity of the infinite immediate mode of thought undeniably belongs to the whole and its parts, since the human intellect is eternal and proves to be a part of God's eternal and infinite intellect. In the second case, the human intellect considered as a whole is formed of adequate ideas that are themselves eternal. Parts and whole thus equally possess eternity.

What is common, moreover, does not constitute the essence of any singular thing.[59] And eternity is a property that constitutes neither the essence of God (since it is not an attribute) nor the essence of singular things (since it can be conceived without Peter, Paul or Simon and belongs equally to each of them).

Finally, common notions can only be conceived adequately.[60] And both the eternity of God and that of the human intellect are the object of adequate knowledge. Does Spinoza not demonstrate in proposition 47 of Part II that 'the human mind has an adequate knowledge of God's eternal and infinite essence'?[61] He insists on this crucial point by recalling in the scholium that 'God's infinite essence and his eternity are known to all.'[62] The eternity of the human intellect can also be perceived in an adequate manner, as the second section of Part V shows. Eternity thus well fulfils the necessary requirements for being a common notion. In this case, whoever reduces it to a genus or a species, a general concept or a particular category,

---

[59] *Ethics* II, 37; CWS I, 474.
[60] *Ethics* II, 38 and 39; CWS I, 474.
[61] *Ethics* II, 47; CWS I, 482.
[62] *Ethics* II, 47 Schol.; CWS I, 482.

falls victim to the error which consists in confusing, under the influence of the imagination, a common notion with a universal.

It thus becomes clear that in Spinoza common notions take the reins from what the scholastics had called communicable attributes. As such, the *Ethics* marks a decisive break from *Metaphysical Thoughts*, for it substitutes this concept for that of a communicable attribute, of which Spinoza was already suspicious but which he nevertheless continued to use, when he claimed, for example, that God 'has always communicated his eternity to the son',[63] and rejected this possibility for creatures. This enigmatic phrase obviously refers to the scholastic division between communicable and incommunicable attributes that Spinoza will consider in the following chapter as more nominal than real.

Consequently, the details of the problematic find themselves modified and must be reformulated. It is no longer a question of knowing whether eternity is a communicable or incommunicable attribute, but of determining if it is one of these universal common notions that belong to all men without exception (whether they be wise or not) or if it is to be placed in the category of common notions specific to certain minds only. The stakes of this question are high, for it concerns the salvation of the ignorant.

Concerning divine eternity, it is clear, based on the scholium of proposition 47 of Part II, that it has to do with what Martial Gueroult calls a universal common notion. Spinoza leaves no room for doubt on this subject insofar as he claims that 'God's infinite essence and his eternity are known to *all*.'[64] The examination of this single case should itself be sufficient to prove that eternity is a property also belonging to all minds, for if we all can conceive the eternity of God, it is by virtue of this common property that we share with him. Human eternity is thus a part of universal common notions and is not the privilege of only some minds. Spinoza establishes this on several occasions, particularly in proposition 23 of Part V and its scholium where he refers to the human mind in general and maintains that '*we* feel and know by experience that *we* are eternal'.[65] By using the first-person plural pronoun, he includes all humans equally and does not exclude the ignorant. Eternity is thus well and truly a notion common to all humans without exception.

One could, however, contest its universal character and place it in the second category of common notions insofar as it seems to be the privilege of

[63] CM II, 10; CWS I, 337.
[64] *Ethics* II, 47 Schol.; CWS I, 482. Emphasis added.
[65] *Ethics* V, 23 Schol.; CWS I, 607–8. Emphasis added.

human minds. In reality, it is not a notion peculiar to certain minds – those
of humans – but to all *mentes*, as the scholium of proposition 13 of Part II
shows, for there is necessarily an eternal idea in God of all things. From
this perspective, all individuals endowed with a *mens* are eternal, from the
simplest animals to the most complex body politic. The State, for Spinoza,
resembles an individual with a soul constituted by the ensemble of its laws.[66]
As a result, if the most well-organised body politic can be dissolved due to
vicissitudes tied to the possibility of the existence of external, destructive
causes – causes that not even the most exceptional wisdom would be able
to foresee – then its soul, like that of humans, contains an eternal part.
Spinoza specifically claims that the law (*la législation*), the soul of the State,
is in itself eternal when the State is well-constituted. In this regard, if a body
politic persists and endures so long as no factor of dissolution threatens it,
its soul is eternal either way. We must therefore distinguish, for the State
as for humans, a mortal part and an eternal part. For these reasons, we can
subscribe neither to the interpretation nor to the translation of Madeleine
Francès,[67] who claims that Spinoza oddly uses 'the term *aeternus* in the weak
sense of perpetual (*perpétuel*) several times' in the *Political Treatise*. The two
concepts are distinct and do not cover the same reality. One pertains to
the soul of the State and everything related to law. The other concerns a
political body's transformations and duration. It is thus entirely illegitimate
either to systematically translate the term *aeternum* that Spinoza uses in the
Latin text with the word *perpétuel* or to consider that he uses it in a meaning
different than usual.

Does this not only mean that all men, whether they be wise or witless, are
equal, but that any old dog is eternal in the same way as Spinoza? It would be
understandable to denounce the absurdity of a system that not only puts all
men on the same level, but also reduces them to the rank of animals. Let us be
careful not to fall into the trap of a crude interpretation. Just because a property is a common notion does not mean that it is equally formed and known
by all humans. Spinoza reminds us of this in the scholium of proposition 47
in Part II. After having shown that God's infinite essence and eternity are
known by all, he clarifies that humans do not have 'so clear a knowledge of
God as they do of the common notions' and explains why this inequality is
tied to an illegitimate incursion of the imagination into the domain of the
unimaginable.[68] In the same manner, humans are all aware of the eternity

[66] *TP* X, 9; *CWS* II, 600.
[67] Note to *TP*, p. 1500, La Pléiade, Gallimard.
[68] *Ethics* II, 47 Schol.; *CWS* I, 483.

of their mind, but they do not conceive it with equal clarity, often mistaking its nature. The scholium of proposition 34 of Part V develops this in more detail: 'If we attend to the common opinion of men, we shall see that they are indeed conscious of the eternity of their Mind, but that they confuse it with duration, and attribute it to the imagination, or memory, which they believe remains after death.'[69] From this angle, common opinion is simply a common notion that is ignorant of itself; it covers the very same ground as a common notion, but under the veil of the imagination. This allows us to better understand why such opinion is so widespread.

The difference between souls therefore does not rest on the fact that some perish while others do not, since they are all more or less eternal on account of the presence in God of an idea expressing the essence of the body *sub specie aeternitatis*. The difference is rooted not in what Alexandre Matheron calls 'eternity in itself' but in 'eternity for itself', which is to say the consciousness and knowledge of the fact that this property indeed belongs to our mind. It is the greater or lesser aptitude of being conscious of oneself, God and things that differentiates souls. From this angle, knowledge of the intellect's eternity is capable of donning a multiplicity of forms that range from the near unconsciousness typical of the ignorant to the clear and distinct consciousness represented by the wise.

It is thus false to believe that Spinozist eternity consists in the abolition of all individuality in the impersonal fusion of the soul in a universal *We* in the style of Giordano Bruno. Of course, memory, that precious asset for securing personal identity, dies along with its share of images. The eternal essence of the human body does not contain ideas and affections that are tied to the body's duration and disappear with it: 'The mind can neither imagine anything, nor recollect past things, except while the body endures.'[70] As such, the idea of an existing body in duration and the idea of a body *sub specie aeternitatis* do not overlap. This lack of identity or overlap may seem problematic, for the human essence that intuitive knowledge would reveal would not express the entirety of our being, but only one of its parts. Despite the partial character of the mind's eternity, however, the essential is saved, for individuation and distinction between beings are not effectuated on the basis of a lived experience (*vécu*) tied to a memory or personal history. Images and memories belong to the body's duration. They are born and die along with it. Self-consciousness, however, does not vanish with the disappearance of memory and the imagination, for it belongs to the intellect.

[69] *Ethics* V, 34 Schol.; CWS I, 611–12.
[70] *Ethics* V, 21; CWS I, 607.

Consequently, since it is possible to continue to conceive the mind without memory and without imagination, we must admit that they are not essential in the Spinozist sense of this term. If they were, then the idea that expresses the essence of the body *sub specie aeternitatis* would have to include memory and the images of every affection linked to duration – something Spinoza definitively rules out.

If the eternity of the intellect is not reducible to an impersonal fusion of modes with substance, it is not for all that personal; this term does not make much sense in a philosophy that begins not with the first person, since there is no conscious subject to start with, but instead with a being subjected to external causes. If Spinozist eternity is neither personal nor impersonal, it is, in contrast to either of those, particular (*particulière*). Knowledge of the intellect's eternity is not actually limited to the comprehension of an essence through its common properties. Proposition 22 of Part V affirms the presence in God of 'an idea that expresses the essence of *this* or *that*[71] human body, *sub specie aeternitatis*'. We are therefore dealing with a particular essence that one must adequately perceive in order to bring about one's salvation. It is obvious that to perfectly know things is to perceive their particular essence. To prove this statement, it is enough to recall that an essence expresses that without which a thing cannot be conceived and, conversely, that which cannot be conceived without the thing. Every essence is, by definition, particular. Spinoza indeed uses this expression twice in the *Treatise on the Emendation of the Intellect*,[72] and further emphasises the special and particular nature of an essence when he clarifies that a good definition is tied to the innermost essence[73] (*intimam essentiam*) of things, preventing it from being confused with propria. Consequently, it is not exactly accurate to claim that the third kind of knowledge delivers the singular essence of things, since this expression does not appear in Spinoza's work. It is certain, by contrast, that such knowledge concerns their particular, innermost (*intime*) essence. Ultimately, the distinction between beings does not consist in a singularisation but in a particularisation proportional to the degree of consciousness of oneself, God and things.

---

[71] *Ethics* V, 22; CWS I, 607. Emphasis added.

[72] See *TdIE* 93 and 98; CWS I, 39 and 40–1: 'But the best conclusion will have to be drawn from some particular affirmative essence (*ab essentia aliqua particulari*), or, from a true and legitimate definition'; 'I have also said that the best conclusion will have to be drawn from a particular affirmative essence.'

[73] See *TdIE* 95; CWS I, 39.

Eternity Felt and Experienced

Despite the infinite diversity of its degrees, consciousness of eternity can be boiled down to three broad figures: eternity imagined, eternity experienced and eternity known. The first form belongs to knowledge of the first kind and attests to the influence of the imagination. It is therefore necessarily inadequate. It consists, to be sure, in being aware of the mind's eternity, but confuses it with an unlimited duration and attributes it to memory.[74] It is therefore doubly lacking, for it introduces into eternity temporal categories that the former excludes and does not attribute this property to the right part of the mind, namely, the intellect. Eternity is thereby conceived as a survival of the subject, weighed down by its past and individual history. This way of being aware of eternity is proper to all humans and constitutes a common opinion. Nothing, however, prevents us from taking the position that it belongs to all souls (*mentes*) endowed with a memory and an imagination. Spinoza does not openly give an opinion on this question and thus cannot be made to confirm extrapolations concerning the possibility of a confused consciousness of eternity in animals. Still, in theory, any being provided with memory and imagination can apprehend, even if only in a strongly inadequate manner, its own eternity insofar as this eternity is based on the presence of an idea in God.

By contrast, the felt and experienced eternity to which the scholium of proposition 23 refers is the privilege of human souls, for it results from demonstrations. It is therefore different from both imagined eternity, insofar as it mobilises the intellect as opposed to memory,[75] as well as the adequately known eternity proper to the sage. Although they are of the intellectual order, this feeling and experience of eternity, shared by all humans, as the use of the personal pronoun 'we' invites us to think, does not grant a perfectly adequate knowledge and is reducible neither to reason nor to intuitive knowledge. If it were, it would imply that all humans have a true knowledge of their eternity – and this is obviously not the case since only the sage

[74] *Ethics* V, 34 Schol.; CWS I, 611–12: 'If we attend to the common opinion of men, we shall see that they are indeed conscious of the eternity of their mind, but that they confuse it with duration, and attribute it to the imagination, or memory, which they believe remains after death.'

[75] *Ethics* V, 23 Schol.; CWS I, 607–8: 'And though it is impossible that we should recollect that we existed before the Body – since there cannot be any traces of this in the body, and eternity can neither be defined by time nor have any relation to time – still, we feel and know by experience that we are eternal. For the mind feels those things that it conceives in understanding no less than those it has in the memory.'

possesses this gift. Experience nevertheless provides certain and convincing teachings or confirmations; it cannot however serve as a substitute for adequate knowledge. Many of Spinoza's typical expressions, such as 'experience teaches us' and 'experience sufficiently proves', testify at the same time to its validity and limitation.[76]

The nature of this feeling and experience of eternity seems mysterious, for it is determined by intellectual causes and rooted in demonstrations, while at the same time not being of a purely cognitive order. To what experience can Spinoza allude when he claims that 'we feel and know by experience that we are eternal'?[77] Ferdinand Alquié confesses his perplexity and incomprehension on this subject because he estimates that, for him, no real experience of thought answers to concepts. 'It is difficult to live this eternity that Spinoza calls living and not dwell, as far as it is concerned, in the realm of pure concepts. The eternity about which Spinoza tells us is perhaps living. But we doubt that it can be lived, or at least lived by man.'[78]

Spinoza claims, however, that humans as a whole have this experience, but that it relates neither to an empirical lived experience nor to a mystic venture outside the sphere of pure concepts. If there is an experience, it has to do with an experience of thought, an experience of the geometrical type linked to demonstrations. To seek to live it like an event affecting sensibility, memory or the entire body is necessarily to be led astray, for it concerns the intellect. Pierre-François Moreau has clearly established the details of the problem and offered the conditions of its resolution: 'Is it possible to describe a structure that would be entirely internal to the soul that could yet have effects analogous to that of the body to produce a feeling? What is this quasi-memorial structure? How does the soul feel demonstrations?'[79]

He solves the conundrum by showing that the feeling and experience of eternity results from the proof (*épreuve*) of the necessity of demonstrations, a test that is not pure, but that is inscribed within the persistent context of previous perceptions which were experienced (*vécues*) as more or less contingent. Of course, at the start, the soul that performs a demonstration 'understands its necessity' and first obtains a result that is not of the order of feeling. 'But at the same time, this necessity stands out from the background of what is not necessary.'[80] The soul perceives this difference and feels it as

---

[76] Moreau 1994b: 227–305. [TN: Translation of quote mine.]
[77] *Ethics* V, 23 Schol.; CWS I, 607.
[78] Alquié 1981: 349–50.
[79] Moreau 1994b: 543.
[80] Ibid.

a tearing away (*arrachement*) from finitude. Moreau therefore distinguishes necessity known from necessity felt on the basis of a differential perception based on the existence of finitude. Therefore, 'the feeling of finitude is the condition for the feeling of eternity and itself *is*, in a sense, the feeling of eternity'.[81]

Moreau is right to distinguish the feeling of eternity from the knowledge of this property by emphasising its relative opacity and universal character which contrasts with the clarity and distinctness of the sage's intuitive or rational comprehension. Still, certain questions remain. It is true that through rigorous contact with demonstrations, humans get used to necessity; but can we reduce the experience of eternity to which the scholium alludes to that of necessity? Is there not here an elision and misunderstanding of eternity's specificity? One can, of course, retort that experience always contains a share of obscurity and that the two concepts can be easily confused due to their similarity. This observation, however, cannot on its own suffice to justify the assimilation of the feeling of eternity to that of necessity for two reasons. The experience of necessity does not necessarily introduce us to eternity. Everything eternal is necessary, but not everything necessary is eternal. Axiom 1 of Part IV reminds us that it is necessary that a finite mode can be destroyed by a more powerful cause. In this case, to experience necessity is to feel durational and not eternal. Necessity is therefore in itself not enough to explain the appearance of a feeling of eternity, for it can just as well beget a feeling of duration. We must nevertheless admit that demonstrative necessity never provides us with an experience of the temporary, for if an idea is true, it is eternally so. From this angle, every demonstration of our finitude and our durational character is at the same time an experience of eternity. It remains to be understood how a demonstration or a true idea can give me the feeling of the eternity of *my* intellect. That the sum of the angles of a triangle are equal to two straight lines, that there is necessarily in God an idea of the essence of my body *sub specie aeternitatis* – how do these ideas give me the feeling of the eternal *existence* of my mind? Let us not forget that eternity is a property of existence. The feeling in question cannot be restricted to the proof of the necessity of an idea or an essence. It is an existential experience that, to be sure, does not resemble a memorable, empirical experience, but that cannot simply be reduced to the examination of an essence. From this angle, the experience of necessity is too vast, for it can concern essences as much as existences. The feeling of eternity and that of necessity thus cannot completely overlap.

[81] Ibid., 544.

The solution proposed by Moreau also raises reservations because of the ambiguity tied to the origin of the feeling of eternity that would be born, according to him, from the conjunction of the perception of demonstrative necessity and that of finitude. The scholium of proposition 23 does not present the feeling of finitude as a condition for the feeling of eternity; it grounds it only in demonstrations. It even excludes reference to anything connected to a memory or experience otherwise linked to time. By relying on the feeling of finitude and earlier perceptions present in the soul, Moreau surreptitiously reintroduces relations to the body, the imagination and duration – relations that Spinoza had ruled out since the scholium of proposition 20. He thus slips from an experience of the intellect to an experience of memory and mixes the two together, whereas Spinoza claims the existence of feelings born exclusively from a conception of the intellect and distinguishes them from those born of memory. In other words, demonstrations alone account for the fact that we feel and experience that we are eternal. The mobilisation of memory and previous perceptions is excluded, for 'it is impossible that we should recollect that we existed before the body – since there cannot be any traces of this before the body, and eternity can neither be defined by time nor have any relation to time'.[82] Recourse to finitude and its combination with demonstrative necessity would seem to better account for the genesis of feelings of immortality or unlimited duration than it does for that of eternity. At any rate, the feeling of finitude as spoken of above is not explicitly presented as an indication of eternity at any point in the Spinozist corpus. For this reason, we cannot subscribe to Moreau's phrase according to which 'the feeling of finitude is the condition for the feeling of eternity'.

The original question thus returns once again, but, taking into account the intellectual and, as it were, geometric, nature of the feeling and experience of eternity, it can now be reformulated in the following terms: how and why do demonstrations make us feel and experience that we are eternal? The feeling considered is clearly not subject to what Kant would call pathological motives. From this angle, it is possible to make an analogy between the Spinozist feeling of eternity produced by the intellect and the Kantian notion of respect, the fruit of practical reason, since they both elude sensible and corporeal determinations. Their paradoxical character as 'non-sensible feelings (*sentiments non sensibles*)' nevertheless makes them appear as incomprehensible monsters.

In an attempt to uncover their origin and nature, we must first of all acknowledge that the feeling and experience of eternity are presented in the

[82] *Ethics* V, 23 Schol.; CWS I, 607.

scholium of proposition 23 as equivalent to an intellectual vision and obser-vation, respectively. To feel is to see and to experience is to observe with the eyes of the mind, which are demonstrations. Between feeling and expe-rience, therefore, there is no fundamental difference in nature – only that observation implies a more attentive and repeated vision. On this basis, the details of the problem can be clearly posed as follows. Knowing that eternity is a property of existence, we must find what, in the nature of the demonstra-tion, makes us experience (*éprouver*) that this characteristic indeed belongs to our mind. In other words, it becomes a matter of determining the nec-essary link between demonstrations and the eternal existence of our mind.

To solve this problem, we must examine the essence of a demonstra-tion and see whether or not it has the property, according to Spinoza, of engendering feelings. A demonstration is an ordered series of adequate ideas deduced from each other that actually produces a feeling in us: the feeling of certainty. How can we know that the demonstration is true and actually deserves its name? If a demonstration is right, the mind knows so surely because truth is the measure of both itself and the false. In other words, demonstrations engender a certainty in us that expresses the internal impact of truth in the intellect. Certainty is the feeling that accompanies the possession of a true idea. Spinoza openly declares this in paragraph 35 of the *Treatise on the Emendation of the Intellect*: 'certainty is nothing but the objective essence itself, i.e., the mode by which we *feel* the formal essence is certainty itself (*modus, quo sentimus essentiam formalem*)'.[83] The presence of the verb *sentimus* that we also find[84] in the scholium of proposition 23 of Part V invites us to maintain that certainty is indeed this infamous sen-timent engendered by true demonstrative series, a feeling that cannot be reduced to affections tied to memory and the imagination. The fact that Spinoza alludes to the experience of certainty and likens it to a vision in paragraph 35 of the *Treatise on the Emendation of the Intellect*[85] should rid us of any further doubt: it is not by means of finitude, but by means of certainty that we feel and experience that we are eternal. Certainty is a feeling, for it

---

[83] *TdIE* 35; CWS I, 18. Emphasis added. [TN: Curley's translation is here modified. It reads: 'the mode by which we are aware of the formal essence'. Jaquet provides the Latin in her version. The French from which she quotes reads: 'c'est-à-dire que la façon dont nous sentons l'essence formelle'.]

[84] Bernard Rousset also points out this similarity in vocabulary. Cf. *TdIE*, commentary, 229.

[85] *TdIE* 34; CWS I, 18: 'Everyone can experience this, when he sees that he knows what Peter is, and also knows that he knows, and again, knows that he knows that he knows, etc.'

expresses the manner by which we are affected by truth. It is not really distinguished from a true idea, but designates the way in which we experience it as true without requiring any other external sign. Demonstrations are thus well and truly capable of producing a feeling and an experience that we can identify under the name of certainty. On several occasions, the author of the *Ethics* mentions this feeling and relates it to conceiving of something *sub specie aeternitatis*, particularly in Part IV in the demonstration to proposition 62 where he claims that 'whatever the mind conceives under the guidance of reason it conceives under the same species of eternity, or necessity (*sub eadem aeternitatis, seu necessitatis specie*) . . . and is affected with the same certainty'.[86] He continues with this association between knowledge and the feeling of certainty that it engenders when he mentions the way we are also affected by the idea of a past, present and future thing. Lastly, in Part V, he again refers to such a feeling and grounds it, as he did in the scholium of proposition 23, in the ability to conceive things *sub specie aeternitatis*: proof, if it were still needed, that certainty is indeed the mysterious affection engendered by demonstrations.

A first difficulty is now lifted; however, the mystery has not yet been fully unravelled, for we must explain why the fact of being certain gives us the feeling of being eternal. *A priori*, the relation between certainty and the mind's eternity is hardly obvious. In truth though, whoever has certainty also has the experience of their own eternity, even if inadequately. What does it mean, according to Spinoza, to be certain if not to know that we know, or, to use one of Bernard Rousset's phrases, 'to know oneself knowing (*se savoir savoir*)'.[87] In other words, all certainty, by virtue of its reflexivity, implies an idea of oneself, of one's own mind that feels the formal essence of a thing. All knowledge is at the same time self-knowledge. Certainty thus includes the idea of the thing and the idea of oneself. It therefore indeed makes us experience the existence of a mind that knows that it knows.

It remains to be understood how it makes us feel this existence as eternal. Every demonstration implies a being that perceives the truth with the idea of itself as the cause. It makes us experience the eternity of our intellect, for a true idea never stops being true. If we have an idea like this, there is indeed something in us that is eternal. Our mind is not a faculty, but an idea composed of several other ideas. When we have a true idea, we feel that this idea constitutes our mind; we therefore experience ourselves as eternal.

---

[86] *Ethics* IV, 62 Dem.; CWS I, 581.
[87] *TdIE*, commentary, 207 and the following.

Furthermore, whoever demonstrates the eternity of their mind does not simply have the feeling that one of their ideas is eternal; they feel that the ordered set (*ensemble*) of adequate ideas that constitutes their mind is eternal. Not only do they know that there is something in them that is eternal, but they know that they themselves are eternal. They are thus aware of themselves, for they not only possess the idea of a thing, accompanied by themselves as the cause, they also have the idea of their own self with themselves as the cause. If the idea is adequate, it attains the highest degree of certainty. Nevertheless, only the sage is aware of themselves and possesses this supreme certainty. The sage perfectly coincides with their ideas in such a way that for them, to be self-conscious, conscious of God and conscious of things is one and the same thing.

Most humans do not attain this level of certainty and self-consciousness. Nevertheless, they all have the feeling of their eternity, for everyone has at least one true idea, as the infamous '*habemus enim ideam veram*' which opens paragraph 33 of the *Treatise on the Emendation of the Intellect* reminds us.[88] From the most banal common notion, which could be symbolised by the axiom 'man thinks',[89] to the third kind of knowledge, each one can be placed on a spectrum of true ideas proportional to the power of one's intellect. As such, everyone experiences certainties, however minimal they may be, and thereby experiences their own eternity. Certainty is not necessarily all or nothing. It contains degrees that vary with the quality of the idea. Spinoza clearly allows this fact to shine through when he claims that 'no one can know what the highest certainty is unless he has an adequate idea or objective essence of some thing', meaning that this feeling is capable of having lesser degrees.[90] The quality of the feeling and experience of eternity is therefore proportional to that of certainty. So, for example, a common notion affects our mind less than an idea deduced from our essence and will give us a certainty and, therefore, a feeling of our mind's eternity that is less lively, even if the demonstration is beyond doubt.[91] This means that a man who only knows the most universal common notions would only have a very weak feeling of the mind's eternity, for he would not know the innermost (*intime*) essence of his body, but only very general properties. Certainty, whatever its nature may be, it is thus unquestionably a feeling of eternity.

---

[88] *TdIE* 33; CWS I, 17.
[89] *Ethics* II, Ax. 2; CWS I, 448.
[90] *TdIE* 35; CWS I, 18.
[91] The scholium of proposition 36 from Part V, in particular, emphasises this point. See *Ethics* V, 36 Schol.; CWS I, 612–13.

This discovery of our eternity is fundamental, for every cognitive edifice hangs on this property of our intellect because it is not true knowledge that is the condition *sine qua non* of the mind's eternity; it is the mind's eternity that is the condition *sine qua non* of true knowledge. It is because we are eternal that we are able to form either rational or intuitive knowledge. All true knowledge necessarily has an eternal character. To conceive things adequately is to conceive them either *sub quadam aeternitatis specie* or *sub specie aeternitatis*. Does Spinoza not claim that reason grants us the power of perceiving things *sub quadam aeternitatis specie*[92] by virtue of its capacity to understand their necessity or by virtue of its object?

Bracketing the problematic use of the adjective *quadam*, we must note that in both cases, the possibility of knowledge *sub specie aeternitatis* hangs on the theory of the mind's eternity. Proposition 31 of *Ethics* V clearly throws this into relief: 'The third kind of knowledge depends on the mind, as on a formal cause, insofar as the mind itself is eternal.'[93] It is because the mind is eternal that it can conceive things *sub specie aeternitatis*. The gnoseological order should not mislead us here. If the discovery of the mind's eternity comes after that of the third kind of knowledge, it is not for all that legitimate to conclude that the former ontologically depends on the latter. The third kind of knowledge does not actually precede the grasping of the mind's eternity but proceeds from it. It is therefore not the cause but the expression of salvation in act. The possibility of intuitive knowledge thus depends on the possibility of the mind's eternity.

The subordination of true knowledge to the existence of an eternal mind is not limited to knowledge of the third kind only. It extends to the second as well. To be clear, proposition 31 only explicitly concerns the third kind of knowledge, but this does not mean that the second kind of knowledge can be the fruit of a mortal mind or that such knowledge does not imply the existence of an eternal mind. Spinoza has indeed specified that '*whatever the mind understands under a species of eternity, it understands not from the fact that it conceives the body's present actual existence, but from the fact that it conceives the body's essence under a species of eternity*'.[94] This totality covers what is conceived by reason as well as what is conceived by intuitive knowledge. There is no possible doubt on this subject since Spinoza clarifies it throughout the demonstration of this proposition. As a result, the mind's eternity turns out to be the cornerstone of any ade-

---

[92] *Ethics* II, 44 Cor. 2; CWS I, 481.
[93] *Ethics* V, 31; CWS I, 610.
[94] *Ethics* V, 29; CWS I, 609.

quate knowledge. The exact nature of our knowledge *sub specie aeternitatis* therefore remains to be understood. We must also determine whether or not there are multiple modalities of it in accordance with different types of knowledge.

4

Sub Specie Aeternitatis

The Nature and Meaning of Conception *Sub Specie Aeternitatis*

Conception *sub specie aeternitatis* only makes sense within the framework of a philosophy which allows for the real possibility of thinking that things are at the same time eternal and durational. It is therefore unsurprising to note that it does not appear in *Metaphysical Thoughts* where the soul is not eternal, but immortal, and does not escape the ranks of duration, endless though it may be. It is no more surprising that the phrase has no antecedent in a good number of authors prior to Spinoza and that research into this subject has not been very successful, for it is the mark of a doctrine that implies the recognition of an actual (*effectif*) ontological status of duration and eternity without reducing them to relative and subjective points of view.

Such a conception is reducible neither to true knowledge in general nor to that of the second or third type. Due to the specificity of its object, it overlaps with them only in part. It is the counterpart to a conception *sub duratione* and concerns an object that can be doubly apprehended. In support of this hypothesis, we must observe that it only concerns things and does not apply to God.[1] Unlike things, substance cannot conceive things as actual in two ways, for substance has no relation to time and place. It does not therefore lend itself to a multiplicity of approaches, as do modes which, due to the nature of their existence, can be envisaged under the angle of either duration or eternity.

---

[1] Cf. the instances of the phrase inventoried in Giancotti's *Lexicon*: *Ethics* II, 44 Cor. 2; *Ethics* V, 22, 23, 29 Schol., 30 Dem., 31 Schol., and 36.

The structure of Part V well confirms the fact that a conception *sub specie aeternitatis* is the counterpart to one *sub duratione* due to the fact that things have this double property of being both durational and eternal. Indeed, the last section of the *Ethics* contains, by Spinoza's own admission, two parts as articulated in the scholium to proposition 20: the examination of what concerns present life and the analysis of what concerns 'the mind's duration without relation to the body'.[2] The phrase only appears when Spinoza decides to turn his attention exclusively to the mind's eternity. It is also striking to note that even within that second division, knowledge *sub specie aeternitatis* continues to be thought in opposition to a conception *sub duratione*, whether it concerns the essence of things or their actual existence. Proposition 22 thus presents itself as the negative version of proposition 21: to imaginative and perishable ideas linked to the duration of the body and its affects, it opposes the idea that expresses the essence of this or that human body with an eternal necessity. The same schema is reproduced in proposition 23, its demonstration and its scholium, proposition 29, and most notably in the scholium thereof where two ways of conceiving the actual existence of things are distinguished.

After having examined the instances of this expression, Filipo Mignini concludes that *sub specie aeternitatis* 'qualifies a modality of knowledge' and that the 'exclusive subject of such knowledge is the human subject'.[3] Proposition 22, however, is an exception, and in fact seems to contradict the claims of the Italian commentator, for the phrase is not tied to a conception of the human mind but concerns an idea that must necessarily be found in God.[4] This exception nevertheless confirms the rule, for if the phrase is not explicitly related to a conception, it is still obvious that it pertains to the activity of knowing. If there is in God an idea expressing the essence of this or that human body *sub specie aeternitatis*, it simply means that the actual essence of that body is conceived as contained in God as following from the necessity of God's nature. Mignini is therefore absolutely right to claim that the phrase characterises a type of knowledge; he is wrong, however, to attribute a monopoly of this cognitive activity to the human subject and to consider that it refers neither to God nor to the attribute of thought nor to infinite modes, whether immediate or mediate. It is hardly legitimate to exclusively grant human subjects knowledge *sub specie aeternitatis* when we

[2] *Ethics* V, 20 Schol.; CWS I, 606.

[3] Mignini 1994.

[4] *Ethics* V, 22; CWS I, 607: 'in God there is necessarily an idea that expresses the essence of this or that human body, under a species of eternity'.

know that our intellect is part of the divine intellect. To say that we conceive things *sub specie aeternitatis* is to say that God perceives them in this way insofar as he constitutes the nature of our mind.

To grasp the exact meaning and value of this type of conception, it is important to analyse its definition, such as it is established in the scholium of proposition 29, and situate it in relation to the earlier texts. Setting aside the disappearance of the adverb *quadam*, which will constitute the object of its own analysis, the presentation of knowledge *sub specie aeternitatis* in Part V of the *Ethics* contains two changes in relation to the *Treatise on the Emendation of the Intellect*. First, we must note that it is not directly opposed to a perception *sub duratione*, as was the case in paragraph 108 of the *Treatise*, but rather to the way of perceiving the actual present existence of things *in relation to a certain time and place*. If it is obvious that this manner of conceiving things implies a relation to duration, should we thereby conclude that the two formulations are necessarily equivalent and interchangeable, or that the *Ethics* brings along noticeable modifications? We must remind ourselves that the use of temporal determinations implies that we conceive duration in an abstract manner, as a sort of quantity, without taking into account the manner by which it follows from eternal things. Nevertheless, it is clear upon an examination of the scholium of proposition 23 that Spinoza assimilates the manner of perceiving things in relation to a certain time and place to a conception *sub duratione*.[5] The major innovation, which too often seems to go unnoticed, resides in the fact that conception *sub specie aeternitatis* is characterised by its lack of reference to place. It is therefore defined not only by its atemporality, as we are accustomed to emphasising, but also by the exclusion of spatial determinations, which partially contain abstractions insofar as they tend to divide and separate that which is by nature indivisible and inseparable. To conceive things in relation to a certain place is to consider them in their spatial juxtaposition and to determine them from the outside by overlooking the immanent relation that unites them to God. In this sense, knowledge *sub specie aeternitatis* consists in grasping things from the inside by prioritising their necessary link to the substance that contains them. For this reason, such knowledge is connected to the second way of understanding the actuality of things.

---

[5] *Ethics* V, 23 Schol.; CWS I, 608: 'Our mind, therefore, can be said to endure, and its existence can be defined by a certain time, only insofar as it involves the actual existence of the body, and to that extent only does it have the power of determining the existence of things by time, and of conceiving them under duration.'

The second change in relation to the *Treatise on the Emendation of the Intellect* concerns the fact that the conception of knowledge *sub specie aeternitatis* does not exactly form a direct counterpart to a conception of the actuality of things *sub duratione* or in relation to a certain time and place. It is not reducible to the mere apprehension of things under the angle of necessity, as they are contained in God and follow from God's nature; it does not strictly overlap with the second way of conceiving things either, but is presented as its true modality. Spinoza implicitly introduces a subdivision within the second category by distinguishing true actual conception, or conception *sub specie aeternitatis*, from the one that for lack of a better word we would be tempted to call false or unreal. Taken to the letter, the text does not give us permission to purely and simply reduce knowledge *sub specie aeternitatis* to the second mode of perceiving the actuality of things.

Are these negligible nuances or crucial changes? To better weigh their significance, we must understand why a conception *sub specie aeternitatis* is not reducible to the mere perception of the immanence and necessity of things. If we consider things in their duration, we can have the experience of a certain necessity because we see, on the one hand, that they do not arise by chance, but are determined to exist and to act by causes that fall under the common order of nature and, on the other hand, that we have the means at our disposal to perceive the way by which they are linked and succeed one another thanks to 'those aids, all of which serve to help us know how to use our senses and to make, according to certain laws, and in order, the experiments that will suffice to determine the thing we are seeking'.[6] Though we cannot have perfectly adequate knowledge of the common order of nature, of our duration and that of other things, we still have enough experience to apprehend necessity. As a result, a vision *sub duratione*, if it does not rely on the contingent and mutilated order of the imagination, but on rigorous experiments (*expériences*), envisages things from the point of view of necessity. Perhaps this allows us to understand why Spinoza uses the expression 'in relation to a certain time and place' instead of *sub duratione* to qualify the first way of conceiving things. Such an expression places greater emphasis on the contingent vision specific to modes of the imagination, in contrast to the necessary approach of the second mode of perceiving the actuality of things. Conception *sub specie aeternitatis* is defined first and foremost by the exclusion of any and all contingency. This is what already stood out in proposition 44 of Part II where perception *sub quadam specie aeternitatis* resulted from that natural property of reason to contemplate things not as

---

[6] *TdIE* 103; CWS I, 42.

contingent, but as necessary. If he had opted for the phrase *sub duratione* in the scholium of proposition 29 of Part V, assimilating the first way of conceiving a thing's actuality to a contingent vision would have been up for more discussion. In any case, this indeed proves that a conception *sub specie aeternitatis* is not reducible to its necessary character, but must be distinguished from a temporal contemplation according to more precise criteria. This seems to be one reason why Spinoza does not purely and simply reduce knowledge *sub specie aeternitatis* to the second way of conceiving things and adds the further requirement of truth.

Establishing a distinction within the second way of conceiving the actuality of things in all likelihood responds to another, more profound motive. To discern it, we must consider ourselves capable of apprehending the necessity not only of existing things but also of non-existing things. Ideas of singular things or non-existing modes are contained in the infinite idea of God[7] and necessarily flow from it. In this respect, things exist insofar as they are contained in God's attributes. We therefore conceive them as actual insofar as substance exists, but we do not perceive them *sub specie aeternitatis*. For a thing to be conceived *sub specie aeternitatis*, it is necessary for it to be true and real, which is to say that it must possess an existence in act (*en acte*) and not only as contained in God's attributes. The use of the adjective 'true', rather than that of 'adequate', in the scholium is not accidental. A true idea is not really distinguished from an adequate idea except that it implies a relation to an existing object in act. By choosing the word 'true', Spinoza places greater emphasis on this link to a real object. Conception *sub specie aeternitatis* therefore cannot be reduced to an adequate grasping of the necessity of things insofar as they are contained in the idea of God; instead, it implies a comprehension of their real existence in act based on the divine essence.

But is to conceive things as they exist in act not also to envisage them in their duration? If this is the case, a conception *sub specie aeternitatis* would amount to a true apprehension of temporal existence. To guard against such a confusion, Spinoza refers to proposition 45 of Part II and its scholium. To exist in act is not to endure but to follow from the eternal necessity of God's nature. Spinoza is blunt on this point:

By existence here I do not understand duration, i.e., existence insofar as it is conceived abstractly, and as a certain species of quantity. For I am speaking, I say, of the very existence of singular things insofar as they are in God. For even if each one is determined by another singular thing

7 See *Ethics* II, 9; CWS I, 452.

to exist in a certain way, still the force by which each one perseveres in existing follows from the eternal necessity of God's nature.[8]

What, then, does true or real actual knowledge in relation to the simple apprehension of the immanence of things and their necessary link to God mean? To adequately understand that things are contained in God is not only to perceive them as parts of a whole and relate them to the *facies totius universi* by drawing attention to the laws that immutably govern them. It is not to follow the inexhaustible chain of finite and determined causes that preside over their existence in the vain hope of eventually reaching the first cause. In a word, it is not to resituate them within *natura naturata*, but within *natura naturans*. True conception of a thing's actuality consists in grasping that the thing is contained in the essence of substance. Now, the essence of God includes existence. It follows, then, that to really conceive things as actual is nothing other than discovering that they include, through the essence of God, existence. True actual conception therefore apprehends things in their eternity, since that is what the property expressing the fact that God's essence includes necessary existence is called. Here, then, is the reason why Spinoza names true actual knowledge *sub specie aeternitatis* and does not simply resort to the synonymous phrase *sub specie necessitatis* that he had used in the demonstration of proposition 52 of Part IV.

To grasp in the most delicate manner the distinctions made in the scholium of proposition 29, it is enough to take the example of a circle and its rectangles, representing God and its modes:

The circle is of such a nature that the rectangles formed from the segments of all the straight lines intersecting in it are equal to one another. So in a circle there are contained infinitely many rectangles that are equal to one another. Nevertheless, none of them can be said to exist except insofar as the circle exists, nor also can the idea of any of these rectangles be said to exist except insofar as it is comprehended in the idea of the circle. Now of these infinitely many [rectangles] let two only, viz. [those formed from the segments of the lines] D and E, exist. Of course their ideas also exist now, not only insofar as they are only comprehended in the idea of the circle, but also insofar as they involve the existence of those rectangles. By this they are distinguished from the other ideas of the other rectangles.[9]

---

[8] *Ethics* II, 45 Schol.; CWS I, 482.
[9] *Ethics* II, 8 Schol.; CWS I, 452–3.

The set of non-existing rectangles and their ideas can be conceived neither in relation to a certain time and place nor *sub specie aeternitatis*. It can, however, be apprehended as actual because it is contained in the circle and exists insofar as the circle exists. The two rectangles, D and E, can, by contrast, be perceived both in relation to a certain time and place and *sub specie aeternitatis*. A spatio-temporal approach will not primarily emphasise the necessary link that connects them to the circle, but will rather call attention to the external agent that has drawn them here and now. It will fasten them to their present genesis under the geometrician's chalk or else to their sudden disappearance at the hands of his eraser, giving the deceptive feeling of a radical contingency. A vision *sub specie aeternitatis* will overlook external determinations and will be sensitive to the proximate cause that produces the rectangles. It will understand that their existence is inscribed in the circle and results from the circle's necessity. Let us nevertheless note that, for the example to be truly pertinent, we must assume that the circle that engenders them, following the manner of God, controls the geometrician's hand. It is likely for this reason that Spinoza begins his scholium by voicing reservations about the example that he goes on to develop and even calls attention to its inadequate character. Let us also beware of believing, on this basis, that we have to wait for the rectangles D and E to exist for us to be able of conceiving them *sub specie aeternitatis*, thereby subordinating this type of approach to chronological details. If the existence of the rectangle is necessary insofar as it is included in the essence of the circle, the categories of present and future lose their meaning. A necessary future is, to our eyes, as present as the present, like the scholium of proposition 62 encourages us to think.[10]

It remains to be understood why Spinoza does not content himself with qualifying this knowledge as eternal and adds the mysterious *sub specie*. This phrase does not serve to deny that things are eternal, but to show that they are only so to a certain extent and under a certain aspect. Indeed, it is necessary to conceive them from the perspective of necessity, as they are contained in God, in order to perceive them as eternal. From the moment they cease being envisaged as such and become connected to the common order of nature, they are thought in relation to a certain time and place and grasped in their duration. Since things can be conceived as actual in two

---

[10] *Ethics* IV, 62 Schol.; CWS I, 581: 'If we could have adequate knowledge of the duration of things, and determine by reason their times of existing, we would regard future things with the same affect as present ones, and the mind would want the good it conceived as future just as it wants the good it conceives as present.'

ways, let us hazard that the infamous *sub specie* serves to delimit and clarify the framework in which they can be apprehended as eternal. In this sense, the expression *sub specie aeternitatis* is a counterpart to turns of phrase like *eatenus* and *eatenus tantum* used in the demonstration of proposition 29 to draw the contours and restrict the sphere of extension of the concept *sub duratione*.[11]

We can now more reliably risk a translation; because the phrase expresses a particular modality of knowledge, the translation must bear the traces of that fact. Now, the cognitive process is presented as a way of seeing, in accordance with a very widespread tradition. On several occasions, Spinoza uses the term 'contemplation' in order to qualify different types of knowledge[12] and adopts the verb *contemplari* when he introduces the notion of perception *sub quadam specie aeternitatis*.[13] He names the third type of knowledge 'intuitive knowledge' and equates it with a synoptic vision.[14] In this case, it is obvious that the term *specie* in the phrase that concerns us is linked to a manner of seeing and should therefore be associated with the verb *specio* that means to look at something (*regarder*). For this reason, we suggest translating the expression *sub specie aeternitatis* with the phrase 'under a gaze of eternity (*sous un regard d'éternité*)'. To conceive things *sub specie aeternitatis* is to consider them with an eternal eye. The expression seems neither inappropriate nor imported. Doesn't Spinoza himself say that demonstrations are the eyes of the mind?[15] It seems surprising, for that matter, that commentators[16] have hardly considered making a connection with this illuminating claim of the scholium of proposition 23.

It is true that the translation proposed by Martial Gueroult well expresses the fact that a conception *sub specie aeternitatis* consists in envisaging things from an eternal point of view, since the term aspect (*aspect*) designates

[11] *Ethics* V, 20 Dem.; CWS I, 609: 'Insofar as the mind conceives the present existence of its body, it conceives duration (*eatenus durationem concipit*), which can be determined by time, and to that extent (*eatenus tantum*) it has only the power of conceiving things in relation to time (by P21 and IIP26).'

[12] See *Ethics* II, 40 Schol. 2; CWS I, 477–8.

[13] See *Ethics* II, 44 Dem. of Cor. 2; CWS I, 481.

[14] See *Ethics* II, 40 Schol. 2; CWS I, 478: 'Given the numbers 1, 2, and 3, no one fails to see that the fourth proportional number is 6 – and we see this much more clearly because we infer the fourth number from the ratio which, *in one glance*, we see the first number to have the second.' Emphasis added.

[15] *Ethics* V, 23 Schol.; CWS I, 607–8.

[16] Mignini (1994) rightly connects the expression *sub specie aeternitatis* with the Latin verb *specio* and suggests translating it with something like the point of view or perspective of eternity, implying a gaze, or a vision of the intellect.

what allows itself to be seen (*ce qui se donne à voir*). It nevertheless contains several shortcomings: it implies that things possess an aspect of eternity, which is of course not false but nonetheless masks the essential, namely that the expression here concerns a conception; it does not sufficiently convey the active character of knowledge insofar as the word aspect refers more to what is offered to a gaze (*regard*) than the act of looking (*regarder*) itself – more, that is, to the object than to the subject. Finally, it is not free from ambiguity, since an aspect can be reduced to a mere appearance whereas a conception *sub specie aeternitatis* is necessarily true. For these reasons, it is preferable to place the accent on the active dimension of a vision (*vision*) of the intellect and to rely on evidence provided by Spinoza himself for translating the phrase. It is not by chance that the allusion to the eyes of the mind intervenes immediately after the demonstration of the existence of an idea expressing the essence of the body *sub specie aeternitatis*.

The reference to '*oculi mentis*' is all the less accidental in that in the *Theologico-Political Treatise* Spinoza again alludes to a gaze (*regard*) of the mind that, thanks to demonstrations, sees invisible things. 'Invisible things, and those which are the objects only of the mind, can't be seen by any other eyes than by demonstrations. Someone who doesn't have demonstrations doesn't see anything at all in these things.'[17] In short, sensible things are visible because they are shown (*se montre*) and invisible things because they are demonstrated (*se démontrent*). Invisible objects are conceived as actual only by the intellect via an eternal gaze thanks to demonstrations whose order and connection reproduce the way in which all things follow from the divine necessity.

One could, nonetheless, object that such a translation is inadequate for it can strictly speaking describe conceptions of the human mind but cannot apply to those of God. Spinoza also uses the phrase in relation to God's ideas, notably in proposition 22 when he claims that 'in God there is necessarily an idea that expresses the essence of this or that human body, under a species of eternity'.[18] To attribute a gaze (*regard*) to God . . . is this not to succumb to a gross anthropomorphism? To that, one could reply that the metaphor is no more out of place than when it is used in relation to human intellect. If Spinoza does not hesitate to say that God contemplates himself,[19] then he should be even less reluctant to speak of a gaze insofar as the human intellect is a part of the divine intellect. We must also note that this proposition does

[17] *TTP* XIII; *CWS* II, 260.
[18] *Ethics* V, 22; *CWS* I, 607.
[19] *Ethics* V, 36 Dem.; *CWS* I, 612.

not bring substance into play but concerns the immediate infinite mode of thought. Finally, the idea that expresses the essence of the body *sub specie aeternitatis* is not presented as an idea *of* God, but as an idea *in* God; it concerns the essence of the human mind rather than that of the divine intellect as a whole.

The affirmation of the existence of eyes of the mind and a gaze of eternity should not be taken as a minor assertion. It constitutes, on the contrary, a crucial thesis, for it is the condition of possibility for that feeling and experience of eternity to which the mysterious scholium of proposition 23 alludes. It is indeed because there are eyes of the mind that we feel and experience that we are eternal. The mind's eternity is not something visible or perceptible by memory or the imagination. In Letter XII, the correspondence with Louis Meyer had already highlighted that it can only be conceived by the intellect. So we can neither feel nor experience it by means of our senses. We therefore cannot remember ourselves as having existed before the body. Neither the eyes nor any other sense instruments can give us a feeling of eternity because everything begins and ends for them with the existence of our body. Through memory and the imagination, we can only feel and experience that we are durational. Under these circumstances, it is clear that the feeling and experience here in question are not connected to the body and are not of the sensible order – for if they were of this nature, they would at most give us an impression of immortality or unlimited duration. For humans to see the invisible, they must be affected in an intellectual manner by means of demonstrations. It is therefore necessary to recognise the existence of a gaze of the mind. The thesis in itself presents nothing new since the Platonic sun,[20] and also finds echoes in Lucretius,[21] Proclus[22] and Boethius.[23]

It remains to be known if this gaze of the soul that adequately conceives things in a necessary manner is unique or if it is liable to take on several modalities that would correspond to different degrees of perception. It is clear that demonstrations can produce a double effect, since they can engender true knowledge and a feeling of eternity, neither of which is reducible to the other. Setting experience aside, can they not also give rise to certain gazes alongside certain gazes (*faire naître certain regards à côté de regards certains*), as the phrase *sub quadam specie aeternitatis* invites us to believe? In

---

[20] Plato, *Republic* VII, 519b, also cited by Moreau.
[21] Lucretius, *De natura rerum*, also cited by A. Suhamy at the Spinoza colloquium, March 1993.
[22] Proclus, *Elements of Theology*, 178, also cited by Mignini 1994.
[23] Boethius, *Consolation of Philosophy*, I, 12.

other words, it becomes necessary to clarify the nature of this gaze of eternity by comparing conceptions *sub specie* and *sub quadam specie aeternitatis* to determine their respective meaning and value.

Sub Quadam Specie Aeternitatis

The expression *sub quadam specie aeternitatis* appears four times[24] in the Spinozist corpus and does not fail to provoke questions as to its exact meaning and value. Commentators have sometimes taken it to be negligible and passed over the term *quadam* in silence, or else have more generally wondered whether the distinction between conceptions *sub quadam specie* and *sub specie aeternitatis* strictly corresponded to that between knowledge of the second and third kind.

It is clear that if this expression is connected to reason, it does not serve to put forth a radical distinction between knowledge of the second and third kinds insofar as it is presented as a property of the intellect in general in the *Treatise on the Emendation of the Intellect*[25] and as it is assimilated, as we have seen, to conception *sub specie aeternitatis* in the demonstration of proposition 29 of *Ethics* V. Reason is thus capable of conceiving things both *sub quadam specie* and *sub specie aeternitatis*. The equivalence between the two conceptions seems beyond doubt. To be persuaded of this, it is enough to compare the terms in which each one of these perceptions is defined. If we follow the scholium of proposition 29 from Part V, it is necessary, in order to form knowledge *sub specie aeternitatis*, to understand in a true way that things are contained in God, follow from the necessity of God's nature, and that their ideas involve God's eternal and infinite essence. Now, perception *sub quadam specie aeternitatis* perfectly fulfils these demands since reason truly grasps the necessity of things as they are in themselves and connects it to that of the eternal nature of God. Corollary 2 of proposition 44 does not explicitly mention the fact that reason conceives things as they are contained in God and involve God's eternal essence; proposition 45, however, establishes this and recalls that existence does not here refer to duration, but to singular things insofar as they are in God.

---

[24] See *TdIE* 108, CWS I, 44; *TTP* VI, CWS II, 158; *Ethics* II, 44 and 44 Dem. of Cor. 2, CWS I, 480–1.

[25] *TdIE* 108, CWS I, 44: The intellect 'perceives things not so much under duration as under a certain species of eternity, and in an infinite number – or rather, to perceive things, it attends neither to number nor to duration; but when it images things, it perceives them under a certain number, determinate duration and quantity'.

Should we for all that take the two formulations for synonyms and consider the adjective *quadam* to be a completely meaningless determination? It is in any case curious to note that the expression *sub quadam specie aeternitatis* only appears in the second corollary of proposition 44 of Part II and then disappears in Part V. Is this a mere coincidence? Either way, the adjective introduces a specification whose significance will have to be weighed. To shed some light on this difficulty, we must not limit ourselves to an examination of the properties common to conceptions *sub quadam specie* and *sub specie aeternitatis*, for such an endeavour will not give us their singular essences. We must rather search for their proximate cause in accordance with the Spinozist demands of a genetic definition. To this end, we must first observe that all knowledge implying an eternal gaze is, by definition, conditional upon grasping the essence of the body *sub specie aeternitatis*.[26] This makes perfect sense insofar as the mind is nothing other than the idea of the actually (in both senses of the term) existing body. In this respect, all its perceptions are grounded either in affections of the body tied to spatio-temporal existence or in grasping the body's essence *sub specie aeternitatis*. From this angle, even the principles of the second kind of knowledge rely on a conception of the essence of the body *sub specie aeternitatis*. Although they do not explain the singular essence of the body, they do in fact involve it, for they cannot be born without apprehension of notions common to my body and another body. The principles of reason are therefore eternal because they express certain properties of the body's eternal essence.

Nevertheless, if all knowledge *sub specie aeternitatis* depends on the perception of the body's essence under the same angle, it is clear that reason cannot, strictly speaking, fully meet this demand, for reason never provides us with the body's essence, but only with common notions. Proposition 37 of Part II establishes this fact once and for all: 'What is common to all things . . . and is equally in the part and in the whole, does not constitute the essence of any singular thing.'[27] Consequently, when reason conceives things *sub specie aeternitatis*, it does so not based on the body's essence, but on its properties. In this case, the adjective *quadam* could refer to this particular angle of approach, which in no way compromises the adequate value of the perception insofar as both the body's essence and its properties are eternal truths. In other words, to conceive things *sub quadam specie aeternitatis* consists in understanding them in their necessity and truth on the basis

---

[26] *Ethics* V, 29; CWS I, 609.
[27] *Ethics* II, 37; CWS I, 474.

of our body's properties; conceiving things *sub specie aeternitatis* also consists in understanding them in their necessity and truth, but based on our body's essence.

An examination of two other texts where the expression *sub quadam specie aeternitatis* appears confirms the above interpretation. In paragraph 108 of the *Treatise on the Emendation of the Intellect*, the phrase is used during an analysis not of the intellect's essence, but of its properties. Its capacity to perceive things *sub quadam specie aeternitatis* stems from one of its properties, that which consists in forming certain ideas, and not from its essence, which is at that point still not fully known. Spinoza, let us recall, seeks a principle that allows him to reach knowledge of eternal things that can grant him perfect happiness. For this, he defines a method whose principal part 'is to understand as well as possible the powers of the intellect, and its nature'.[28] His approach can be easily accounted for since we can only know eternal things by means of what is eternal in us. We must therefore grasp the essence of what is eternal in us, namely, the intellect. For this reason, Spinoza sets out to discern its innermost (*intime*) nature. Now, insofar as its definition is not entirely clear in itself, Spinoza seeks to get closer to it by way of its properties. If we come to know the properties clearly and distinctly, the definition will be clarified. In fact, we cannot truly understand the properties without understanding the essence of the thing since the former are consequences of the latter. To perceive the exact nature of a consequence, it is clear that we must know its cause. Knowledge of a property therefore involves the essence of the thing. We understand better when reason is able to pass from a conception *sub quadam specie aeternitatis* to a conception *sub specie aeternitatis*. It is enough for reason to develop and explain the essence of the thing implied in each one of its properties. Here, then, is why, in Part V, Spinoza no longer uses the adjective *quadam* when he recalls that reason perceives things *sub specie aeternitatis*. It is actually on the basis of a clear and distinct analysis of the body's properties that reason reaches the essence that they involve. Any comprehension of properties is inseparable from that of essence. Consequently, there is neither a break nor a difference in nature, but a difference of degree between conceptions *sub quadam specie* and *sub specie aeternitatis*.

Chapter VI of the *Theologico-Political Treatise* also supports this interpretation. Spinoza, in his critique of the idea of miracles, establishes that only the universal laws of nature allow us to know the essence and existence of God. 'But since (as we've already shown) the laws of nature extend to

---

[28] *TdIE* 106; CWS I, 43.

infinitely many things, and we conceive them under a certain species of
eternity, and nature proceeds according to them in a definite and immutable order, to that extent they indicate to us God's infinity, eternity, and
immutability.'[29] Spinoza refers to an earlier demonstration: the laws of
nature can be conceived *sub quadam specie aeternitatis*, for they involve an
eternal necessity. They are divine decrees or concepts, since willing and
conceiving are one thing for God. Nothing in nature can come to contradict them, for that would violate the decree, God's intellect, and God's
nature, thereby decreasing God's power. God himself cannot act against his
own laws, for to do so would be to deny God's own nature; an unthinka-
ble absurdity that would amount to saying that God is not God. The laws
have a universal extension and are not limited to only certain things, for
the power of nature is the very power of God and, by virtue of God's infinity, this power extends to all that is conceived by God's intellect. For this
reason, no miraculous exception can come to disrupt natural laws. This
allows us to understand that the laws of nature can be contemplated under
a gaze of eternity. If Spinoza says that they are conceived by us *sub quadam
specie* and not simply *sub specie aeternitatis*, it is because they are common
notions. They thus allow us to know our essence and that of God only on
the basis of common properties that they convey. Spinoza says so clearly:
God's essence and existence are not perceived directly, but through the
intervention of the fixed and immutable order of nature; they are deduced
from common notions.

The approach followed to illuminate God's nature is the same as the one
that was recommended in the *Treatise on the Emendation of the Intellect*. It is
on the basis of properties and their connection with essence that adequate
knowledge of God's nature is formed. The adjective *quadam* here thus
indicates that specific determination that leads us to apprehend essence
through common notions, a determination that vanishes as soon as we
truly understand. To know the property of a triangle according to which the
sum of its angles is equal to that of two straight lines is to know its nature.
This property is indeed a consequence of its essence and cannot be truly
conceived without its cause being adequately perceived. There is therefore
no need to maintain that conceptions *sub quadam specie* and *sub specie
aeternitatis* are really distinct, for they go perfectly hand in hand with each
other.

The problem would be resolved if Spinoza had not introduced two vari-
ants on his typical formulation. In *Ethics* II, he uses the expression '*sub hac*

---

[29] *TTP* VI; CWS II, 158.

specie aeternitatis' to qualify the manner in which reason perceives things.[30] He also uses the phrase *sub eadem aeternitatis seu necessitatis specie*[31] in Part IV when he attempts to demonstrate that the mind, under the guidance of reason, 'is affected with the same certainty . . . whether the idea is of a future or a past thing, or of a present one'.[32] Should we grant a specific value to these expressions? Or, considering them insignificant, draw our investigation to a close?

The first phrase is presented as an equivalent to the expression *sub quadam specie aeternitatis* since it appears during the first demonstration of the second corollary and concerns the natural capacity of reason to perceive the necessity of things such as it is in itself. The demonstrative *hac* here indicates that the eternal contemplation in question is none other than the true perception of the necessity of things such as they are contained in the eternal nature of God. We cannot invoke the presence of *hac* in the first part of the demonstration and that of *quadam* in the second to mark a distinction between two forms of conception, for both arguments aim to establish the same corollary, namely that reason, by nature, perceives things *sub quadam aeternitatis specie*. It is therefore false to believe that *hac* would serve to positively highlight the eternity of a perception while *quadam* would be limited to negatively emphasising its atemporality by showing that it escapes time.

As for conception *sub eadem aeternitatis seu necessitatis specie*, it is explicitly assimilated to perception *sub quadam aeternitatis specie*, since through the demonstration, Spinoza makes direct reference to the second corollary of proposition 44.[33] *Eadem* marks the fact that the mind confers the same necessity to things when it conceives them from an eternal viewpoint. The present, in this case, has no greater influence on us than the past or future and does not affect us more intensely. Chronological determinations cease to matter, making way for axiological considerations alone that themselves invite us to forgo a minor present good for the benefit of a greater future one.

Ultimately, the different phrases used by Spinoza to qualify conception *sub specie aeternitatis* do not testify to a desire to mark out distinctions

---

[30] *Ethics* II, 44 Dem. of Cor. 2; CWS I, 481: 'Ergo de natura rationis est res sub hac aeternitatis specie contemplari.' 'Therefore, it is of the nature of reason to regard things under this species of eternity.'

[31] *Ethics* IV, 62 Dem.; CWS I, 581: 'Quicquid mens ducente ratione concipit, id omne sub eadem aeternitatis, seu necessitatis specie concipit . . .'. 'Whatever the mind conceives under the guidance of reason, it conceives under the same species of eternity, or necessity . . .'.

[32] *Ethics* IV, 62; CWS I, 581.

[33] See *Ethics* IV, 62 Dem.; CWS I, 581.

between types of more or less adequate approaches to the necessity of things. They therefore cannot be understood as progressive stages of a cognitive approach that would go from a confused representation *sub duratione* to a clear and distinct perception *sub specie aeternitatis*. Whether it is exercised on the basis of the examination of properties or of essences, eternal vision is entirely adequate. At the same time, the mystery surrounding the relation and connection between an existence *sub specie aeternitatis* and an existence *sub duratione* grows stronger. It thus becomes crucial to analyse the relations between eternity and duration to be able to determine how the two types of existence can be reconciled.

Part II
From Eternity to Duration

5

Eternity and Temporality

In the Greek tradition, the relationship between time and eternity takes the form of a mysterious passage from the world of perfect and immutable being to its pale copy, the world of becoming in perpetual change. The moving image of eternity for Plato, a consequence of the processual movement of the One for Plotinus, time is often the result of a degradation of the chain of beings that is exhausted in being unfurled. Even though duration is in league with the existence of modes and constitutes the property (*propre*) of beings that are not self-caused, it does not appear as the indication of an ontological impoverishment in Spinoza. Modes are not the beneficiaries of necessary existence, but they do enjoy a necessity of existing. All things, when conceived *sub specie aeternitatis*, include, through God's essence, existence – at least if we follow the demonstration of proposition 30 from *Ethics* V. The eternity of modes is well and truly a reality that is reducible neither to a participation nor to an imperfect imitation. At the same time, through a curious reversal in perspective, it is not the mind's eternity that constitutes a real conundrum, but the appearance and existence of duration. This looks a bit like the mysterious, contingent residue of history of which Hegel speaks, a residue that does not shake the necessity of the process but remains rebellious to it. It is nonetheless clear, to Spinoza's eyes, that the feeling of contingency is the deceptive fruit of a confused understanding and that the existence of duration itself answers to a necessity. Given this situation, it is important to determine why and how eternal modes can endure.

To this end, we must, before anything else, clear away the obstacles that prevent us from understanding the relationship between duration and eternity and that thereby lead to confusion. The first is tied to an apparent difficulty of Spinozist thought which seems to temporalise the intemporal. The second concerns a reworking of the concepts of duration and time in relation to the scholastic tradition. So long as the details of the problem go unclarified, the existence of duration will lead to vain speculations improperly based on the idea of a genesis or a passage from the eternal to the temporal.

The Problem of the Temporalisation of Eternity

The Details of the Problem

The first thing that an examination of the relation between duration and eternity encounters is what we could call the paradox of a temporalisation of eternity. On the one hand, eternity excludes any reference to a temporality, even an infinite one. Spinoza always takes care to distinguish eternity from a duration without beginning or end[1] and further clarifies that it allows for neither chronological succession[2] nor a division between past, present and future. From this angle, he does not display much originality, for it resonates with classical characteristics of the *aîon* such as Plato formulated it in the *Timaeus* by castigating, like Spinoza, the inadequate use of temporal categories applied to eternity. Plato had already recalled that 'the past and future are created species of time, which we unconsciously but wrongly transfer to the eternal essence; for we say that he "was", he "is", and he "will be", but the truth is that "is" alone is properly attributed to him, and that "was" and "will be" are only to be spoken of becoming in time'.[3] It is equally clear for Spinoza that 'eternity can neither be defined by time nor have any relation to time'.[4]

On the other hand, Spinoza makes use of a temporal register to describe the properties of eternity on multiple occasions. In particular, he employs adverbs or phrases that invite one to reduce eternity to sempiternity. So, for example, the expression *to always exist* is used as a synonym for eternal being in proposition 21 of *Ethics* I: 'All the things which follow from the absolute nature of any of God's attributes have always had to exist and be infinite (*semper et infinita existere*), or are, through the same attribute, eternal and infinite.'[5] If we follow certain commentators, the presence of temporal references to describe eternity is not accidental but constant. Bernard

---

[1] See on this subject CM II, 1; CWS I, 317–18; *Ethics* I, Def. 8 Exp.; CWS I, 409.

[2] CM II, 1; CWS I, 316: 'For since his being is eternal, i.e., in it there can be nothing which is before or after, we can never ascribe duration to him, without at the same time destroying the true concept which we have of God.'

[3] Plato, *Timaeus*, 37e–38a.

[4] *Ethics* V, 23 Schol.; CWS I, 607.

[5] *Ethics* I, 21; CWS I, 429.

Rousset will even come to devote a study to 'the expression and temporal signification of eternity'.[6] He surveys several occurrences of chronological vocabulary in the last pages of the *Ethics* to show that Spinoza temporalises eternity by treating it as a particular form of duration subject to succession and becoming.

Should we in that case subscribe to the thesis according to which Spinoza conceives eternity as a 'continuous and constant temporality',[7] a 'necessary perpetuity',[8] or should we instead place the emphasis on its irreducible atemporality? The Spinozist doctrine seems contradictory, for it is impossible to simultaneously maintain that eternity 'cannot be explained by duration or time'[9] and define it with the help of this very register. The problem seems all the more intractable as it brings the coherence of Spinozism into play, whatever the chosen solution may be, for if we opt in favour of a temporalisation of eternity, we are forced to acknowledge the incoherence or failure of an endeavour aiming to strip this property of any chronological reference. In this light, several warnings intended to prevent confusion appear either as hollow fantasies or pious pledges. Conversely, if we instead refuse to reduce eternity to a particular type of duration, in accordance with Spinoza's stated intentions, then we run into the presence of a formidable duality for a monist philosophy, for the essential atemporality of eternity seems radically opposed to the fundamental temporality of duration.

Critique of the Theory of a Temporalisation of Eternity

If we focus our attention on the meticulousness with which Spinoza attempts, on several occasions, to distinguish eternity from an unlimited duration, then it obviously becomes impossible to think for a moment that it is only a variant of sempiternity. The idea of a 'temporalisation' of eternity proves to be all the more inadequate insofar as it renders incomprehensible the critiques that Spinoza directs to those who have committed the error of conceiving this property as a particular species of duration.[10] If he denounces the attribution to God of a duration founded on the observation of an increase in the length of God's creation since the creation of Adam, it is not merely to then fall victim to the same reproaches. When he claims that

---

[6] Rousset 1968: 70–8.
[7] Ibid.
[8] Ibid.
[9] *Ethics* I, Def. 8 Exp.; CWS I, 409.
[10] Cf. CM II, 1; CWS I, 317.

'the chief attribute, which deserves consideration before all others, is God's eternity, by which we explain his duration',[11] he immediately clarifies his formulation by specifying that 'so as not to ascribe *any* duration to God, we say that he is eternal'.[12]

Eternity cannot be reduced to some form of duration, whatever this form might be, for the good reason that it is not the property of an existence taken in isolation, but rather expresses the necessary relation between existence and essence. 'Duration', however, 'is an affection of existence, and not of the essence of things.'[13] 'For no one will ever say that the essence of a circle or a triangle, insofar as it is an eternal truth, has endured longer now than it had in the time of Adam.'[14] Neither the indefinite nor the infinite character of an existence can account for Spinozist eternity. Only grasping the necessary link between existence and essence allows one to apprehend it. If God is eternal in *Metaphysical Thoughts*, it is because its essence is not distinguished from its existence. The *Ethics* will not go back on this point. If finite minds are themselves eternal and no longer simply immortal, it is precisely because their existence is conceived as necessarily following from the essence of God.[15] Consequently, as duration is a property that applies exclusively to existence and implies no link with essence, it is not of the same nature as eternity and is not capable of providing us with the latter's exact content.

Given the above, the presence of temporal expressions to qualify eternity continues to be enigmatic. Should this paradox be attributed to a deficiency in vocabulary, as a remark in *Metaphysical Thoughts* suggests?[16] This explanation is even more seductive to the extent that it is supported by Spinoza's own conception of the imaginative and inadequate character of language. For this reason, we must be attentive to the ambiguity and equivocity of words before accusing Spinoza of incoherence, and refrain from coming to hasty conclusions, for several expressions lend themselves to a double interpretation.

In this respect, some commentators assert that Spinoza, by affirming, for example, that 'all the things which follow from the absolute nature of any of God's attributes have always had to exist (*semper existit*)',[17] supports the

---

[11] CM II, 1; CWS I, 316.
[12] Ibid. Emphasis added.
[13] Ibid.
[14] Ibid.
[15] *Ethics* V, 30 Dem.; CWS I, 610.
[16] CM II, 1; CWS I, 317: 'We are accustomed, on account of a defect of words, to ascribe eternity also to things those essence is distinguished from their existence . . .'.
[17] *Ethics* I, 21; CWS I, 429.

idea that modal eternity boils down to a sempiternity. Alan Donagan[18] goes even further: he reckons that substance, too, exists in time, relying, in particular, on the demonstration of proposition 11 from *Ethics* II where Spinoza observes that 'an infinite thing must always exist necessarily (*semper necessario existere*)'.[19]

We must note, however, that the expression 'infinite thing' does not here apply to substance but to immediate and mediate infinite modes as the reference to propositions 21 and 22 of Part I suggests. It thus cannot secure the assimilation of God's eternity to a sempiternity or an existence in time. The presence of the word *semper* is no more decisive. If it is true that the adverb *always* (*toujours*) implies a reference to duration, to the extent that it evokes a continuity and a permanence, it can also designate that which is without reference to a past or a future and that instead expresses an absolute presence as opposed to a mere temporal present. Plotinus made this point in his chapter of the *Enneads* dedicated to eternity and time. To maintain that the eternal being can know neither before nor after, he declares that it always is (*est toujours*). To guard against any error, however, he specifies that he does not use this adverb in its typical sense:

> Observe that such words as 'always', 'never', 'sometimes' must be taken as mere conveniences of exposition: thus 'always' – used in the sense not of time but of incorruptibility and endlessly complete scope – might set up the false notion of stage and interval . . . There is, of course, no difference between Being and Everlasting Being; just as there is none between a philosopher and a true philosophy: the attribute 'true' came into use because there arose what masqueraded as philosophy; and for similar reasons 'everlasting' was adjoined to 'Being', and 'Being' to 'everlasting', and we have the tautology of 'Everlasting Being'.[20]

In light of Plotinian analyses, it becomes possible to clarify Spinozist thought and to suggest an interpretation of proposition 21 of *Ethics* I stripped of any chronological references. When Spinoza maintains that 'all the things which follow from the absolute nature of any of God's attributes have always had to exist and be infinite, or are, through the same attribute, eternal and infinite',[21] he does not temporalise eternity. To *always exist* here means to

[18] Donagan 1979.
[19] *Ethics* II, 11; CWS I, 456.
[20] Plotinus, *Enneads* III, 7, 6, 20–35.
[21] *Ethics* I, 21; CWS I, 429.

be necessarily in act, in opposition to being contingent. Spinoza's aim is to show that what stems from the absolute nature of an attribute cannot have a determinate duration by virtue of the immutable necessity that links effects to causes. The expression to *always exist* is thus not used to affirm a duration, but to deny it. This interpretation seems to be in better keeping with the spirit of proposition 21, for it is fully compatible with the affirmation of eternity that follows it and does not introduce any incoherence or distortion into the utterance.

Commentators have always based themselves on proposition 23 of *Ethics* V to establish the inescapably temporal character of Spinozist eternity. 'The human mind cannot be absolutely destroyed with the body, but something of it remains (*remanet*) which is eternal.'[22] The verb *remanet* is interpreted in a temporal sense as meaning what persists (*subsister*) after death; it can, however, also refer to [the result of] a mathematical operation of subtraction, implying a logical and not chronological process.[23] It would then designate what remains once we have taken away memory and the imagination, namely, the intellect. In this case, the intellect is not conceived as the part that enjoys a posthumous destiny when the other parts perish. It is eternal and does not begin to be so after the destruction of the body. There is thus no need to mark out periods within its existence by distinguishing what is anterior or posterior to the existence of the body and imagination. If we avoid the temporal connotations of the Spinozist vocabulary to retain only its logical sense, then, the difficulties vanish, for it is no longer possible to accuse the author of the *Ethics* of temporalising eternity despite himself.

Supporters of this thesis, however, do not base themselves only on lexical considerations. They also claim that Spinoza, in the economy of his system, openly supports the interpretation of eternity in temporal terms. Does he himself not introduce his conception of the mind's eternity by saying that 'it is time now to pass to those things which pertain to the mind's duration without relation to the body'?[24] The expression 'mind's duration' does not, however, allow us to presuppose the nature of the exposition which follows. Spinoza comes to complete the examination of all that concerns the duration of the mind in relation to the present existence of the body and he logically follows his reflection with a study of the mind's duration without relation to the body's present existence, without yet resolving the question of whether the term is itself adequate insofar as it still does not envisage

[22] *Ethics* V, 23; CWS I, 607.
[23] See Hallett 1930: 35 and the following.
[24] *Ethics* V, 20 Schol.; CWS I, 606.

things *sub specie aeternitatis*. This does not, however, prevent him from subsequently denying that it involves a duration, as he had done in *Metaphysical Thoughts* when he began by claiming that eternity was the principal attribute that allows us to explain God's duration only to then clarify his formulation and refuse the imputation of a duration to God.[25] He follows, it seems, the same path in the *Ethics*, for not only will he no longer use the term duration to designate the mind's eternity, he will also take care to highlight that we can only grant duration to the mind during the actual existence of the body. 'But we do not attribute to the human mind any duration that can be defined by time, except insofar as it expresses the actual existence of the body, which is explained by duration, and can be defined by time, i.e. (by IP8C), we do not attribute duration to it except while the Body endures.'[26] We must finally note that, if he opens his reflection with a remark announcing his intention to treat *the mind's duration without relation to the body*, he closes it, in the scholium of proposition 40, by omitting any reference to this concept. 'These are the things I have decided to show concerning the mind, *insofar as it is considered without relation to the body's existence*.'[27]

Bernard Rousset nevertheless maintains that Spinoza temporalises eternity, for he himself explicitly admits that the eternal part has existed before and will exist after the body, thereby introducing chronological points of reference.[28] The commentator relies on three citations of the *Ethics* to show that 'it indeed involves an existence anterior and posterior to that of the body and imagination: "we have existed before the body"; "this love for God has had no beginning"; and "the sage never ceases to be"'.[29]

The first phrase, taken from the scholium of proposition 23 from Part V, cannot serve as an argument in favour of the theory of eternity's temporalisation, for Spinoza does not say 'we have existed before the body', but 'it is impossible that we should recollect that we existed before the body', which is quite different.[30] The concept of anteriority does not directly apply here to the eternal existence of the mind. Spinoza's aim is not to show that the mind exists before the body, but rather to affirm the possibility of an experience of eternity that memory would be incapable of recounting insofar as the

---

[25] CM II, 1; CWS I, 316: 'The chief attribute, which deserves consideration before all others, is God's eternity, by which we explain his duration. Or rather, so as not to ascribe any duration to God, we say that he is eternal.'

[26] *Ethics* V, 23 Dem.; CWS I, 607.

[27] *Ethics* V, 40 Schol.; CWS I, 615. Emphasis added.

[28] Rousset 1968: 72.

[29] Ibid.

[30] *Ethics* V, 23 Schol.; CWS I, 607.

latter is dependent on both the body's duration[31] and inadequate temporal categories. To say that we do not remember having existed before the body does not therefore mean that the eternal element in us is anterior to the body's existence, even though our imagination inclines us to believe so.

Neither does the second phrase prove that Spinoza defines eternity by relying on the concepts of anteriority and posteriority. If 'the love for God has had no beginning', it becomes precisely impossible to assign a limit before which it did not yet exist and upon which it is developed. Now, in the absence of a fixed point of reference, before and after are categories emptied of any content. The absence of a beginning does not permit us to either reduce eternity to intellectual love or to a duration unlimited in both directions, for Spinoza has taken good care to forbid such an assimilation.[32]

Finally, the last phrase according to which 'the sage . . . never ceases to be (*nunquam esse desinit*)'[33] does not in any way allow us to justify the introduction of a distinction between before and after because what it emphasises is continuity. Like the adverb *semper*, the adverb *nunquam* can express a necessity that is not of a chronological order. Thus, the eternity of the sage should not be understood as a succession of presents, but as a self-presence (*présence de soi*). The sage indeed does not cease to be, for he is conscious of himself and of God.

Still, proponents of the theory of a temporalisation of eternity in Spinoza point to one last piece of apparently indisputable evidence in support of their reading. Eternity, by their lights, indeed dons a temporal character since it is progressively acquired bit by bit in the development of our adequate knowledge. Bernard Rousset maintains this position when he writes that eternity 'is even more temporal than immutability: it is becoming and transition, if it is true that Spinoza posits an acquired and progressive eternity tied to the development of our knowledge and love and that the joy which is based on this love and beatitude corresponds to a variation of our power'.[34] It is obvious that the more we adequately understand, the more we are active and the greater we increase our power, but this in no way means that the mind's eternity is gradually acquired. We must not confuse the discovery here and now of the eternal character of the mind with its eternity in act. If we conceive things *sub specie aeternitatis*, we cannot maintain that the

---

[31] See *Ethics* V, 21; CWS I, 607.
[32] *Ethics* I, Def. 8 Exp.; CWS I, 409: an eternal existence 'cannot be explained by duration or time, even if the duration is conceived to be without beginning or end'.
[33] *Ethics* V, 42 Schol.; CWS I, 617. Translation modified.
[34] Rousset 1968: 73.

mind acquires an eternity or advances toward it. The notions of beginning, of emergence (*naissance*) and growth constitute pedagogical fictions[35] and do not express a reality. Concerning this point, Spinoza recalls that 'the mind has had eternally the same perfections which, in our fiction, now come to it'.[36] An eternal existence is an existence *tota simul* where all is given in act.[37] This goes for the human mind just as well as for substance. It is also the reason why the eternity of substance is equated with infinite existence in act.[38] Though infinite, the existence of substance is a complete (*achevée*) existence, and we know well why Spinoza reduces eternity and the other three characteristic propria of a necessary being to one single property, perfection.[39] If everything is given in act, nothing can be lacking or come to be added. Plotinus had already underscored this fact: 'a close enough definition of Eternity would be that it is a life limitless in the full sense of being all the life there is and a life which, knowing nothing of past or future to shatter its completeness, possesses itself intact forever'.[40] As a result, there can be neither increase nor loss, neither change nor progress, in eternity's midst.

The idea of an eternity that is progressively acquired also leads to irresolvable contradictions, for it would mean that we could add properties to our essence bit by bit as we develop our knowledge. Our essence and its properties would thus not be eternal but would be constituted in duration. Spinozism would thereby become an existentialism *avant la lettre* since existence would precede essence and God would, like us, have to paradoxically await the evening our lives in order to form an idea of our essence.

Ultimately, Spinoza conceives of eternity as intemporal and is careful not to give it properties characteristic of duration. Martha Kneale,[41] however, claims that it is impossible to distinguish eternity from time by asserting that eternity is *tota simul*, for *simul* is a temporal notion.[42] In time, things appear either successively or simultaneously. While it denies the existence of chronological succession, the idea of simultaneity is never fully exempt

---

[35] *Ethics* V, 31 Schol.; CWS I, 610–11.

[36] *Ethics* V, 33 Schol.; CWS I, 611.

[37] Spinoza claims this in a very clear manner in paragraph 102 of the *TdIE*: in the series of eternal things, everything is simultaneous. *TdIE* 102; CWS I, 42.

[38] CM II, 1; CWS I, 318.

[39] See *Ep.* XXXV and *Ep.* XXXVI.

[40] Plotinus, *Enneads* III, 7, 5, 25–7.

[41] Kneale 1979.

[42] If in paragraph 102 of the *TdIE* Spinoza uses the adverb *simul* in relation to eternal things ('Ibi enim omnia haec sunt simul natura'), he never, in the *Ethics*, defines eternity as existence *tota simul*, as Vittorio Morfino rightly observes.

from temporal connotations, for it implies that the parts of time – past, present and future – happen together. Simultaneous things arise at the same time, not outside of time. Eternity conceived as existence *tota simul* is thus indeed in time and is not truly distinguished from sempiternity.

It is nonetheless possible to reply to Kneale with the claim that the adverb *simul* does not necessarily imply a reference to time. So, for example, in mathematics, the parts of a set can be said to be *tota simul*, for they are given all at the same time as soon as the set is itself posited. Simultaneity here refers to a logical order of necessary coexistence and not to a chrono-logical order.

Reasons for the Presence of Temporal Expressions

The fact remains that the vocabulary sometimes contains ambiguities, so much so that we should ask why Spinoza did not simply refrain from using expressions that lead to such confusion. Such an enterprise is indeed possi-ble, as the absence of temporal references in the definition of eternity itself makes clear. The author of the *Ethics* did not need to use adverbs like always or categories like before and after to make us clearly and distinctly under-stand the nature of eternity. If he uses terminology marked by chronological significations on several occasions, it is likely with a very specific intention that we must determine. It seems simplistic to think that all such expressions are to be attributed to a deficiency in vocabulary. Language, it is true, is tied to the imagination, but it is always possible to correct its inadequate charac-ter, if only by refraining from using equivocal terms or by specifying the strict meaning that one gives them. Spinoza, for that matter, takes advantage of these methods quite frequently, often giving explanations designed to ward off any confusion.

If he uses verbs like *remaneo* or adverbs like *semper* and *nunquam* without taking care to determine their exact meaning, it is because he allows for the possibility of a double reading. Such a hypothesis is not out of place, for it is possible to conceive things in two ways: *sub specie aeternitatis* and *sub duratione*. Spinoza allows for this double understanding when he claims that we conceive things as actual in two ways: 'either insofar as we conceive them to exist in relation a certain time and place, or insofar as we conceive them to be contained in God and to follow from the necessity of the divine nature'.[43] The second way of conceiving corresponds, when it is adequate, to a conception *sub specie aeternitatis*. When Spinoza says that 'the human

---

[43] *Ethics* V, 29 Schol.; CWS I, 610.

mind cannot be absolutely destroyed with the body, but something of it remains which is eternal',[44] the verb *remanet* can legitimately take the sense of subsisting after death if we conceive things in relation to a certain time and place; it must be disentangled from any chronological connotation, however, if we envisage things *sub specie aeternitatis*.

The fact remains that the first way of conceiving things is inadequate and imperfect and only concerns modes capable of a spatio-temporal approach. Now, Spinoza sometimes indifferently uses vocabulary traditionally laden with chronological connotations and applies them to beings that do not allow for any relation to either time or place, to which testifies, in particular, proposition 21 from *Ethics* I. Despite its inadequate character, the first form of conception can nevertheless serve as an aid to thought and can prove favourable to comprehension, as long as its fictive and hypothetical character is acknowledged. The scholium of proposition 31 from *Ethics* V clearly emphasises this fact. We can conceive our eternity in relation to a certain time and place and pretend that the mind now comes to acquire it and begins to understand things *sub specie aeternitatis* to explain the arduous path of salvation more easily.

Ultimately, Spinoza does not temporalise eternity as it is true that the presence of chronological references is explained by the necessity of conceiving things both *sub specie aeternitatis* and *sub duratione*. This double possibility of understanding things implies that eternity and duration are both real properties that are irreducible to one another such that it is equally vain to reduce eternity to a refined form of duration as it is to reduce duration to a degraded form of eternity. The atemporality of the first is not, however, opposed to the temporality of the second; it would be less erroneous to say that the one transposes in an eternal register what the other exposes in a temporal register. The first pitfall being avoided, the second remains to be eliminated by examining what in the Spinozist definition of duration constitutes an obstacle to understanding its relationship with eternity.

The Problem Surrounding the Reworking of the Concept of Duration

The knot of difficulties resides in the particular status of the concept of duration – a concept that, contrary to appearances, in fact takes on two distinct meanings. Typically, Spinoza assigns this term the original meaning provided in definition 5 of *Ethics* II, but he will occasionally use it in a more traditional

---

[44] *Ethics* V, 23; CWS I, 607.

sense, keeping with the meaning in use among the scholastics. The confusion between these two semantic levels inevitably leads to misunderstandings and aporias insofar as the first encompasses any form of temporality while the second is radically distinguished from eternity and can in no manner explain it. To untangle the knot of relations between the two concepts, we must discern the exact nature of duration by clarifying the older foundations of this notion as well as the reorganisation that Spinoza brings to it.

In classical thought, duration designates, in a generic sense, the mode by which a being perseveres in its existence. It has three distinct species: time, *aevum* and eternity. From this point of view, eternity is not opposed to duration, since it is a modality of it, but is rather opposed to aeviternity and temporality. So, unlike what Spinoza will say in chapter 1 of the second part of *Metaphysical Thoughts*, nothing should prevent him from attributing duration to God on the condition that it be an eternal duration. Suarez, for example, considers *aevum* and eternity to be particular forms of duration and sets himself the task of extracting specific characteristics from each. Eternity is a perfect and complete duration: 'Aeternitas essentialiter exigit quod sit duratio totius esse totiusque perfectionis et operatonis rei aeternae (Eternity essentially requires that it be a whole duration, wholly perfect and an operation of the eternal thing).'[45] *Aevum* is a permanent duration, immutable and necessary, but it does not imply existence *tota simul*. 'Aevum essentialiter est duratio permanens natura sua immutabilis, seu necessaria (Aevum is essentially a permanent duration that is by its nature unchangeable or necessary).'[46] The existence of three different species results from the necessity of finding measures of duration suitable for different types of beings. The distinction between eternity, aeviternity and temporality is thus rooted in the nature of things and is grounded on their variable or immutable character. In the same way that there are different measures of quantity for solids and liquids, there are measures of duration in accordance with a being's essence. This is what Heereboord means when he shows that there must be three measures, since there are three types of beings: beings subject to change according to their nature and affections (namely, humans); beings invariable so far as their substance is concerned but variable so far as their affections are concerned (namely, angels); and beings invariable when it comes to both their substance and affections (namely, God).[47] Spinoza will

---

[45] Suarez, *Disputationes Metaphysicae*, XXVI, 925.10.

[46] Ibid., XXVI, 943.9.

[47] Heereboord, *Meletemata Disputationum ex philosophia selectarum*, Vol. 1, 94: 'Dei aeternitate: Nam oportet mensuram esse proportionatam rei mensuratae: Ideoque quemad-

set himself apart from this tradition by simultaneously rejecting the generic character of duration, the attribution of temporality in accordance with the type of being, and the reference to the concept of measure.

The Problematic Abandonment of the Generic Concept of Duration

Spinoza's originality lies in his refusal to consider duration as a genus subdivided into species or as the central concept around which three forms of temporality would be organised. He abolishes the primacy of duration and relieves it of its generic role by assigning it a function that had traditionally been reserved for time. He breaks the traditional schema by ceasing to conceive of eternity as a particular form of duration, instead granting it an autonomous status, emancipated from any temporal determination. The specificity of the author of the *Ethics* therefore essentially concerns his desire to define a sphere proper to each concept. In neither Descartes nor Leibniz does one find such a clear refusal to think eternity by referring it to duration. In the *New Essays on Human Understanding*, Philalethes[48] claims that 'the ideas of time and of eternity really have a common source, for "we can, in our thoughts, add [certain] lengths of duration to one another, as often as we please"'.[49] Thus, the idea of eternity can be extracted from an indefinite addition of lengths of time to each other. From this point of view, Leibniz very closely approaches Locke's position, for whom the idea of eternity is a result of the addition of lengths, to infinity, of a certain duration. He is, nevertheless, against a purely empirical construction of the concept of eternity, for after Philalethes' remark, Theophilus immediately specifies that 'But to derive the notion of eternity from this we must also conceive that the same principle applies at every stage, letting one go a stage further. It is this thought of principles which yields the notion of the infinite, or the indefinite, in possible progressions. Thus, the senses unaided cannot enable us to form these notions.'[50]

The concern with making a rigorous distinction between the two concepts does not, however, lead Spinoza to a radical break with the scholastic tradition, for he continues to sometimes use, as an exception, the term

---

modum aliam mensuram pro rebus liquidis, aliam pro solidis, ita aliam debemus habere mensuram pro homine, aliam pro angelo, aliam pro deo: mensura qua mensuramus hominis esse, dicitur tempus: qua angeli aevum, qua dei aeternitas.'

[48] [TN: Philalethes constitutes a spokesperson for Locke in Leibniz's work. See Remnant and Bennett's Introduction to Leibniz's *New Essays* (p. x).]

[49] Leibniz, *New Essays*, Book II, Chapter 14, 27.

[50] Ibid.

duration in its generic sense, conforming with its scholastic use. Several examples testify to this fact in the *Short Treatise*, where Spinoza is not only unhesitant to use the expression eternal duration[51] but also clearly establishes the existence of several types of duration in accordance with the perishable or inalterable nature of the object to which the soul is attached. This is the point that chapter 23 of Part II, which deals with determining whether the soul is mortal or immortal (on the basis of an examination of its essence, the causes for its change and the causes for its duration), throws into relief. 'If the soul is united with the body only, and the body perishes, then it must also perish.'[52] Its duration is thereby limited and temporary; inversely, if it is united 'with another thing, which is, and remains, immutable, then, on the contrary, it will have to remain immutable also'. In this case, its duration would be eternal.

Spinoza does not only maintain the scholastic terminology in the *Short Treatise*, for he presents eternity as the principal attribute that allows us to explain God's duration in the first chapter of the second part of *Metaphysical Thoughts*. It is obvious that he here uses this term in its generic sense and that he in no way confers it the meaning previously determined in chapter 4 of the first part. Duration defined as 'an attribute under which we conceive the existence of created things insofar as they persevere in their actuality' cannot actually pertain to God.[53] Spinoza, it seems, is aware of the ambiguity of his formulation, for he changes his wording to guard against interpretive errors. He begins by saying that 'the chief attribute, which deserves consideration before all others, is God's eternity, by which we explain his duration' and reconsiders, adding: 'or rather, so as not to ascribe any duration to God, we say that he is eternal'.[54]

In the same way, when he opposes eternity to a determinate duration in the demonstration to proposition 21 of *Ethics* I, and implicitly connects it to an endless duration,[55] it is clear that he does not attribute to duration the same meaning as that which he will ascribe to it in the fifth definition of Part II. He uses the concept in a generic sense, since he compares forms of duration and does not restrict them to the indefinite continuity of existence.

[51] *KV* II, 24; *CWS* I, 142.
[52] *KV* II, 23; *CWS* I, 141.
[53] *CM* I, 4; *CWS* I, 310.
[54] *CM* II, 1; *CWS* I, 316.
[55] *Ethics* I, 23 Dem.; *CWS* I, 430: 'anything else which follows necessarily from the absolute nature of some attribute of God, cannot have a determinate duration, but through the same attribute is eternal'.

Spinoza's borrowing of the scholastic vocabulary is perhaps not limited to the above: could one not see in the *Ethics* a legacy of that scholastic usage at the heart of the scholium of proposition 20 from Part V where Spinoza declares his intention to pass 'to those things which pertain to the mind's duration without relation to the body'?[56] This phrase, as we have seen, cannot mean that the mind continues to endure, that is to say that the mind continues to persevere in existence in an indefinite manner after the destruction of the body, for the three propositions that follow demonstrate precisely the contrary. 'But we do not attribute to the human mind any duration that can be defined by time, except insofar as it expresses the actual existence of the body, which is explained by duration, and can be defined by time, i.e. (by IIPC), we do not attribute duration to it except while the body endures.'[57] It can no more be understood as an assimilation of the mind's eternity to duration, such as it is strictly defined at the beginning of Part II, for Spinoza explicitly rejects this interpretation. 'We nevertheless feel that our mind, insofar as it involves the essence of the body under a species of eternity, is eternal, and that this existence it has cannot be defined by time or explained through duration.'[58] It is therefore not out of the question to think that the term duration here takes on a generic sense in accordance with its scholastic use, which would be justified by the necessity to not pre-suppose the nature of the mind's temporality without relation to the body, given that the mind's eternity has not yet been demonstrated at this point.

Consequently, it is clear that Spinoza sometimes permits a use of the concept of duration in its scholastic meaning, as a letter contemporary with the writing of the *Ethics* addressed to Hudde in the middle of June 1666 also confirms – a letter where he does not refrain from speaking of the duration of the attribute of extension.[59] However, we cannot use this as an argument to show that eternity blends into (*se confond avec*) duration. Nor can we use it as an argument for denouncing the inconsistencies of the system – for traces of the survival of a broad traditional meaning alongside a more restricted and rigorous meaning of the concept are rare, and essentially confined to the earlier works.

---

[56] *Ethics* V, 20 Schol.; CWS I, 606.
[57] *Ethics* V, 23 Dem.; CWS I, 607.
[58] *Ethics* V, 23 Schol.; CWS I, 608.
[59] *Ep.* XXXVI [to Hudde]; CWS I, 27.

The Abandonment of a Temporality Proportionate to Types of Beings

Not only does Spinoza redefine the sphere of duration by narrowing its field of extension, he also stops making the attribution depend on a duration or an eternity in the nature of beings and stops distinguishing between forms of temporality adapted to different ontological types. Of course, in *Metaphysical Thoughts*, he does not significantly break from Suarezian custom, for though he abandons the concept of *aevum*, he still affirms a sympathy between a being's temporality and its nature. Indeed, in that work, the distinction between duration and eternity is the result 'of our earlier division of being into being whose essence involves existence and being whose essence involves only possible existence'.[60] The *Ethics*, by contrast, marks a major development since the dichotomy that had reserved eternity for substance and duration for modes is shattered; the two concepts are no longer defined by the division between substantial and modal nature. Eternity is no longer explicitly tied to substance. Duration, understood as indefinite continuity in existence,[61] is not presented as a determining characteristic of modes, and is itself not by definition tied to them. At the same time, the traditional details of the relations between the two concepts are turned upside down, for they no longer closely fit the contours of ontological distinctions. If the same being can combine temporal and eternal existence, then the determination of the relationship between duration and eternity can no longer limit itself to an examination of the links between a substance and its modes, but requires an analysis of the interplay (*l'articulation*) between these two ways of being within the same individual.

The Abandonment of Reference to Measure

Spinoza also breaks new ground by no longer conceiving of eternity and duration as measures appropriate to different types of being, distinguishing himself in this manner from Aquinas and Heereboord. For Spinoza, time alone retains this status. Still, the break is less straightforward than it seems. Aquinas himself draws attention to the improper character of the term measure when it is applied to God, and Heereboord agrees wholeheartedly: 'Ac quamvis Deus proprie loquendo non habeat mensuram, quia tamen aliter ejus durationem intelligere non valemus dicimus eum mensu-

---

[60] CM I, 4; CWS I, 310.
[61] *Ethics* II, Def. 5; CWS I, 447.

rari aeternitate per quam apprehendimus durationem divini esse.'[62] Eternity is therefore not truly reducible to a measure, for God's immensity allows for no such thing. To say that eternity is the measure of the divine being is only a manner of speaking of God's duration, which does not correspond to any reality.

Spinoza, for his part, does not proscribe all recourse to quantitative evaluation. If he completely abandons the idea that eternity is a measure of divine duration, he preserves, by contrast, the idea that time is a measure of the duration of finite things. As created things are made known to us through the intermediary of duration, it is hardly surprising to see that we pay extreme attention to this affection, that we compare degrees of the longevity of beings, and that we create modes of thinking designed to measure that longevity. This can be gleaned from chapter 10 of the second part of *Metaphysical Thoughts*, a chapter dedicated to creation. Still, Spinoza expresses reservations on this subject, for immediately after having recalled that 'time is the measure of duration', he revises it by adding 'or rather, is nothing but a mode of thinking'.[63] This specification responds, it seems, to a double imperative. It is meant to guard against the error that would consist in hypostatising time by granting it either an objective reality or the status of a point of reference actually existing outside of thought. It also serves the role of rectifying what is inadequate in the use of the term measure. Strictly speaking, measure is a mode of thinking that pertains to continuous quantity, whereas number pertains to discrete quantity and time to duration.[64] It is not illegitimate to represent duration as a species of continuous quantity because, by definition, it expresses perseverance in existence. However, this 'indefinite continuation of existing'[65] is not reducible to a measurable quantity without supposing a certain abstraction. Existence does not actually consist of a mere quantity of efforts, but is also evaluated with the yardstick of the quality of its power. Further, it should not be conceived in an isolated manner, independent of the necessity of God's nature. Nevertheless, any measure implies a delimitation and, hence, a certain separation. It thus requires that one disregard the inseparable link between substance and its modes. Spinoza himself recognises this fact in a scholium:

---

[62] Heereboord, *Meletemata Disputationum ex philosophia selectarum*, VI, *De Dei Aeternitate*, 94.

[63] CM II, 10; CWS I, 334.

[64] CM I, 1; CWS I, 300.

[65] *Ethics* II, Def. 5; CWS I, 447.

By existence here I do not understand duration, i.e., existence insofar as it is conceived abstractly, and as a certain species of quantity. For I am speaking of the very nature of existence, which is attributed to singular things because infinitely many things follow from the eternal necessity of God's nature in infinitely many modes. I am speaking, I say, of the very existence of singular things insofar as they are in God.[66]

Together, these two reasons allow us to understand why the term measure, when applied to time, will tend to disappear in favour of the concept of determination.[67]

By abolishing this referent, Spinoza renders vain any attempt to search for a common measure between duration and eternity. Neither commensurable nor incommensurable, both properties nevertheless coexist in a being who feels, imagines and thinks. After having thus cleared away the major obstacles which prevented us from grasping the relationship between the two concepts, it now becomes necessary to analyse how Spinoza determines and redefines the nature of duration and its relation to eternity across his work.

---

[66] *Ethics* II, 45 Schol.; *CWS* I, 482.

[67] This is what results from the scholium of proposition 62 of Part IV of the *Ethics*: 'If we could have adequate knowledge of the duration of things, and determine by reason their times of existing, we would regard future things with the same affect as present ones, and the mind would want the good it conceived as future just as it wants the good it conceives as present.' See *CWS* I, 581.

6

The Nature and Origin of Duration

Duration in *Metaphysical Thoughts*

The Essence of Duration

In the appendix to Descartes' *Principles of Philosophy*, the distinction between duration and eternity is organised around the division 'of being into being whose essence involves existence and being whose essence involves only possible existence'.[1] Possible, here, is not to be taken as contrary to necessary, for strictly speaking, everything is subject to the necessity of divine law. Spinoza takes great care to specify that 'possible and contingent signify only a defect in our knowledge about a thing's existence'.[2] 'A thing is called possible, then, when we understand its efficient cause but do not know whether the cause is determined.'[3] In this respect, it is hardly surprising that the origin of duration seems obscure, since it is linked to the problematic concept of possible existence. Consequently, an elucidation of its nature presupposes an analysis of the reasons for our ignorance, reasons that explain why we perceive as merely possible what is really necessary. Possibility and contingency are not affections of things, but testify to a weakness of our intellect, for if we perceive the existence of an efficient cause and thereby acquire the conviction that the thing is not impossible, we cannot therefore conclude with certainty that it will inevitably be produced, since we do not know if this cause is determined. If everything is necessary, how is it that we are kept in such a state of ignorance, seeing the indeterminate instead of the

[1] CM I, 4; CWS I, 310.
[2] CM I, 3; CWS I, 310.
[3] CM I, 3; CWS I, 308.

determinate? Logically, if we know the efficient cause, namely God, without which nothing could be conceived, we must infer that the effect follows from it. Why don't we manage to deduce the necessity of a thing's existence when its efficient cause is given? And why do we limit ourselves to envisaging the existence of the thing as merely possible? This weakness of our power of knowing stems from the fact that the existence of a created thing does not depend on its essence and is not contained in it. In itself, the essence has no necessity, for it is also created by God and 'depends on the eternal laws of nature'.[4] The thing's existence is subordinated to God and more specifically to 'the series and order of causes'.[5] It is not immediately created by God but implies the infinite chain of intermediary causes. Consequently, for us to be able to perceive this existence as necessary, we must conceive the whole order of nature. Spinoza confirms this observation in the second part of his appendix, in chapter 9 dedicated to the examination of God's power. 'For if men understood clearly the whole order of Nature, they would find all things just as necessary as are all those treated in Mathematics.'[6] As long as we are not capable of embracing in a single glance, through intuitive knowledge, the entire infinite chain of causes which, from God to created things, determines a thing's existence, we will consider it as merely possible and have to wait to arrive at a certainty in relation to its causes which unfold and succeed from one another in the order necessary to produce it. Since we cannot easily have a *tota simul* vision of the infinite series of productive causes, we discover this series successively and progressively. We therefore conceive existence under the angle of duration and not under that of eternity. For this reason, the concept of duration is connected to that of possible existence.

After having shown that the distinction between duration and eternity stems from the division of Being into Being whose essence includes existence and Being whose essence only includes possible existence, Spinoza presents duration as 'an attribute under which we conceive the existence of created things insofar as they persevere in their actuality'.[7] Duration therefore expresses a thing's perseverance in being, and is a property not of the thing's essence but of its existence. This definition is quite classic. Suarez, to take only one example, claimed that duration expresses permanence in being and only applies to the existence of things: 'Duratio (quae

[4] CM I, 3; CWS I, 307.
[5] Ibid.
[6] CM II, 9; CWS I, 332.
[7] CM I, 4; CWS I, 310.

permanentiam in esse significat) aliquid reale est, et solum existentibus rebus conveniens (Duration (which means permanence in being) is something real, and only pertains to the existence of a thing).'[8] The 'pope of metaphysics' also maintained that duration is not really distinguished from the existence of things: 'Duratio sola ratione distinguitur ab existentia rei durantis (Only reason distinguishes between duration and the existence of the thing enduring).'[9] Now, Spinoza himself also claims that 'duration is only distinguished by reason from the whole existence of a thing'.[10] If existence and duration conversely explain each other and designate a single and same thing, it becomes inappropriate to speak of existence in duration. Such a formulation implies that duration is a milieu in which existence comes to be inscribed and takes place. Duration thus finds itself hypostasised and appears as an abstract element prior to existence. Spinoza avoids this questionable formulation, for it is a source of confusion and a ferment of false problems.[11] By detaching duration from existence, we come to wonder how the former could have arisen from the midst of eternity. We therefore come to be surprised by Spinoza's seemingly suspicious silence concerning its enigmatic genesis. In doing so, we inadvertently forget that such a question is nonsensical, for it amounts to falsely separating duration from existence, without which it cannot be conceived.

By reducing duration to the existence of things that persevere, Spinoza actually grants it the status of an affection. He uses this very expression in the first chapter of the second part when he claims that 'duration is an affection of existence, and not of the essence of things'.[12] Here again, he shares this idea with the scholastic tradition. Heereboord, for instance, presents temporality as an affection of a being that follows from existence and is demonstrated through it: 'Temporalitas est entis affection quae sequitur existentiam & per eam demonsratur.'[13] The presence of the same concept of affection should not however leads us to believe that Spinoza purely and simply adopts Heereboord's analyses, for he actually puts forth a reversal

[8] Suarez, *Disputationes Metaphysicae* 26, 921, 1.

[9] Ibid., 914, 5.

[10] CM I, 4; CWS I, 310.

[11] For this reason, we cannot subscribe to Appuhn's translation of the phrase 'easque sub duratione concipiendi', which appears at the end of the scholium of proposition 23 from *Ethics* V, with 'conceive them (the existence of things) in duration', and prefer to it that of Pautrat: 'conceive them under duration', which is more faithful to the spirit and letter of the text'.

[12] CM II, 1; CWS I, 316.

[13] Heereboord, *Meletamata Pneumaticae*, Book II, Cap. VIII.

from the gnoseological point of view. It is no longer duration that is demonstrated through existence, but existence that is demonstrated through duration. The author of *Metaphysical Thoughts* indeed specifies that by affection he understands what Descartes calls attribute and declares in chapter 3 of the first[14] part that 'affections of being are certain attributes, under which we understand the essence or existence of each thing, [the attributes], nevertheless, being distinguished from [being] only by reason'.[15] Now, article 52 from Part I of Descartes' *Principles*,[16] to which Spinoza explicitly refers, shows that the attribute is what reveals the existence of a substance and allows us to be assured of its actual presence in the world. Without the perception of an attribute, we would not be able to know that a substance exists. It is not sufficient that it exists in and through itself without the aid of any created thing for us to notice it; it is also necessary that we be affected by at least one of its properties. Since nothingness does not have properties, grasping one single attribute attests with certainty to the existence of a substance. As a result, if duration is an affection or an attribute, in the Cartesian sense of the latter term, it becomes the privileged medium through which we discover the actual presence of a thing. In this sense, things do not exist in, but through duration; we know that we exist because we endure. Without the intervention of duration, we would not be able to be aware of our existence since the latter does not stem directly from our essence. It is likely for this reason that Spinoza will say in chapter 4 of the first part of *Metaphysical Thoughts* that duration is '*the* attribute under which we conceive the existence of created things insofar as they persevere in their actuality'.[17]

It remains to be understood why Spinoza equates duration with a form of perseverance in being. Duration is the property (*propres*) of beings whose essence only includes a possible existence. Created things, unlike God, do not have their own power capable of engendering and keeping them in

---

[14] TN: Jaquet's original text references the second part, but the quote can only be found in the first.

[15] CM I, 3; CWS I, 306.

[16] 'Yet substance cannot be initially perceived solely by means of the fact that it is an existing thing, for this fact alone does not per se affect us; but we easily recognise substance from any attribute of it, by means of the common notion that nothingness has no attributes and no properties or qualities. For, from the fact that we perceive some attribute to be present, we [rightly] conclude that some existing thing, or substance, to which that attribute can belong, is also necessarily present'. Descartes, *Principles of Philosophy*, I, 52.

[17] CM I, 4; CWS I, 310. [TN: Emphasis added by Jaquet and differs from Curley's translation (the latter opts for the indefinite article 'an').]

being, for their essence is distinct from their existence and does not include it. They therefore need God's support to exist and be preserved.

> In order that we may better understand what eternity is, and how it cannot be conceived without the divine essence, we need to consider what we have already said before, viz. that created things, or all things except God, always exist only by the power, or essence, of God, and not by their own power. From this it follows that the present existence of things is not the cause of their future existence, but only God's immutability is. So we are compelled to say that when God has first created a thing, he will preserve it afterwards continuously, or will continue that same action of creating it.[18]

Spinoza here espouses the Cartesian theory of continuous creation and claims that things are said to endure when their future existence is not contained in their present existence. We can represent their perseverance in being as a juxtaposition of logically and chronologically independent moments whose continuity is assured by God's immutability.

If present time has no connection with the future, it implies 'not so much that God preserves things as that he creates them'.[19] Everything is, so to speak, in perpetual beginning. This fact allows us to understand why duration, unlike eternity, is divisible into parts and can be conceived as bigger or smaller, more or less. If each moment does not depend on the preceding one, it becomes possible to distinguish one from the other, to conceive each separately and, consequently, to divide duration, to measure it with time and to make comparisons. Paradoxically, the inauguration of chronological order and temporal succession are made possible by the absence of real connection between past, present and future. In eternity, by contrast, it is the presence of an indissoluble link between all properties of existence that forbids the introduction of a distinction between before and after as well as any utilisation of the category of succession, for an eternal being by definition possesses an essence that includes existence. To posit essence in its infinite totality is *ipso facto* to posit existence in its infinite totality. God's existence encompasses everything in its presence, such that the future (*l'avenir*) is not to come (*à venir*) but is already there (*déjà là*). It thus becomes impossible to put forth chronological distinctions, for the present is so filled (*gros du*) with the future that the two overlap entirely. For a necessary being, present existence

---

[18] CM II, 1; CWS I, 317–18.
[19] CM II, 11; CWS I, 339.

is the cause of future existence, but the effect is so tied to the cause and contained in it that it is no longer possible to distinguish one from the other, to separate one from the other, unless one mutilates it and misconceives its nature. Recourse to temporal categories testifies to an inadequate perception that divides the indivisible and separates the inseparable. When it comes to created things, by contrast, present existence is not the cause of future existence; there is inevitably a discontinuity between the two, a discontinuity that only the preservative (*conservatrice*) action of God can abolish by filling in the gaps in duration via his immutable decrees. Temporal division is here legitimate, on the condition that we do not believe that duration is by nature divisible. If we consider things abstractly, by cutting them from the ties that unite them to substance, their duration lends itself to the operation of division, since there is no necessary connection between past, present and future. By contrast, if we link their existence to the substance that produces and preserves them, their duration is necessarily continuous and indivisible, for God cannot fail to lend his support. From this point of view, it does not seem that the essence of duration is completely different from that of eternity, for the preservative action of God is not a perpetuation that would imply that we can distinguish a before from an after, but a work wherein 'at each moment God continually creates a thing, anew as it were'.[20]

The Relationship between Duration and Eternity

The grounds for the distinction between duration and eternity in *Metaphysical Thoughts* makes the analysis of the relationship between the two concepts far less problematic than in the *Ethics*, for created things are not at the same time durational and eternal. Eternity is the privilege of being whose essence includes existence and only pertains to God. Indeed, Spinoza does not attribute eternity, but immortality, to the human mind, which is to say an indestructability tied to the immutability of the divine laws that preserve such a mind at each moment. The mind thus enjoys a continuous and unlimited duration by virtue of the laws of nature, which imply that no substance can be destroyed. Of course, 'he who has the power of creating a thing, has also the power of destroying it',[21] and in this sense the human mind can be called mortal, but 'a philosopher does not ask what God can do by his supreme power, but judges the nature of things from the laws that God has placed in them. So he judges to be fixed and settled what is inferred

[20] CM II, 11; CWS I, 339.
[21] CM II, 12; CWS I, 341.

from those laws to be fixed and settled, though he does not deny that God can change those laws and everything else'.[22] Since we do not have a clear and distinct idea by which we conceive that a substance can be destroyed, we must therefore reasonably claim that the mind is immortal and demonstrate this from the immutability of divine laws. It is clear, however, that the mind's immortality cannot be confused with divine eternity and that it can be spoken of in terms of duration. Spinoza elsewhere carries out his demonstration of the mind's eternity by claiming that 'from all this we infer clearly that God's immutable will concerning the duration of souls has been manifested to men not only by revelation, but also by the natural light'.[23] Duration, even if immortal, belongs only to those beings whose essence only includes a possible existence, and there can be no interference nor communication between the two forms of temporality.

In the *Ethics*, Spinoza goes back on this idea, abolishing the divine monopoly on eternity and profoundly modifying the relationship between the two concepts. To understand his own doctrine, it is especially important to analyse its stages, particularly in the pivotal text which constitutes the letter to Louis Meyer dated 20 April 1663. The limited comparison with *Metaphysical Thoughts* will not aim to mark a development in Spinoza's thought – since the purpose of that work was not to express the ideas of its author – but will instead serve as a point of comparison in order to better discern the Spinozist position and its specificity in relation to the tradition.

Eternity and Duration in Letter XII

Changes in Relation to *Metaphysical Thoughts*

In this infamous piece of writing, the difference between duration and eternity stems from the distinction between substance and mode and corroborates the division made in chapter 4 of the first part of *Metaphysical Thoughts*. Nevertheless, Spinoza does not exactly employ the division of Being into Being whose essence includes existence and Being whose essence includes only possible existence. The attribution of duration or eternity to a thing still concerns the nature of its essence, but the concept of possible existence no longer explicitly appears in the definition. This disappearance is likely due to the fundamentally inadequate character of the idea of possibility in a system where everything is necessary.

[22] CM II, 12; CWS I, 341–2.
[23] CM II, 12; CWS I, 342.

Louis Meyer's correspondent continues to reserve eternity for substance and duration for modes; however, the separation between beings is less rigid than it was in *Metaphysical Thoughts*. At first glance, Spinoza's claims belie this impression, for it is clearly specified that 'we conceive the existence of substance to be entirely different from the existence of modes'.[24] In the first case, it is true, essence implies existence; in the second, the examination of the essence of modes does not permit one 'to infer from the fact that they exist now that they will or will not exist later, or that they have or have not existed earlier'.[25] However, the letter introduces a dissymmetry that dissolves the exclusive character of the possession of eternity by substance. If it is inconceivable to attribute duration to substance in any manner, since Spinoza himself explicitly restricts its field of application by specifying that 'it is *only* of modes that we explain the existence by duration', it is not inconceivable to extend eternity to modes.[26] If one reads the text to the letter, Spinoza does not say: 'by eternity we can only explain the existence of substance', but 'the existence of substance is explained by eternity',[27] breaking an otherwise strict symmetry and opening up the possibility for the application of eternity to modes. It is necessary, in all rigour, to acknowledge that Spinoza does not explicitly grant this property to modes; nevertheless, he is much less formal than in *Metaphysical Thoughts*, where the infinite existence called eternity could only be attributed to God and in no way to created things.[28]

Besides these modifications, such as the disappearance of the concept of the possible and a relaxing of the limits of the sphere of extension of eternity (which may seem minor by comparison), the letter introduces one major innovation: division into parts stops being an intrinsic property of duration, instead becoming the product of an operation of the imagination. In *Metaphysical Thoughts*, Spinoza maintains that duration is 'composed of parts'[29] and confesses its real divisibility alongside that of matter. He in no way presents divisibility into parts as an abstraction.

This change in perspective proves to be the product of a break with Cartesian thought and a desire to shed light on a blind spot within it. Even though he considers the real division of matter to be a sufficiently

---

[24] *Ep.* XII [to Louis Meyer]; CWS I, 202.
[25] Ibid.
[26] Ibid. Emphasis Jaquet's.
[27] 'Per Durationem enim Modorum tantum existentiam explicare possumus; Substantiae vero per Aeternitatem.' Ibid.
[28] CM II, 1; CWS I, 318.
[29] CM I, 4; CWS I, 310.

established fact, the author of *Metaphysical Thoughts* nevertheless confesses that it remains incomprehensible. 'For there are many things exceeding our grasp which we nevertheless know to have been done by God – e.g., there is that real division of matter into indefinite particles, which we have already demonstrated quite clearly (IIP11), though we do not know how that division occurs.'[30] There, Spinoza adopts Descartes' thesis which claims, in articles 34 and 35 of Part II of the *Principles*, that 'although we cannot comprehend how this indefinite division occurs, we must not on that account doubt that it does occur'. In short, partition is knowable (*connaissable*) but incomprehensible (*incomprehensible*). In Letter XII, Spinoza goes back on this position and instead affirms the indivisibility of extension and duration in themselves, not only because the opposite thesis is incomprehensible, but because it leads to irresolvable incoherencies and contradictions. 'Hence they talk utter nonsense, not to say madness, who hold that extended substance is put together of parts, or bodies, really distinct from one another. This is just the same as if someone should try, merely by adding and accumulating many circles, to put together a square or a triangle or something else completely different in its essence.'[31] When it comes to duration considered in itself, it is neither divisible nor composed of parts. Supposing that it was: either it would be infinitely divisible, or else it would be composed of indivisible elements. In the first case, we fall into the inextricable paradoxes designed by Zeno himself:

> When someone has conceived duration abstractly, and by confusing it with time begun to divide it into parts, he will never be able to understand, for example, how an hour can pass. For if an hour is to pass, it will be necessary for half of it to pass first, and then half of the remainder, and then half of the remainder of this. So if you subtract half from the remainder in this way, to infinity, you will never reach the end of the hour.[32]

In the second case, duration would be composed of indivisible moments (*instants*). But there too, we must not confuse it with time and represent it as a sum of moments. The moment is a lack (*néant*) of duration, and it is not by adding noughts (*néants*) that we manage to engender a being. 'For composing duration of moments is the same as composing number merely by adding noughts.'[33] So, those who would like to avoid the aporias tied to

---

[30] CM I, 3; CWS I, 310.
[31] *Ep.* XII [to Louis Meyer]; CWS I, 202.
[32] *Ep.* XII [to Louis Meyer]; CWS I, 203.
[33] *Ep.* XII [to Louis Meyer]; CWS I, 204.

the infinite divisibility of duration by claiming that duration is composed of moments have run from Charybdis into Scylla. It is therefore necessary to avoid both the belief that duration is in itself divisible and the confusion of duration with time.

Divisibility and Indivisibility: Grounds for the Distinction between Duration and Eternity

At the same time, duration and eternity no longer seem to be of truly different natures since they are both fundamentally indivisible. If this is the case, then what is it that distinguishes them from one another? It is the abstract possibility of being divided into parts and measured by time that turns out to be the essential criterion on which the *Ethics* will not go back. While eternity does not lend itself to any partition or temporal determination, duration can be split, considered as finite, and is measurable by time when we conceive it abstractly. But in the name of what can the one be fragmented and the other not? In what exactly does this abstract or superficial conception consist, according to Spinoza's own terms? Eternity is indivisible, for it expresses nothing other than the necessary existence of substance and cannot be thought without it. Now, since substance is indivisible, so too, consequently, is eternity. The *sine qua non* condition of divisibility resides in the possibility for a thing to be thought, in a certain way, independently of substance. Unlike duration, eternity absolutely cannot be conceived without substance. Spinoza references the fact that 'when we conceive quantity abstracted from substance and separate duration from the way it flows from eternal things, we can determine them as we please'.[34] How are we to explain this dissymmetry between the two concepts since duration, like any affection, cannot really be conceived without substance and proves to be indivisible in itself? The prohibition of dividing things and approaching them temporally is, in truth, tied to their infinity. We can at leisure delimit the existence and duration of modes, 'conceive [them] as greater or less, and divide [them] into parts – without thereby destroying in any way the concept we have of them. But since we can conceive eternity and substance only as infinite, they can undergo none of these without our at the same time destroying the concept we have of them.'[35]

It remains to be understood how the infinity of substance renders null and void, under penalty of destruction, any attempt at dividing it up, for *a*

[34] *Ep.* XII [to Louis Meyer]; CWS I, 203.
[35] *Ep.* XII [to Louis Meyer]; CWS I, 202.

priori, the infinite is not necessarily indivisible. To avoid any error, we must remind ourselves of the cautionary note with which the correspondent to Louis Meyer opens his letter:

> Everyone has found the problem of the infinite very difficult, indeed insoluble. This is because they have not distinguished between what is infinite as a consequence of its own nature, or by the force of its definition, and what has no bounds, not indeed by the force of its essence, but by the force of its cause. And also because they have not distinguished between what is called infinite because it has no limits and that whose parts we cannot explain or equate with any number, though we know its maximum and minimum . . . If they had attended to these distinctions, I maintain that they would never have been overwhelmed by such a great crowd of difficulties. For then they would have understood clearly what kind of infinite cannot be divided into any parts, or cannot have any parts, and what kind of infinite can, on the other hand, be divided into parts without contradiction.[36]

Spinoza thus distinguishes between three types of infinity: the first is unlimited by virtue of its nature and allows for absolutely no division, for that would imply that it is composed of finite parts, which is contrary to its essence. The second, though it is also unlimited, does not take its infinity from itself, but from its cause. Compatible with division, it could absolutely pertain to mediate or immediate modes or to singular things that are infinite through the force of substance. Finally, the third type of infinity, or the indefinite, is innumerable (*indénombrable*). For this reason, every temporal determination is improper and ends up leading to irresolvable problems like that of attempting to know what God did before creation.

As for the existence and duration of modes, they do not belong to the ranks of infinity by nature, but to the category of things that, when they are conceived in an abstract manner, can be divided into parts and considered as finite. To understand what allows us this abstract conception, we must specify the conditions of validity for the method of delimiting and measuring duration. The divisible character of duration is not an intrinsic and essential property, but the result of an operation of the imagination. We can only divide and temporally determine modes when we consider their essence and duration independently of the actual (*effectif*) order of nature. Such an approach necessarily contains a degree of abstraction, for thought, or rather

---

[36] *Ep.* XII [to Louis Meyer]; *CWS* I, 201.

the imagination, separates the mode from substance without which, however, it cannot be conceived. For this reason, Spinoza underscores the inadequate character of the notion of time that does not allow us to truly give
an account of the nature of modes and their duration. 'And if the modes of
substance themselves are confused with beings of reason of this kind, or aids
of the imagination, they too can never be rightly understood. For when we
do this, we separate them from substance, and from the way they flow from
eternity, without which, however, they cannot be rightly understood.'[37] If
we stop imagining the duration of modes and if we conceive them through
the intellect, we will find them to be neither divisible nor determinate.

The Status of Time

At the same time, time increasingly becomes a way of thinking about problematic foundations. It was already related to beings of reason in *Metaphysical
Thoughts*. 'Time, therefore, is not an affection of things, but only a mere
mode of thinking, *or*, as we have already said, a being of reason. For it is a
mode of thinking that serves to explain duration.'[38] Spinoza distinguishes
between three types of modes of thinking, those that allow us to memorise
things, like genus and species, those that allow us to explain them, like
number and measure, and finally those that allow us to imagine them,
like extremity or limit (*fin*).[39] He puts time in the category of modes of
explicative thinking whose function is to determine things by comparing
them with others. Thus, time serves to determine the duration of things by
comparing it to that of things that possess invariable movement. Because
of this, time is not an idea, for no existing object corresponds to it. Spinoza
is explicit on this point: 'So it is evident that these modes of thinking are
not ideas of things, and can not in any way be classed as ideas. So they also
have no object that exists necessarily, or can exist.'[40] Without a real *ideatum*,
time cannot be an idea; it belongs to the category of beings of reason. In this
respect, every idea is a mode of thinking, but not every mode of thinking is
an idea.

How do we get the impression that time actually exists as a reality outside
of our mind, possessing the status of an idea? From where does this impression come? Spinoza explicitly explains why beings of reason 'are not ideas of

[37] *Ep.* XII [to Louis Meyer]; CWS I, 203.
[38] CM I, 4; CWS I, 310.
[39] CM I, 1; CWS I, 300.
[40] CM I, 1; CWS I, 300–1.

things' though they 'are taken for ideas of things':[41] 'The reason why these modes of thinking are taken for ideas of things is that they arise from the ideas of real beings so immediately that they are quite easily confused with them by those who do not pay very close attention. So these people also give names to them, as if to signify beings existing outside our mind, which Beings, or rather Nonbeings, they have called beings of reason.'[42] In short, the mistake consists in believing that time is an idea due to a confusion of its nature with that of duration. While time may be a being of reason, it no less possesses the reality of a mode of thinking whose relevance is unquestionable in Metaphysical Thoughts, for it explains duration all the more legitimately inasmuch as it is composed of parts and by nature lends itself to temporal division.

In Letter XII, by contrast, the rejection of the thesis concerning the real divisibility of duration leads, as a result, to a change in the status of time. If we pay attention to vocabulary, we observe, to be sure, that Spinoza continues to conceive time as a mode of thinking; he assimilates it on several occasions to a being of reason[43] and never speaks of it as an idea, but as a notion.[44] A shift in meaning has occurred, however, in relation to chapter 1 of the first part of Metaphysical Thoughts, for time is presented as a mode of the imagination; it had previously been one of the ways of thinking that allowed us to explain things, a way of thinking that Spinoza distinguishes from memory aids, on one hand, and aids of the imagination, on the other.

To weigh the significance of this change, we must indeed discern the difference between explicative and imaginative functions and understand why time is released from the first to be assigned to the second. To explain a thing is to lay out its hidden contents. An explanation can be adequate when it correctly displays what had been concealed and is based on the nature of the thing without betraying that nature. In this respect, in Metaphysical Thoughts, the use of the categories of past, present and future may allow us to explain duration in a relevant manner, since the latter is composed of parts that must be distinguished. Time is thus a mode of thinking peculiarly well adapted to reality, for it limits itself to exhibiting what is contained in the thing itself. For this reason, it can be an honest aid to the intellect and need not be limited to serving memory and the imagination. No one would think of contesting the fact that certain modes of thinking intended to explain

[41] Ibid.
[42] CM I, 1; CWS I, 301.
[43] Ep. XII [to Louis Meyer]; CWS I, 203.
[44] Ibid.

things can in fact give rise to adequate knowledge. The champion of this category, number, offers dazzling proof of this fact, unless one were to consider arithmetic in its entirety as a 'master of error and falsity'.

In Letter XII, by contrast, duration is no longer composed of parts; temporal divisions no longer fit the contours of real division. Chronological distinctions thus lose their explanatory virtue and become mere agents of the imagination charged with furnishing a sensible representation and facilitating a certain comprehension. Time therefore has more to do with the imagination. Does this mean that it is to be put away in the museum of chimeras and that the application of chronological categories to existence is as inappropriate for modes as it is for substance? In reality, the degree of inadequacy is not the same: legitimate for modes, the application becomes illegitimate for substance. From a general perspective, it is true that only the conception of things in an eternal manner by the intellect is adequate, but we must distinguish between two types of beings: those that can only be understood by the intellect and those that can be understood by the intellect and the imagination. Substance and its eternity concern the first case and prohibit any abstraction and all imaginative conceptions. Modes and their duration fall under the second case and therefore lend themselves to the imagination. The determination of duration by time results, to be sure, in an abstraction, but this step owes its legitimacy to the nature of things.

One question nevertheless lingers: why can some beings be imagined and not others? The reason for this fact is that there are things that cannot be grasped by the imagination without us also destroying the concept we have of the thing, thereby falling into inextricable difficulties. Thus, the nature of substance forbids any division whether it be spatial or temporal, given that its essence cannot be distinguished from its existence. The introduction of chronological determinations would lead to an absurdity, for it would amount to temporalising an essence and giving an historical dimension to an eternal truth. Such is not the case for modes: since their existence is not included in their essence, it becomes possible to consider them in isolation and to conceive of them as longer or shorter 'without destroying the concept we have of them'. In short, it is the possibility of distinguishing essence from existence that justifies recourse to temporal aids on the condition that they be confined to their status of modes of thinking, and not confused with properties of things. Unlike that of substance, the present existence of modes is not the cause of their future existence. As a result, different moments of existence can be separated, for they do not depend on each other, but on the cause that preserves them. Consequently, if we dwell only on a present effect, an abstraction made from the chain of causes that produces it, it is possible to distinguish it from that which precedes it and that which follows it as well as represent existence as composed of a succession of stages. Temporal determination is therefore grounded in the nature of things: it is because a mode's existence is not included in its essence that it becomes possible to consider it as a quantity measurable by time. Such an operation, however, is an abstraction which still contains an inadequate part, for if my existence is not contained in my essence, it is nevertheless contained in that of God. In this respect, my essence and my existence cannot be truly divorced from one another.

The change in the status of time in Letter XII should not be interpreted as a devaluation of this concept since, for one part, explanatory and imaginative functions do not necessarily exclude one another and, for another, modes of thinking that serve to imagine things contain neither more nor less inadequacy than others. Here again the case of number is conclusive, since it becomes, in its turn, a mode of imagination just like time. Arithmetic operations quite rightly claim exactitude; it is simply necessary to guard against believing that they express real properties of things. In this respect, they can be called adequate and not true. Truth or falsity indeed assumes conformity to a thing. Since time, unlike duration, is not a property of existing beings, it must not be confused with real things. It is not the type of idea that can be considered true or false. Spinoza emphasised this fact, for that matter, in a passage from *Metaphysical Thoughts* where he had determined the status of modes of thinking like species: 'Still, these modes of thinking cannot be called ideas, nor can they be said to be true or false, just as love cannot be called true or false, but only good or bad.'[45] Time and number in Spinoza resemble what we today call pure operational concepts that concern a form of validity but do not have truth value. Their sphere of validity stops at the boundaries of the imaginable; beyond this opens the realm of pure understanding in which all imaginative incursion comes at the price of irresolvable contradictions.

It is therefore hardly surprising to note that the concept of time occupies a minor place in the *Ethics*. It is, in fact, of no help in understanding things like substance and eternity that can only be grasped by the intellect. Instead, it incites confusion. It would be better to guard against recourse to it not only to apprehend the nature of substance but also for correctly understanding modes. It is likely for this reason that Spinoza grants it a more and more modest place within his philosophy and will not mention it in his definition

[45] CM I, 1; CWS I, 301.

of duration in the *Ethics*, unlike the steps he takes in other works.[46] Time only has a rightful place in the domain of the imagination. From this point of view, the *Ethics* follows the beacons of Letter XII, for references to temporal determinations only intervene precisely when Spinoza considers questions related to the affections of the body and the imagination, as the scholium of proposition 44 from Part II, for example, demonstrates. Time will retain its status as an aid of the imagination, for it cannot be determined adequately by reason.[47] Time is not an idea that expresses the nature of external things; it is an image that instead indicates how their duration affects us. Spinoza here forms a part of the Platonic tradition and in a sense completes the mission of time's derealisation that had been initiated in the famous definition from the *Timaeus*. From the moving image of eternity, Chronos becomes 'an aid of the imagination'[48] intended to explain duration. The ontological status that is granted to it is without contestation different in the two authors – for in the *Timaeus*, the moving image of eternity, despite its fallen character, is still an extra-mental reality, while in the *Ethics*, time is nothing outside of our mind, but this while possessing a positivity and fertility of which physics is an ample guarantor. In short, the derealisation does not have the same meaning in the two authors: a devaluation in Plato linked to the precarity of images, a revaluation in Spinoza for whom images can be powerful aids to comprehension. Setting aside these differences – which, to the extent that Plato also recognises a positivity to images, should not be overemphasised – it is interesting to note that the Spinozist genesis of the concept of time is inspired by certain aspects of the Platonic model. Chronos, indeed, is conceived by the demiurge as the imitation, adapted to perishable things, of the motion of the eternal celestial spheres. Now, in Spinoza, time is a mode of thinking created on the basis of comparison between a thing's duration and a standard chosen among 'other things which have a certain and determinate motion'.[49] Even though the author of *Metaphysical Thoughts* never explicitly mentions celestial periods, we must observe that in both cases it is the sphere of invariable motion that serves as a model and scaffold for the genesis of time. The scholium of proposition 44 from *Ethics* II confirms this

---

[46] Pierre-François Moreau claims that the rarefication of references to time is not the effect of a disavowal, but is explained by the fact that this concept, fundamental for physics, is not central in a work dedicated to *Ethics*. It may be objected, however, that *Metaphysical Thoughts* is not an exposition of physical principles either, and yet the analysis of time still figures prominently in chapters 1 and 4 of the first part.

[47] The scholium of proposition 62 of Part IV reminds us of this point.

[48] *Ep.* XII [to Louis Meyer]; CWS I, 203.

[49] CM I, 4; CWS I, 310.

connection, since it is with reference to the sun that the imaginative ideas of time and contingency will be created:

> Moreover, no one doubts but what we also imagine time, viz. from the fact that we imagine some bodies to move more slowly, or more quickly, or with the same speed. Let us suppose, then, a child, who saw Peter for the first time yesterday, in the morning, but saw Paul at noon, and Simon in the evening, and today again saw Peter in the morning. It is clear from P18 that as soon as he sees the morning light, he will immediately imagine the sun taking the same course through the sky as he saw on the preceding day, or he will imagine the whole day, and Peter together with the morning, Paul with the noon, and Simon with the evening. That is, he will imagine the existence of Paul and Simon with a relation to future time . . .[50]

Ultimately, the ontological status of time is not uncertain, for if it should not be confused with that of real things existing in act, then it has the same characteristics as that of images, capable of increasing or decreasing one's power of acting.

The Interplay between Eternity and Duration

The nature of the relationship between duration and eternity is yet to be understood. Letter XII offers us some indications on this subject, since Spinoza, while explaining the genesis of the ideas of time and measure, references the manner by which duration follows from eternal things. 'Next, from the fact that when we conceive quantity abstracted from substance and separate duration from the way it flows from eternal things, we can determine them as we please, there arise time and measure.'[51] Duration therefore follows in a certain manner from eternal things. This enigmatic phrase gives rise to three problems: what are these mysterious 'eternal things' on which duration depends? What does the verb follow (*suivre*) mean here? And finally, in what manner does duration follow from eternal things?

We must admit that Spinoza hardly clarifies the nature of these famous eternal things, leaving the door open for speculation. The term thing is more often applied to modes in the Spinozist vocabulary and is not typically used to describe substance. That duration derives uniquely and directly

[50] *Ethics* II, 44 Schol.; CWS I, 480–1.
[51] *Ep.* XII [to Louis Meyer]; CWS I, 203.

from the eternal substance therefore seems to be ruled out. The phrasing in Letter XII corroborates this interpretation insofar as it does not exactly place duration and quantity on the same plane. While the idea of measure comes from the fact that we conceive of quantity *apart from substance*, that of time implies that we disregard the way in which duration follows *from eternal things*. It is therefore tempting to think that under this expression Spinoza intends immediate and mediate infinite modes, but, if that were the case, then why does he not designate them by name instead of contenting himself with a term as vague as that of things? Such an enigma could be partially explained by the fact that Letter XII does not once mention the existence of mediate and immediate infinite modes. Must we, in light of the above, conceive of 'eternal things' as a substitute for or an embryonic form of a later theory of infinite modes? Such a hypothesis is not absurd, for it is striking to note that Spinoza no longer invokes these eternal things in the *Ethics*, whereas he dedicates a relatively detailed analysis to them in the *Treatise on the Emendation of the Intellect*, a work in which the doctrine of infinite modes makes no appearance. In fact, occurrences of the phrase 'eternal things' become extremely rare in the *Ethics*. According to Giancotti's *Lexicon*, the expression *res aeterna* only appears there once.[52] Moreover, it is used in the singular and accompanied by an indefinite article. It therefore does not exactly take on the same meaning as it does in the plural. Comprehending the phrase in the *Ethics* does not, for that matter, pose the same problem, for it is clear in the scholium of proposition 20 of Part V that love for an eternal thing refers explicitly to God. The inventory of the *Lexicon*, however, is not exhaustive, for definition 8 from Part I also mentions an 'eternal thing'.[53] It is nevertheless obvious that Spinoza is once again referring to God in this definition. Apart from these two particular occurrences, the reference to eternal things well and truly disappears in the *Ethics*.

By contrast, the phrase appears multiple times in the *Treatise on the Emendation of the Intellect*,[54] once in the singular, and several times in the plural. In the singular, this mysterious eternal thing is presented as an object of love and likely refers to substance; in the plural, eternal things appear as a source of knowledge and are associated with the fixed and immutable

---

[52] *Ethics* V, 20 Schol; CWS I, 605: 'Deinde Amorem gignit erga rem immutabilem, et aeternum . . .'.

[53] 'Per aeternitatem intelligo ipsam existentiam quatenus ex sola rei aeternae definitione necessario sequi concipitur.'

[54] *TdIE*, 10; CWS I, 9: 'Sed amor erga rem aeternam . . .'.

laws governing nature. In both cases, however, nothing allows us to claim with certainty that eternal things are anything other than infinite modes. In fact, in paragraph 10 of the *Treatise on the Emendation of the Intellect*, Spinoza alludes to love for an eternal thing in opposition to attachment to perishable things; he does not further determine the nature of this object, for he does not yet know, at this stage of his research, if such a good exists. He simply posits the necessary conditions for the acquisition of a highest good (*une félicité suprême*), without yet assuming the success of his enterprise. It is, however, beyond doubt that the term eternal thing designates, by anticipating, a perfect being.

In paragraphs 99 to 105, where Spinoza more precisely develops the concept of *res aeternae et fixae*, the expression 'eternal things' cannot designate substance in its unity due to the multiplicity that it introduces; even so, that does not imply that it refers to only infinite modes. It can just as well be applied to *natura naturans* as to universal (and even particular) *natura naturata*. This is the position maintained by Errol Harris, for example, in his work *Salvation from Despair*,[55] where he assimilates eternal things to the infinite essence of God, its attributes and its modes. Ultimately, for him, there is no need to delimit the sphere of extension of this concept by considering that it only encompasses infinite modes or, at a push, the attributes of God. In support of his interpretation, it is necessary to recognise not only that substance is an eternal thing, but that finite modes are equally so in a certain measure, if we believe propositions 22 and 23 from *Ethics* V.[56] Must we therefore conclude that this concept simply has a very broad scope and covers the entirety of eternal beings, substance and modes included? On the contrary, it seems that with this expression Spinoza designates a more precise and determined reality. To prove this claim, it is enough to examine the clarifications provided concerning the nature of order in paragraphs 99 to 104 of the *Treatise on the Emendation of the Intellect*. For all our perceptions to be ordered and unified, it is necessary to search for a being that would serve as the cause of all things, and then to deduce all our ideas by proceeding in accordance with the series of causes, from one real thing to another real thing. Spinoza then notes that 'by the series of causes of real beings' he 'do[es] not here understand the series of singular, changeable things, but only the series of fixed

---

[55] See Harris 1973: 23 and the following.

[56] *Ethics* V, 22: 'Nevertheless, in God there is necessarily an idea that expresses the essence of this or that human body, under a species of eternity'; 23: 'The human mind cannot be absolutely destroyed with the body, but something of it remains which is eternal.' *CWS* I, 607.

and eternal things'.[57] Eternal things are thus constituted in a series, being defined as real, singular, physical beings and thereby distinguished both from abstractions and from mutable singular things. Spinoza insists on the fact that they can, though singular, function as universals or genera by virtue of their presence and extremely great power. For this reason, the concept of eternal things does not necessarily cover everything that is eternal. In fact, for it to be able to serve as a genus, it must be provided with a vast enough range and express universal common notions, or at least notions common to certain parts and the whole. What is strictly singular in an eternal being, if such a property exists, would therefore not fall under the category of eternal things. Conversely, since those eternal things are called singular, they necessarily belong to the category of finite modes and can neither refer to substance nor to infinite modes, for a singular thing is, by definition, a finite thing. The two expressions are, for that matter, used synonymously – for example, at the beginning of proposition 28 from *Ethics* I.[58] With these considerations in mind, although the phrase 'eternal things' can sometimes take on a broader meaning and apply both to God or universal *natura naturata*, it must be understood, in the Letter to Louis Meyer, in a more restricted sense and be presented as the equivalent of what the *Treatise on the Emendation of the Intellect* calls the series of real causes and beings and what we find in the *Ethics* in the form of the infinity of finite causes or the determination of an eternal mode of thought by another mode of the same kind.[59] The increasing scarcity of reference to eternal things in this last work would thus neither be explained by a disavowal nor by a loss of interest, still less by the existence of a more elaborate theory of infinite modes. These infamous eternal things remain implicitly present and are replaced by the infinite chain of finite causes.

It is now necessary to clarify the mysterious manner by which duration follows (*suit*) from eternal things. In Latin, the verb *fluo* pertains to the ideas of flow and source, meaning to flow (*s'écouler*) and stem (*découler*) from an origin. It expresses the necessary link that unites a cause to its effect and implies both a logical and chronological relation. The verb *to follow* (*suivre*) translates these two aspects well, since it evokes both succession and

---

[57] *TdIE* 100; *CWS* I, 41.

[58] *Ethics* I, 28; *CWS* I, 432: 'Every singular thing, or any thing which is finite and has a determinate existence . . .'.

[59] Vittorio Morfino notes the disappearance of the term 'series' for the benefit of that of 'connection' in the *Ethics*. He sees in this evidence for a change in the nature of Spinozist causality which stops being thought in accordance with a lineal, serial order in order to be conceived as a complex entanglement. Cf. Morfino 2012: 148–65.

deduction. Must we, however, attribute this double meaning to it, insofar as it seems, rigorously speaking, impossible for duration to succeed something that is eternal? Such an attribution would seem to amount to surreptitiously introducing temporal categories of before and after into the heart of eternity with no regard for Spinoza's repeated warnings on this topic.[60] Whoever thereby imagines the appearance of duration as a gradual passage from the intemporal to the temporal misunderstands eternity's specificity and irremediably condemns themselves to aporias. But even if we restrict the semantic field of the verb *to follow* so as to grant it a purely logical or ontological meaning, the problem is not for all that resolved. In what manner does duration stem from eternal things?

The verb *fluo* implies a relation of order and inscription into a series. Consequently, to understand how duration follows from eternal things is to understand the type of order that unites them to each other. On this subject, Letter XII offers little in the manner of details. By contrast, it is possible to shed some light on this phrase under the glow of paragraph 100 from the *Treatise on the Emendation of the Intellect* where Spinoza makes a clarification concerning the notion of the order and series of real things. He effectively distinguishes between three types of order: the series of eternal things, the series of singular changing things and the series of ordered experiences. Duration does not primarily fall within the jurisdiction of the order of singular changing things, nor of the laws of experience, but of the series of eternal things and their effects. This implies, as a result, that one's understanding of duration is not principally tied to the perception of change and the vicissitudes of life. Spinoza's conception, in this sense, is original, since it turns away from the tradition which typically associates the existence of duration, or rather of time, with change and the mobility of things. At most, the series of changing things gives us the confused feeling of things' durations and limits. It is also interesting to note that the essence of duration does not depend in the first instance on experiential laws, for this allows us to understand why Spinoza does not reduce duration to succession. To make the essence of duration depend on the laws of eternal things is not to stress the presence of a successive order, 'for there, by nature, all these things are at once'.[61] Only a proper use of our senses and the conducting of experiments according to strict laws can serve as a guide for us to grasp the order of things 'one before the other'.[62] This is why Spinoza never highlights

---

[60] CM II, 1; CWS I, 316; *Ethics* I, 33 Schol. 2; CWS I, 437–9.
[61] *TdIE*, 102; CWS I, 42.
[62] Ibid.

the successive character of duration, even to the point of passing over it entirely in the definition he presents at the beginning of *Ethics* II. There again, he demonstrates a great originality, for philosophers generally agree to distinguish duration from eternity by insisting on its successive character. Thomas Aquinas, for example, thinks that eternity can be recognised by two properties: an absence of limitation and absence of succession, while time is in itself successive.[63] Suarez wholeheartedly agrees with the Thomist stance, underscoring the fact that duration designates nothing other than existence as it is envisaged successively and that there is no real distinction between the concepts of duration and succession.[64] The connection between duration and succession seemed so obvious that it becomes inconceivable to represent them separately from one another. Hume, incidentally, will openly declare it: "Tis a property inseparable from time, and which in a manner constitutes its essence, that each of its parts succeed another, and that none of them, however contiguous, can ever be co-existent.'[65] For Spinoza, succession is not an essential characteristic of duration, and cannot therefore be allowed to define the nature of duration. This fact may seem odd, and we can indeed question why Spinoza principally links duration to the order of eternal things rather than to that of experience. This decision is, in reality, due to the fact that duration is, in itself and as adequately understood by the intellect, not successive, for it is indivisible and is not composed of really distinct parts. It is simply the pure, indefinite continuation of existence; it can, unlike eternity, lend itself to the division put forth by the imagination insofar as it turns out to be compatible with the distinction of successive moments due to the type of infinity proper to it. A thing that endures, as we have seen, is not infinite by nature and does not belong to the type of infinity which is absolutely indivisible – the type of infinity proper to substance. Ultimately, if duration follows from the series of eternal things and does not fall within the jurisdiction of the successive order of experiences, it does not maintain a link of chronological nature with its cause. The verb *fluo* thus could not take on the sense of succeeding; for this reason, it would be better to translate it with the phrase 'stems from' (*découler*) instead of 'follows' (*suivre*) in order to avoid any ambiguity.

Duration therefore seems to be a consequence of eternal things; it follows from the necessity of substance producing an infinity of things in an infinity

---

[63] Aquinas, *Summa Theologicae*, First Part, Quest. 10, art. 1.
[64] Suarez, *Disputationes Metaphysicae*, XXVI, 916, 2–3: 'Duratio non distinguitur ab existentia per connotationem successionis in se.'
[65] Hume, *A Treatise on Human Nature*, Part II, Section II.

of modes. It stems from eternal things and not simply from God, for the existence of finite modes depends, by definition, not only on substance, but also the laws of eternal things and the infinite series of causes which presides over its genesis. The way in which it follows from eternal things must be consistent with the nature of causality that prevails in this domain. Now, in the series of eternal things, everything is simultaneous; as a result, the existence of duration is posited at the same time as that of substance. Once the cause is given, the effect necessarily ensues. The presence of eternal things therefore implies, *ipso facto*, that of duration. However, the exact nature of the causality that joins them remains enigmatic. Is it a matter of a proximate or remote causality? A mediate or immediate causality? Letter XII does not provide a precise answer on this point, but it is possible to clarify the mysterious manner by which duration stems from eternal things with the help of a passage from the *Theologico-Political Treatise*[66] where Spinoza explains the interplay between the universal doctrine of Scripture and the provisional precepts adapted to particular circumstances.

Eternity and Duration in the *Theologico-Political Treatise*

The Details of the Problem

The following passage from chapter 7 is crucial, for it constitutes one of the rare moments where Spinoza confronts, in a direct and central manner, the problem of the relationship between duration and eternity. The analysis of the relationship between the eternal principles of religion and teachings which prove valid only temporarily is not merely an example but can serve as an archetype. It concerns, to be sure, the particular domain of Scriptural interpretation; nevertheless, our extrapolation is not inappropriate to the extent that it heeds a certain Spinozist caution. Doesn't the author of the *Theologico-Political Treatise* recall that the method he applies to Scripture is the same as that which prevails in the general study of nature?

> To do this we also need a method and order like the one we use for interpreting nature according to its history. In examining natural things we strive to investigate first the things most universal and common to the whole of nature: motion and rest, and their laws and rules, which nature always observes and through which it continuously acts. From these we proceed gradually to other, less universal things. In the same way, the first

[66] *TTP* VII; CWS II, 169.

thing we must seek from the history of Scripture is what is most universal, what is the basis and foundation of the whole of Scripture, and finally, what all the Prophets commend in it as an eternal teaching, most useful for all mortals.[67]

Based on this passage, the interplay between the temporal content of Scripture and its universal teaching is only a particular reflection of that which exists more generally in nature between eternal laws and historical details.

A comparison of these passages with Letter XII is all the more justified insofar as Spinoza uses, to explain the link between eternal teachings and provisional precepts, an expression quite close to that which he employs with Louis Meyer to describe the relationship between duration and eternity. 'Once we rightly know this universal teaching of Scripture, we must next proceed to other, less universal things, which nevertheless concern how we ordinarily conduct our lives and which flow (*derivo*) from this universal teaching like streams (*tanquam rivuli derivantur*). Examples would include all the particular external actions of true virtue, which can only be put into practice when the occasion for them arises.'[68] The verb *derivo* is in a way reminiscent of the infamous *fluo* in Letter XII. They both evoke the idea of a flow, of a flux, of a derivation from a source. *Derivo*, however, carries an additional precision, for it also implies a diversion, suggesting the presence of an obstacle or of an intention which modifies the initial flow to adapt it to particular ends. It is, for example, used to designate the diversion of a flow of water or of any property for its own benefit. The fact that Spinoza adds that the less universal teachings derive like streams from the more universal ones allows us to understand that the initial source is spread out and divided into several particular tributaries. The terminology is here quite similar to that used by Plotinus to describe the movement of procession from the one to the multiple. On several occasions, the author of the *Enneads* uses the metaphor of a source which gushes and disperses itself into smaller threads as it flows. The analogy with Plotinus comes to an end there, however, for the dispersal into streams is, for Spinoza, not the result of the water flow's exhaustion, but of the necessity of its adapting itself to particular circumstances. The existence of provisional teachings is tied to a local history and to an external context, while the eternal doctrine is universal and etched into the heart's interior. In short, the appearance of duration corresponds to the emergence

[67] *TTP* VII; CWS II, 175–6.
[68] *TTP* VII; CWS II, 176.

of a plural causality, particular and external to a unique, universal and internal causality.

It therefore becomes clear that eternity and duration do not maintain a relation of opposition or incompatibility. Neither property excludes the other, for they do not belong to the same order. One has a universal reach, the other a particular one. Duration is not, for all that, an avatar of eternity adapted to particular things. It does not have to do with replacing a universal law with a particular law. Provisional precepts do not suspend the course of universal principles which are themselves eternally valid and genuinely applicable in history when circumstances and individuals are amenable to them. Whether eternal or temporary, each has its own domain and validity.

Does this mean that the heterogeneity of these two spheres is radical? And that the eternal sphere and temporal sphere absolutely do not communicate with one another? This is impossible – for if it were the case, one could not stem from the other. The difference between duration and eternity is not one of nature, but of degree. Spinoza lets this be clearly understood since he uses this expression to describe the method of interpretation of nature. From more universal realities, it is necessary 'to proceed gradually to other, less universal things'.[69] Once we know that the most universal realities correspond to Scripture's eternal doctrine and the least universal ones to provisional teachings, no doubt can remain: the link that unites eternity to duration is that of a gradual progression. We pass from the first to the second by degrees that range from the most universal to the least universal. We must therefore recognise the existence of a process that goes from eternity to duration, since Spinoza himself uses the verb *procedo*.[70] It is true that he does not explicitly say that the least universal proceeds from the most universal, but that *we* proceed by degrees from one to the other, in conformance with the method required for correctly interpreting Scripture. Nevertheless, if the order and connection of ideas is the same as the order and connection of things, to say that we proceed from the most to the least universal amounts to affirming the existence of a progression between the two. There can therefore be no radical break or absolute discontinuity between eternity and duration. The process[71] from the eternal to the provisional (*temporaire*) takes the form of a derivation linked to the presence of obstacles. This is

---

[69] Ibid.: '. . . et ex his graditim ad alia minus universalia procedimus'.

[70] See preceding note.

[71] We thank André Lécrivain for having suggested we render the verb *procedo* with the substantive 'process' rather than that of procession, the latter being too burdened with Neo-Platonic connotations.

what transpires very clearly in one of the examples that Spinoza develops to illustrate his aim.

Example of the Interplay between the Eternal Teachings and Provisional Precepts of Scripture

The comparison carried out between the universal doctrine of Scripture, Mosaic law and the particular moral teaching of Christ, which encourages one to turn the other cheek, has exemplary value, for not only does it testify to the acuity and pertinence of the exegetical method, it also perfectly allows us to understand the nature of the relationship between duration and eternity. The universal doctrine of Scripture rests on fundamental eternal teachings, like the love of God and one's neighbour. Christ's teaching, which recommends loving one's neighbour as oneself, is an eternal truth, which is to say it expresses a necessity. Eternal truths, however, are not always perceived as such in an adequate manner. It is not easy to understand that it is just as necessary for a man to love his neighbour as it is for a triangle to have three angles equal to two right angles. The ignorance and obstinacy of humans are an obstacle to pure thought's immediate comprehension of eternal truths. They therefore apprehend them as derived laws. What distinguishes a law from an eternal truth? Their content is identical, for it expresses a necessity. The law, however, is an inadequately perceived eternal truth, because it is not considered as a necessity emanating from the nature of the thing, but as an imperative instituted by the will of a ruler.

The eternal principle of love of one's neighbour undergoes a first derivation when it takes the form of a law. Men obey it not because they have understood that its violation is an evil (*mal*) in itself, but because they either desire love for themselves or fear God's reprisals. The Mosaic law of an eye for an eye, for example, is eternal and derived from the doctrine of love for one's neighbour. It is less universal, however, for it reveals the way in which Moses and the Hebrews understood this love and adapted it to communal life. An eye for an eye seems like a divine commandment that leads to inevitable consequences when it is transgressed. So, we attach less value to the action in itself than to its consequences. The very formulation of the rule 'an eye for an eye, a tooth for a tooth', testifies to this since it does not explicitly advocate for the love of one's neighbour but determines the nature of the penalties imposed on the one who flouts it. The law corrects external actions and limits the harm (*mal*) done to the other but does not change the internal dispositions of the soul. There is thus indeed a derivation which explains that only the Hebrews could identify with this law, or at least that it is not universally adopted. The law therefore has a less general reach than the eternal truth, even though there is no difference in nature between them.

But sometimes the course of justice is diverted, because men live in corrupt cities that go adrift. We must therefore extract moral teachings that flow (*couler*) from the source and define provisional precepts. This is what Christ did when he told people to turn the other cheek, which is to say accept injustice. This precept is not erected into law, otherwise it would contradict the law of Moses. It is not universal and does not challenge the law of an eye for an eye which is valid for all eternity. Christ gave a sage piece of advice to oppressed men in a corrupt city. It is, indeed, vain, to demand justice from totally unjust men or to make justice for oneself. We must recognise that the law of an eye for an eye is not always appropriate given the particular circumstances. Must we respond to one holocaust with another, demanding reparations by the hangmen when the same persecutors are still in power? It would be better to accept injustice when we cannot avoid it and take some time (*temporiser*) – a phrase we must hear literally, for this attitude of non-resistance is only valid for certain periods of oppression. When one is unable to correct the external actions of others, so corrupt as they are, one must at least attempt to save one's soul by not ceding to hate or vengeance, by preventing the escalation of harm that would come from constantly one-upping the violence received from the other. Unlike the law of Moses, the Christian precept only holds in particular circumstances and in a provisional manner. 'Indeed, in a good republic, where justice is preserved, everyone is bound, if he wants to be thought just, to exact a penalty for injuries in the presence of a judge.'[72] Spinoza does not justify this last attitude with reference to base feelings of vengeance, but with the desire to defend justice and prevent evil from becoming advantageous in the eyes of bad men due to its perceived impunity. It is thus necessary to carefully distinguish eternal teachings from those which are valid only for a specific time if we do not want to destroy true religion. For this reason, Spinoza relies, on the one hand, on the Gospel according to Saint Matthew to prove that Christ himself did not present his teachings as a law capable of challenging the Mosaic commandments and, on the other hand, on the Book of Lamentations to show that the famous precept had been used temporarily by Jeremiah in a period of ruin and decadence.

---

[72] *TTP* 7; *CWS* II, 177.

General Implications of the Example

This examination of the interplay between the eternal principles and provisional teachings of Scripture is particularly illuminating, for it allows us to shed new light on the relationship between duration and eternity. First, it reveals to us that the existence of temporal things is in no way at odds with the existence of eternal things. The moral precept, 'turn the other cheek', is not completely cut off from the Mosaic source; on the contrary, it stems from it like a consequence adapted to a particular circumstance, for the eternal principle 'an eye for an eye, a tooth for a tooth' only applies in the hearts of men insofar as it makes it more possible for them to protect themselves from corruption and injustice. Now, paradoxically, in certain circumstances, the best means of resisting injustice is to give in to it. The acceptance of external injustice protects internal justice, for it prevents the heart from being eroded by a ferocious hate and an immoderate desire for vengeance. In this sense, in his moral teaching, Christ did not disavow the law of an eye for an eye, but fulfilled it exactly where circumstances were the most hostile to it. He maintains a principle of justice by giving up on the temporarily impossible task of correcting the external actions of men to devote himself to the improvement of their internal dispositions. His provisional teaching is thus indeed derived from the law of an eye for an eye and carries traces of its source, even though the nets of justice are thin in such decadent cities.

Secondly, the analysis of the example allows us to better discern the nature of the process from the most universal to the least universal that follows three steps. First, the foundation and source of true religion and the universal *Ethics* are the knowledge and love of God that Christ teaches. The son of God adequately understood the nature of this sovereign good and introduced it as an eternal truth and not as a law. For this reason, he did not teach as a legislator, but as a doctor. Secondly, from the original source of true life derives the law of an eye for an eye – a law that bridges the gap between the immutable and the temporal and consummates the inscription of duration in eternity. The law indeed contains an eternal aspect, since it emanates from a divine revelation to Moses, and a provisional aspect, for it is historically adapted to the Hebrews and is addressed to carnal man, concerned as he is with temporal joys. Third and finally, the Christian precept unfolds entirely in a historical setting; it nevertheless fulfils eternal doctrine by delivering men from servile submission to the law. In short, it constitutes the exception which confirms the rule. A teaching valid for a time here functions as an eternal truth. Spinoza actually underscored that Christ, in teaching things to his disciples as if they were eternal truths and not laws, 'freed them from bondage to the law. Nevertheless, he [didn't abolish the law for them, but] confirmed and established it more firmly, and wrote it thoroughly in their hearts.'[73] It is therefore interesting to note that a precept valid for a time only here better realises eternal principles than the law of an eye for an eye. Everything happens as though the eternal only coincided with itself by way of the temporal and not by way of the eternal. In this specific case, the temporal, far from being a fallen or defeated reality, in some way salvages the eternal and fulfils it in history.

Based on the above analysis, it becomes possible to sketch a table of different figures of the relationship between the two properties. There are cases where temporal existence and eternal existence perfectly coincide, when historical actions are wholly the expression of the knowledge and love of God. Christ is the perfect illustration of this type of existence, and with him there is no need to strictly distinguish between what belongs to duration, on the one hand, and eternity, on the other. His story is itself eternity. The sage also tends to coincide perfectly with the eternal. There are cases where the durational and the eternal meet and unfold in parallel, even though there is a possible distinction between the historical character of existence and its eternal aspect. Moses, the law-abiding Hebrew, or all the obedient citizens of a just State, enter this figure. The parallelism remains so long as the law is not tarnished or destroyed. By contrast, in a tyrannical state where men are corrupted, chaotic history does not closely fit the contours of eternity, but drifts away from immutable principles, instead proclaiming the triumph of hate and death. Not every distance, however, testifies to a separation from or ignorance of eternity. Thus, it was by taking distance from the law of an eye for an eye that Christ grew closer to eternal doctrine and fulfilled it. It is the apparent divergence that allows for convergence and restores the principles. In short, the relationship maintained between duration and eternity can take at least four forms: coincidence (symbolised by the life of Christ), conformity (represented by the figure of Moses), divergence (embodied by ignorant, unrighteous people) and corrective gap[74] (of which Jeremiah was the instigator before Christ).

[73] *TTP* IV; *CWS* II, 134.
[74] TN: The French reads '*l'écart convergent*'. As becomes clear throughout Jaquet's analysis of this figure and its examples, she uses this phrase to refer to situations in which something that seems to go against or further departs from eternity actually helps steer a course back toward coincidence with one's eternal essence. In this sense, there is still a gap between eternity and time, essence and existence, but a gap which narrows due to some corrective measure that may be saddening, painful, or apparently divergent

Drawing attention to the nature of the ontological link between duration and eternity has crucial epistemological consequences from the point of view of a philosophy of history. If temporal events flow like streams from an eternal source, they cannot be understood without being related to their foundation. In other words, the constitution of a rigorous history presupposes comprehension of eternal principles which give that history meaning, rescuing it from the obscurity of apparent contingency or chaotic becoming. In short, no history worth the name is without a reflection on eternity. Absent a key to the eternal vault, it is impossible to measure the real meaning and significance of an act or speech. Spinoza openly presents this principle as an imperative. Particular actions must be clarified and measured by the universal doctrine of Scripture.[75]

Both examples that Spinoza gives in support of his method show that only eternal principles render the real intelligible and avoid historical misinterpretations. We have seen how the precept 'turn the other cheek' must be understood with reference to the eternal doctrine of the love of God and one's neighbour, like a provisional teaching designed to preserve justice in one's soul when States are stricken with injustice. Without this eternal perspective, Christ's advice seems not only incoherent and incompatible with the Mosaic law but gives rise to misunderstandings that prove seriously harmful for faith and true religion. Such advice can be interpreted as an attitude of cowardice or submission to a power of greater strength, thereby discrediting believers accused of obeying a slave morality. Separated from its temporal context and interplay with eternity, the meaning of particular acts becomes veiled and distorted. This is what emerges in a still more salient way from the analysis of the first example mentioned by Spinoza.[76] Considered in isolation, the phrase 'Blessed are those who mourn, for they will be comforted', can be understood as an invitation to martyrdom, an exaltation of suffering and an encouragement of masochism or vulgar miserabilism. In isolation, it leaves the nature and object of mourning completely in the shadows. By contrast, it takes on its full meaning when connected to the eternal doctrine. The texts actually teach that only the kingdom of God and its justice merit human concern. 'By mourners' Christ 'understands only those who mourn for the kingdom of God and the justice men have neglected. For this is the only thing they can mourn, who love nothing but

---

from the eternal doctrine. For these reasons, I have chosen to translate the phrase with the linguistically inaccurate but conceptually accurate 'corrective gap'.

[75] *TTP* VII; *CWS* II, 176.
[76] Ibid.

the divine kingdom, or righteousness, and who completely disdain what for-tune may bring.'[77] What matters for religious history equally applies to his-tory in general, and even more so in the political domain which cannot be understood without eternal principles. This point also explains why Spinoza insists so strongly on the eternal legislation which constitutes the soul of the State.

Ultimately, chapter VII of the *Theologico-Political Treatise* clarifies the nature of the relationship between duration and eternity by revealing the existence of a process from the most universal to the least universal and a derivation tied to particular circumstances. However, it leaves the exact causal mechanism by which the gradual procession from the eternal to the temporal works in the shadows. Is it a continuous or discontinuous process? Is it possible to determine a transitional moment where the eternal source splits into temporal streams, thereby assigning a beginning to the derivation? Many questions remain unresolved. And we only find their answers in the *Ethics*.

Eternity and Duration in the *Ethics*

In this last work, the details of the problem are reconfigured, for duration stops being presented as the result of a gradual movement from the most to the least universal. Any and all trace of Neo-Platonism disappears insofar as Spinoza does not allude to any procession and no longer resorts to the metaphor of the source and streams. The ideas of progression and derivation do not in fact allow us to fully account for the origin of temporal phenom-ena; they tend to sidestep the paradox of their appearance, reducing the latter to a type of metaphysical sleight of hand that conceals the nature of their cause. How could eternal things engender duration? Everything that follows from an eternal and infinite thing is by nature eternal and infinite, as propositions 21, 22 and 23 from Part I show. Could duration derive directly from attributes? This is impossible, for 'all the things which follow from the absolute nature of any of God's attributes have always had to exist and be infinite, or are, through the same attribute, eternal and infinite'.[78] Does it therefore come from infinite immediate modes? Proposition 22 deters us from believing in this option since 'whatever follows from some attribute of God insofar as it is modified by a modification which, through the same attribute, exists necessarily and is infinite, must also exist necessarily and be

[77] *TTP* VII; CWS II, 177.
[78] *Ethics* I, 21; CWS I, 429.

infinite'.[79] Infinite mediate modes seem like the last refuge, but there too, it is clear they cannot be the proximate cause of duration, for they are eternal. We are thereby in the hands of an antinomy: on the one hand, duration follows from eternal things and turns out to be the effect of divine power; on the other hand, it cannot stem directly from eternal things, otherwise it would be eternity.

Spinoza does not evade the difficulty and does not claim that duration is determined by God, God's attributes, or universal *natura naturata*, as they are all infinite and eternal. To resolve the aporia, we must consider that duration is a property of existence that results from eternal things not by virtue of their infinite causality, but insofar as they are affected by finite and determinate modifications. The demonstration of proposition 28, which turns out to be the key to the relationship between duration and eternity, establishes this fact:

> Whatever has been determined to exist and produce an effect has been so determined by God (by P26 and P24C). But what is finite and has a determinate existence could not have been produced by the absolute nature of an attribute of God; for whatever follows from the absolute nature of an attribute of God is eternal and infinite (by P21). It had, therefore, to follow either from God or from an attribute of God insofar as it is considered to be affected by some mode. For there is nothing except substance and its modes (by A1, D3, and D5) and modes (by P25C) are nothing but affections of God's attributes. But it also could not follow from God, or from an attribute of God, insofar as it is affected by a modification which is eternal and infinite (by P22). It had, therefore, to follow from, or be determined to exist and produce an effect by God or an attribute of God insofar as it is modified by a modification which is finite and has a determinate existence.[80]

God is thus indeed the efficient cause of duration, for without God no effect could be produced, but God is not the absolutely proximate cause of it since duration does not immediately follow from God's nature.

Must we therefore conclude that substance is the remote cause of duration? This designation is inappropriate if it refers to a cause that is in no way linked to its effect, for everything that is is in God and cannot be conceived without God. For this reason, Spinoza undertakes a terminological

---

[79] *Ethics* I, 22; CWS I, 430.
[80] *Ethics* I, 29 Dem.; CWS I, 432.

clarification in the scholium to proposition 28. He agrees to the use of the expression 'remote cause' only to distinguish the production of singular things from those which stem immediately from the absolute nature of God, but he makes it clear that he is thereby deviating from the custom which understands a remote cause to have no link to its effect.

In all rigour, it would be more accurate to say that duration is the fruit of what the scholastics called a subsidiary instrumental cause. Spinoza mentions this form of causality in the *Short Treatise* and distinguishes it from principal causality, mainly following Heereboord. The author of the *Hermeneia* divides the notion of efficient cause into two categories: principal and subsidiary. The principal cause is that which produces the effect with its own force. The subsidiary cause is subdivided into three: *causa procatartica*, *proegumena*, *instrumentum*. The subsidiary instrumental cause is that which accommodates the effects of the principal cause when one is dealing with affections concerning particular things.[81] God is generally the principal cause of his works, but God cannot, by virtue of his infinity, directly rule over the numerous and particular production of finite effects. God thus works through the intervention of a subsidiary instrumental cause. Spinoza joins the professor of Leyde on this point when he declares that 'God is a principal cause of the effects he has created immediately, such as motion in matter, etc.', and that the subsidiary cause only intervenes when it comes to particular things.[82] While denying it even the slightest role in the production of infinite immediate effects, Spinoza nonetheless acknowledges the existence of a subsidiary causality restricted to the sphere of particular *natura naturata* and clarifies his remarks with the help of the famous incident of the Red Sea where God parts the waves with a strong wind. Without this wind-powered agent serving as a subsidiary instrumental cause, the divine action would be an incomprehensible miracle. It is also, incidentally, the reason why Spinoza, in chapter VI of the *Theologico-Political Treatise*, pays particular attention, in an analysis of the same passage of *Exodus*, to the natural causes which serve as relays for divine commandments and shows that their omission inclines awestruck men to cry miracle and become superstitious.

---

[81] Heereboord 1657: 106–9; quoted in Gueroult 1968: 247: 'causa efficiens alia est principalis, alia minus principalis. Causa principalis est quae sua virtute effectum producit . . . Causa minus principalis est triplex, causa procatartica, causa proegumena, instrumentatum. Instrumentatum est quod causa principalis in ipsa rei affectione subvenit . . . Causa procatartica est quae causam principalem efficientem extrinsecus incitat ad agendum. Causa principalis proegumena est quae causam principalem intus disponit, vel etiam proritat, ad agendum.'

[82] *KV* I, 3; *CWS* I, 80–1.

So we must believe that although the circumstances of miracles and their natural causes are neither always nor all fully described, nevertheless the miracles did not happen without them. This is established also by Exodus 14:27, where it is related only that it was simply by the command of Moses that the sea rose up again, and there is no mention of a wind. Nevertheless, in the Song it is said (15:10) that it happened because God blew with his wind, i.e., with a very strong wind. So this circumstance is omitted in the story, and for this reason the miracle seems greater.[83]

In the same manner, if we conceal the role of subsidiary causes, the appearance of duration seems like a miracle, for we have a hard time seeing how it could emerge from divine eternity. It is therefore through the intermediary of a finite modification that God engenders duration.

Spinoza, it is true, does not refer to subsidiary instrumental causality in the *Ethics* and only holds onto the distinction between proximate and remote causality with reluctance. The reason for his silence might be his refusal to let any doubt linger concerning divine efficacy and his desire to show that nothing can be conceived without God. The idea of an instrumental causality relieving the principal cause in the production of finite effects can lend itself to an error insofar as it introduces a duality rather incompatible with Spinoza's monism alongside a form of subordination of substance to an agent that would come to help it in its incapacity to immediately engender the finite. This does not mean that Spinoza disavowed his analyses in the *Short Treatise* or broke with Heereboord's classification; he merely avoids references liable to producing misunderstandings, as witnessed elsewhere by his reluctance to use the expression remote cause. In any manner, subsidiary instrumental causality is here helpfully replaced by the infinity of finite causes.[84]

Still, some might question the legitimacy of basing the genesis of duration on the model of the existence of singular things. In fact, proposition 28 does not explicitly concern duration, but establishes the necessity of an infinity of finite causes to determine singular things to exist and to act. What right do we have to apply a determination valid for singular things to duration? This

---

[83] *TTP* VI; *CWS* II, 163.

[84] In light of this, we wholly subscribe to Martial Gueroult's claims when he writes in relation to divine causality in the *Ethics*: 'as for the subsidiary instrumental cause, it does not disappear, but is reduced, as in the *Short Treatise*, to the infinite series of finite causes (or things) that are effects of God and that constitute the common order of nature' (1968: 254).

application is legitimate insofar as duration is nothing other than existence understood in its indefinite continuity. Duration, let us recall, is an affection that is not really distinguished from existence. To begin to exist is to begin to endure. For this reason, the problem of duration's appearance is tied to that of the production of singular things and should not be treated separately from that production. Consequently, the enigma concerning the relationship between eternity and duration can only find its resolution in the more general framework of the examination of causal relations between the finite and the infinite. Such an examination allows us two things: first, to better understand why the analysis of the way duration follows from eternal things had not been the subject of a central development and, second, to interpret Spinoza's strange silence on this subject as an economic principle rather than a blind spot or an admission of helplessness.

It remains to be seen if proposition 28 is enough to entirely explain the appearance of duration, for the causal process it describes could also apply to the eternal existence of modes. Doesn't the scholium of proposition 40 from Part V invite this interpretation to the extent that it seems to also bring into play an infinity of finite causes from a completely non-temporal perspective? Spinoza indeed claims that 'our mind, insofar as it understands, is an eternal mode of thinking, which is determined by another eternal mode of thinking, and this again by another, and so on, to infinity; so that together, they all constitute God's eternal and infinite intellect'.[85] In this case, what allows us to conclude with certainty that proposition 28 only concerns the temporal existence of modes instead of referring to their eternal existence? The stakes of the question are sizeable, for if the demonstration covered a general scope and could be extended to the eternal causality of finite modes, it would not allow us to solve the specific problem of the cause of their duration. The initial enigma would therefore return once again.

Proposition 28 clearly does not apply to the eternal existence of modes. Simple considerations of vocabulary suffice to show this: the expressions 'singular things' and 'finite things' always describe modes subject to duration and the pressure of external causes. We no longer find these terms under Spinoza's pen when he dedicates himself to the examination of the human intellect's eternity. Additionally, the infinity of finite causes cannot account for the mind's eternity: a finite cause can only produce finite effects. The causality that presides over the existence of eternal modes, whether they are finite or infinite, is not of the same nature as that which prevails in proposition 28. A mode is eternal only insofar as it is tied to the absolute nature

85 *Ethics* V, 40 Schol.; CWS I, 615.

of the attribute and, through the essence of God, includes existence. In the scholium previously invoked, Spinoza does not refer to proposition 28 to explain the existence of eternal modes, but to proposition 21 according to which 'all the things which follow from the absolute nature of any of God's attributes have always had to exist and be infinite, or are, through the same attribute, eternal and infinite'.[86] Proposition 28 does not involve God in its absolute nature, but in its essence as it is modified by a finite affection. 'What is finite and has a determinate existence could not have been produced by the absolute nature of an attribute of God; for whatever follows from the absolute nature of an attribute of God is eternal and infinite.'[87] His intention is, then, not to account for the eternity of modes (otherwise he would have invoked the absolute nature of the attribute), but to clarify the nature of temporal existence by revealing the causality that is proper to it. For this reason, it is legitimate to present proposition 28 as the key to the existence of duration.

Have we nevertheless not stumbled from Charybdis to Scylla? For if duration results from eternal things, not by virtue of their infinity causality, but insofar as they are affected by finite and determinate modifications, the problem of its appearance is not yet resolved – it is merely displaced. A formidable question still hangs in the air: how could a first finite modification arise from attributes and infinite modes?

Proposition 28 alone undoes this difficulty by dismissing the idea of a passage or jump from the infinite to the finite and resolves the false problem of a beginning by showing that there is no first finite cause. A search for such a thing is destined for failure, for it transforms the presupposition of the existence of a beginning into a certainty, losing itself in vain speculation. Our tendency to anthropomorphism leads us to believe that everything has a beginning and an end. It also leads us to reject any hypothesis contrary to this prejudice. But to hell with beginnings! Every finite modification 'had also to be determined by another, which is also finite and has a determinate existence; and again, this last (by the same reasoning) by another, and so always (by the same reasoning) to infinity, q.e.d.'[88] Spinoza clearly distinguishes between two types of causality: the infinity of infinite causes and the infinity of finite causes. We must refrain from confusing the two, lest we run into pitfalls that go along with the interference of heterogeneous elements. If every finite modification is produced by another which is in turn engendered

---

[86] *Ethics* I, 21; *CWS* I, 429.
[87] *Ethics* I, 28 Dem.; *CWS* I, 432.
[88] Ibid.

in the same manner, it becomes impossible to stop in the chain of causes and assign a beginning to duration. Spinozist duration therefore approximates sempiternity, for it has never started to be, but has been and will be.

A property inseparable from the existence of finite modes, duration is the product of the infinity of finite causes. It is an affection touching every individual included in the *facies totius universi*. Its indefinite character, however, leaves the question of the exact reach of its domain open. In other words, it turns out to be necessary to examine the limits of its domain and to determine whether those limits strictly coincide with the sphere of finite modes.

7

The Sphere of Extension of Duration

Attributes and Duration

For most commentators, it goes without saying that attributes are, like God, not subject to duration, and that the problem of duration's appearance is not one that would fall within the sphere of *natura naturans*. Still, a curious passage found in a letter to Hudde[1] seems to call this all too obvious conclusion into question. On the occasion of explaining the concept of imperfection, Spinoza gives an example pertaining to extension to illustrate what he means by privation. 'For although extension, for example, may deny thought of itself, this in itself is not an imperfection in it. But if it were deprived of extension, that would show an imperfection in it, as would really be the case if it were limited. Similarly, if it lacked *duration*, position, etc.'[2] Not only does duration not carry the stigma of finitude, but it must belong to extension for the latter to attain its perfection. Extension without duration would be imperfect, which is to say that it would lack what was by nature owed to it.[3] How should we understand this enigmatic claim? Doubly enigmatic, in fact, insofar as it invites us to locate the appearance of duration within *natura naturans* itself and to grant it the status of a property specific to extension, just like position and quantity. Must we conclude from this statement that the attribute of extension is by nature inclined to endure,

---

[1] See *Ep.* XXXVI [to Hudde]; *CWS* II, 28–32.

[2] Ibid., 29. Emphasis Jaquet's.

[3] See *Ep.* XXXVI [to Hudde]; *CWS* II, 30: 'Here I should like you to note what I said just now about the term imperfection, namely, that it signifies that something is lacking to a thing which pertains to its nature.'

thereby distinguishing itself from thought to which such a characteristic is not imputed in the letter?

We must first of all note that this property, of which extension cannot be deprived without becoming imperfect, is, unlike position, by no means the privilege of this attribute. Duration is, according to Letter XII, a characteristic of the existence of modes in general, including those of thought. In the *Treatise on the Emendation of the Intellect*, Spinoza also specifies that ideas have 'their own duration in the mind',[4] thereby confirming that extension does not have a monopoly on indeterminate duration.

This being the case, how are we to understand the letter to Hudde which attributes duration to extension, whose essence is not distinct from its existence? What meaning does the term duration take on here? The attribute of extension can be said to endure neither in the sense that this term takes on in *Metaphysical Thoughts*, nor in the sense granted to it in the *Ethics*, for in the first case, duration only pertains to a being whose 'essence involves only possible existence'.[5] Yet, 'each attribute of a substance must be conceived through itself',[6] and has no need of support from another to be produced. In this respect, it includes necessary existence, though this latter concept cannot be deployed independently of substance. Neither does the attribute of extension allow for 'an indefinite continuation of existing',[7] for its existence is by nature determinate, infinite in its kind, and knows no point of limitation, since no external cause can come to annihilate it.

We could easily resolve the problem by observing that Hudde's correspondent never explicitly attributes duration to the *attribute* of extension (the word does not actually appear in the letter), but seems rather to mean extension in a more general sense, for he uses expressions like 'the term extension' or defines it as 'a certain type of being'. These lexicological considerations, however, only provide a false sense of clarification, as the context enjoins one to think that Spinoza considers extension to be something that constitutes the essence of God. He grants it every property of an attribute (infinity and perfection in its kind), and compares it with the other attribute we know (thought) to clarify what he means by perfection and imperfection.

Some light can be shed on the difficulty if we pay attention to the sense of the term duration in the letter itself. The privation of duration constitutes an imperfection insofar as it introduces a determination, a limitation. To

---

[4] *TdIE*, 82, note d; CWS I, 36.
[5] CM I, 4; CWS I, 310.
[6] *Ethics* I, 10; CWS I, 416.
[7] *Ethics* II, Def. 5; CWS I, 447.

possess duration here means to have an indeterminate existence, in contrast to a determinate and finite existence. From this point of view, if extension does not endure, it is necessarily imperfect, for it lacks what by nature belongs to it. If it includes necessary existence, we cannot deny its duration without contradiction. Spinoza clearly highlights this point: 'if the term extension involves necessary existence, it will be as impossible to conceive extension without existence as it is to conceive extension without extension'.[8] It must therefore be in full possession of an indeterminate duration.

Even if the term duration had taken the sense of a temporally determinate or determinable period, which is obviously not the case here, it would be no less true that extension without duration would be imperfect, for according to the famous proposition 16 from *Ethics* I, 'from the necessity of the divine nature there must follow infinitely many things in infinitely many modes (i.e., everything which can fall under an infinite intellect)'.[9] The absence of extended modes knowing a determinate duration would constitute an imperfection to the extent that substance would not have produced all that is in its power to produce and would not have achieved the realisation of everything possible. It is evident that in the letter to Hudde, duration is not a synonym for a determined period of time; but this hypothesis merited examination as a cross-check since it shows, in a decisive manner, that in every instance, extension deprived of duration would be imperfect.

The presence of the term duration there remains no less surprising, for one would rather expect to find the term eternity under Spinoza's pen. Is this to say that in 1666, he conceived eternity under the form of an indeterminate duration and that he will go back on this idea in the *Ethics* by proscribing the assimilation of that concept to any form of temporality, even if unlimited in both directions? In truth, the term duration here takes on a generic sense, such as we had found it on several occasions in the Spinozist corpus. It encompasses all forms of temporality. When he declares that extension deprived of duration would be imperfect, Spinoza does not presume an eternal, aeviternal or temporal quality for it, but instead aims to show that a limitation would be incompatible with the nature of the attribute. Behind this refusal of a privation of duration or position likely looms the critique of a world limited in space and in time. According to pre-Galilean cosmology, the world is finite in space and limited to a fixed sphere beyond which there is nothing but imaginary space. It is also limited in time, endowed with a beginning dating back to its creation several thousand years ago, and an end

---

[8] *Ep.* XXXVI [to Hudde]; CWS II, 29.
[9] *Ethics* I, 16; CWS I, 424.

attached to the Last Judgment, beyond which there is nothing. Now, for Spinoza, it is contradictory to conceive of a world with a finite and determinate position and duration: whatever the vastness of a space and length of a time, it is always possible to conceive of a greater one. In this light, the enigmatic passage from Letter XXXVI becomes quite clear: the correspondent of the 'very wise Hudde' does not mean to deny the eternity of extension or affirm the appearance of duration within this attribute. He merely seeks to dismiss any determination indicative of a privation, any determination incompatible with the nature of extension. The word duration does not here have its typical, strict sense, but a broader reach like it did in the scholastics.

To eliminate lingering doubts, we must only consider the way in which Spinoza makes use of this term in a similar demonstrative schema found in an earlier letter addressed to Hudde on 10 April 1666. To prove the eternity of necessary being, he uses a *reductio ad absurdum* in an effort to denounce the contradictory character of the attribution of a determinate duration to God. 'So to undertake this task I shall first show briefly what properties a being possessing necessary existence must have, namely: (1) That it is eternal. For if a limited duration were attributed to it, that Being would be conceived as not existing beyond that limited duration, or as not involving necessary existence, which would be contrary to its definition.'[10] Spinoza thus grants an eternity to necessary being and implicitly connects it to an indeterminate duration. From this angle, it is evident that the aim of his demonstration is not to grant duration to God, and that the term takes on a generic sense.

The Duration of Infinite Modes

Origin and Nature of the Problem

If *natura naturans* is eternal and does not tolerate duration, *natura naturata*, by contrast, lends itself to temporal determination. To what extent, exactly, remains to be seen. It is typically admitted that duration is the property of singular things and the whole of particular *natura naturata*. But by what right do we restrict its domain to finite modes only and exclude universal *natura naturata* from its sphere of extension? Several clues invite us to wake from our dogmatic slumber on this subject. *Metaphysical Thoughts* already raises suspicions: doesn't every created thing fully possess duration? Even though Spinoza makes no allusion to *natura naturata* in that work, it would

---

[10] *Ep.* XXXV [to Hudde]; CWS II, 27.

seem reasonable to place infinite modes in the category of created things and to attribute duration to them, since they cannot take the privilege of self-causation away from God, nor can they have an essence which includes existence.

But it is Letter XII above all that carries out a vigorous attack against the idea that duration is the sole privilege of finite modes. When Louis Meyer's correspondent claims that 'for it is only of modes that we can explain the existence by duration', he does not explicitly exclude in his verbiage infinite affections of substance. To be sure, he does not openly maintain that all modes fall under the same system, but lacking a deliberate prohibition or more extensive clarifications, he indirectly authorises the attribution of duration to the whole of *natura naturata*. The infinity of mediate and immediate modes does not constitute a sufficient argument for claiming that Spinoza here only intends to speak of finite modes, for this infinity is neither the cause nor the condition of possibility for their eternity. Infinity is a derived effect which follows from the absolute or modified nature of an attribute in the same way as eternity does. Proposition 21 from *Ethics* I clearly shows that the eternity of a mode does not result from its infinity but 'follows from the nature of the attribute'. The properties are therefore separated from each other and do not derive from one another. Infinity, ultimately, changes nothing of the matter at hand and does not grant an absolute privilege when it comes to eternity. Finite or infinite, modes remain modes. In the absence of reservations excluding infinite affections, is it really illegitimate to include all modes and maintain that God's infinite intellect and motion and rest endure, together with the *facies totius universi*? Spinoza, it is true, never explicitly says so, but it is not absurd to ask whether *natura naturata* in its entirety might not share, in this respect, the lot of singular things.

Before settling this question, it is indeed important to grasp the details of the problem: it is not an issue of calling into question the eternity of infinite modes and reviving the argument surrounding the fruitless search for intermediary categories. Rather, it has to do with determining whether infinite modes can be eternal and endure, as finite modes can. In other words, can we and should we extend what is valid for the finite, in accordance with the same modal status, to the infinite?

Letter XII does not provide the elements required for an answer, for Spinoza's silence on the subject of infinite modes opens the door for a plurality of interpretations. It is possible to assert that the author of the letter did not mean all modes and excluded universal *natura naturata* in particular. It is also plausible to retort that if Louis Meyer's correspondent did not include all modes, he would have likely specified this fact in order to guard against any potential confusion.

It would be tempting to resolve the issue by showing that it does not arise for the good reason that in 1663 the conception of infinite modes had not yet been elaborated. This eventuality is not to be excluded right away, for Spinoza remains oddly mute on this question. If he had already had a solid conception on this subject, he probably would have used it to illustrate the distinction between different types of the infinite.

However, the hypothesis according to which Spinoza could not have meant to include infinite modes under the pretext that he had not yet conceived of them encounters two insurmountable pitfalls. For one part, the *Short Treatise*, which we generally agree to consider as earlier, incontestably presents an embryonic theory of infinite modes: Spinoza dedicates a chapter to universal *natura naturata* and mentions two creatures that depend immediately on God: 'motion in matter, and intellect in the thinking thing'.[11] For another part, Letter IX, addressed to Simon de Vries, constitutes a commentary on the first propositions of the future *Ethics* and presents the divine intellect as an infinite mode: 'I think I have demonstrated clearly and evidently enough that the intellect, though infinite, pertains to *natura naturata*, not to *natura naturans*.'[12] It is not therefore possible to avoid the difficulty raised by Letter XII, since in April of 1663, Spinoza already had a conception of infinite modes. For lack of sufficiently decisive clues to resolve it, the enigma still lingers. The problem thus returns in the *Ethics* where it is posed in a crucial manner since infinite modes form the object of a concise but nonetheless undeniable development.

The Criteria of Duration

To solve the problem methodologically, one should, rather than tracking the always questionable presence of a chronological vocabulary applied to infinite modes, instead determine whether universal *natura naturata* indeed possesses the properties inherent to duration, verifying them alongside the criteria given in definition 5 of *Ethics* II.

The fact that this definition is formulated alongside the study of the nature and origin of the mind invites us to believe that it uniquely concerns finite modes and that it was not necessary for understanding the existence of infinite modes in Part I. But before thereby concluding that infinite

---

[11] *KV* I, 9; CWS I, 91.
[12] *Ep.* IX [to de Vries]; CWS I, 195.

affections should be exclusively placed under the banner of eternity along-side substance and its attributes, we must make sure that they are not char-acterised by 'an indefinite continuity of existence'. Now, if we follow the explanation of definition 5 from Part II to the letter, infinite modes seem inclined to endure, for their existence seems to fulfil both requisite con-ditions for being indefinite. They are determinate neither by nature, since they are not self-caused, nor by the nature of their efficient cause, since God necessarily posits their existence, but does not necessarily eliminate it.

The test, however, is hardly conclusive, for if we stick to this superficial consideration of definition 5, we can note that substance also meets the criteria required for a thing to endure. In fact, divine existence can be deter-mined neither by the nature of substance, since it is absolutely infinite and allows for no limitation whatsoever, nor by its efficient causality which is complete self-affirmation and includes no seed of destruction whatsoever. God is the cause of itself: this implies, according to definition 1 of Part I, that its nature can only be conceived as existing. Logically, we must conclude that God endures, which is absurd since Spinoza refuses God this property over and over again. The case of God here provides us with a counter-example which, short of entirely disproving the hypothesis of a duration for infinite modes, puts it back on the stand and forces us to consider the nature of the indefinite in a more extensive manner.

To discern exactly what this term covers, we must examine the three definitions of this notion sketched by Spinoza. The first, observing Cartesian principles, equates the indefinite to that 'whose limits (if it has any) cannot be discovered by the human intellect'.[13] The indefinite designates what the intellect perceives as unlimited not by virtue of the thing's nature but by virtue of the finite character of the intellect's apprehension. The term there-fore includes both what is unlimited in itself and what is unlimited simply for us. In other words, the indefinite is not synonymous with the indeterminate or the unlimited, for it can include what is in itself unlimited without our knowing it.

Even though he does not explicitly disavow the Cartesian definition from the *Principles*, Spinoza, in Letter XII, makes some sensible changes to his first go at the concept since he attributes the unlimitedness less to an incapacity of the intellect than to the nature of the thing which does not lend itself to a determination. Certain things are said to be indefinite 'because they cannot be equated with any number, though they can be conceived to be greater or

---

[13] *PP* II, Def. 4; *CWS* I, 263.

lesser'.[14] The indefinite amounts to a form of uncountable infinity and no longer unites only the unlimited in itself and the unlimited for us, but also everything that is numerically unlimited and indeterminable. There are, for example, scales containing a maximum and a minimum that are called indefinite because the space contained between them exceeds any possible number.

As for the definition in the *Ethics*, it also emphasises the impossibility of a determination and ties it more to the nature of the thing than to any fault of the intellect, in accordance with the analyses of Letter XII. What is indefinite can in reality be limited just as well as unlimited, but we ourselves are unable to tell, for it depends neither on the thing nor on its cause. What makes an existence indefinite rather than unlimited is essentially the possibility of the existence of a cause that would come to put an end to it. This cause of destruction can find itself neither in the mode itself nor in the attribute that engenders the mode. It is therefore necessarily external. At the same time, duration is not numerically determinable with certainty, for it does not depend on the essence of the thing, but fluctuates in accordance with the vicissitudes of the existence and its encounters with external causes. An indefinite existence is therefore recognisable by three major signs: First, its nature does not limit it, but this does not imply that it is necessarily unlimited. If it were necessarily and absolutely unlimited by nature, it would be infinite and not indefinite. Second, it is not numerically determinable, for even though the duration of the existence can consist of a minimum and a maximum, a being longer or shorter, it is impossible in light of the essence of the thing to conclude from this that it will persevere in its being for any definite number of years. Third, an indefinite existence does not exclude the possibility of an external cause of destruction.

Let us now apply these criteria to infinite modes and see what results from it. We must note that they do not perfectly fulfil the first condition required for possessing an indefinite existence. Unlike finite modes, whose nature taken in itself does not include a limit, but does not exclude the existence of external constraints, infinite modes are necessarily unlimited. Their absence of limit does not come from an incapacity on behalf of the intellect to run through the chain of causes and reach their eventual limits. Rather, it results from their infinite nature. Their unlimited character is apodictically deduced from their essence and constitutes a positive property that the intellect can know and apprehend. No further do they fulfil the second criterion. Their existence contains neither minimum nor maximum, and can be conceived

---

[14] *Ep.* XII [to Meyer]; CWS I, 205.

neither as bigger nor smaller since it is infinite. The third condition, in turn, is also not met. An infinite mode, like any individual thing, perseveres in its being and does not carry in itself the seeds of its own destruction, for it is a complete affirmation of itself. Substance as an efficient cause posits its existence and does not remove it. Ultimately, unlike what happens for finite things, the existence of an external destructive cause is excluded by virtue of the infinity of modes.

To the question 'do infinite modes endure?' we must therefore necessarily answer in the negative and remind anyone who would raise doubts of Spinoza's warning concerning the confusion between different types of infinity in Letter XII. Universal *natura naturata* falls under the category of beings infinite through their cause and not that of indefinite things. To think that infinite modes enjoyed an indefinite existence by virtue of their unlimited character would be to fall into the second trap that Spinoza denounces from the outset of the letter. The error, which consists in equating the unlimited and the indefinite, stems from 'not distinguish[ing] between what is called infinite because it has no limits and that whose parts we cannot explain or equate with any number, though we know its maximum and minimum'.[15]

Consideration of Objections

Still, the thesis according to which infinite modes do not endure seems to be called into question by some observations of a Greek researcher, Yannis Prélorentzos,[16] who bases his analysis on proposition 24 of *Ethics* I and its corollary where Spinoza demonstrates that the essence of things produced by God includes neither their existence nor their duration and explains that God alone can be the cause of either of them. Now, the concept of produced things encompasses finite modes just as well as infinite modes. In this respect, one would have to extend duration to the entirety of *natura naturata*. This is at least what Prélorentzos proposes on the basis of a study of the ontological field of application of the corollary of proposition 24. In relying on two passages[17] concerning infinite modes that explicitly appeal to that corollary, he asserts that Spinoza places universal *natura naturata* in the category of produced things, as to which the scholium of proposition 28 testifies, and notes that the sphere of extension of duration widens out to include the

---

[15] *Ep.* XII [to Meyer]; CWS I, 201. [TN: Jaquet's text mistakenly cites *Ep.* XI.]
[16] Prélorentzos 1992: 297–303.
[17] *Ethics* I, 28 Schol.; 29 Dem.; CWS I, 432–3.

entirety of the modal domain. The second concerns modes in general and is not entirely convincing even by the confession of Prélorentzos himself who places himself under the banner of Martial Gueroult to admit that Spinoza equally means to include infinite affections.[18] By contrast, the first lends significant credence to the thesis of a duration of infinite modes, for in the scholium of proposition 28 of Part I, where he picks up a scholastic distinction in order to modify it, Spinoza demonstrates that God is absolutely the proximate cause of infinite modes by referring not only to proposition 15 but also to the corollary of proposition 24:

> Since certain things had to be produced by God immediately, viz. those which follow necessarily from his absolute nature, and others (which nevertheless can neither be nor be conceived without God) had to be produced by the mediation of these first things, it follows: I. That God is absolutely the proximate cause of the things produced immediately by him, and not [a proximate cause] in his own kind, as they say. For God's effects can neither be nor be conceived without their cause (by P15 and P24C).[19]

Now, the corollary of proposition 24 claims that God is the cause of the existence of things and their duration. If the essence of things produced by God does not include existence, it follows that 'God is not only the cause of things' beginning to exist, but also of their persevering in existing.'[20] Consequently, if we rigorously apply this corollary to the particular case of infinite modes, 'their essence can be the cause neither of their existence nor of their *duration*, but only God, to whose nature alone it pertains to exist'.[21] Spinoza thus seems to indeed attribute a duration to infinite modes. Prélorentzos, however, does not risk adopting such a conclusion. He limits himself to noting the existence of a problem, for the affirmation of a sempiternity of infinite modes seems, to him, incompatible with the demonstration of their eternity, and he concludes by denouncing a serious lack of rigour on behalf of Spinoza's text on this point.[22]

---

[18] See Prélorentzos 1992: 301: 'This is very highly probable, and in any case, Martial Gueroult admits it.'

[19] *Ethics* I, 28 Schol.; CWS I, 432–3.

[20] *Ethics* I, 24 Cor.; CWS I, 431.

[21] Ibid. Emphasis Jaquet's.

[22] Prélorentzos 1992: 303: 'In any case, if the affirmation according to which the eternity of infinite modes is ultimately a sempiternity is erroneous, it is at least certain that the very text of the *Ethics* testifies to a serious lack of rigor on this precise question.'

Prélorentzos cannot manage to resolve the difficulty, for he assumes that the existence of an unlimited duration of infinite modes compromises their eternity by marring it with chronological determinations. We must, to be sure, comply with Spinoza's prior warnings and reject the idea that the eternity of infinite modes is reducible to a sempiternity, but it is not necessary to pose the question in terms of a contradictory opposition, as if it were an immediate given that universal *natura naturata* only accommodated one type of temporality. Don't finite modes testify to the possibility of a being at once eternal and durational? This clarification, however, does not invalidate the remarks concerning the ontological field of application of duration. It is therefore important to verify whether the connection between the scholium of proposition 28 and the corollary of proposition 24, a comparison which Spinoza invites us to undertake, actually challenges the conclusion according to which infinite modes are not subject to duration.

We should first of all note that Prélorentzos' analyses rest on two presuppositions. The first consists in admitting that the corollary of proposition 24 introduces the concept of duration in a sense that would be in strict conformity with the definition that will be established in Part II and that it uniquely concerns the actual present existence of envisaged modes and not their eternal existence. The second consists in thinking that in the scholium of proposition 28, the expression 'things immediately produced by God' only designates infinite modes, that the indefinite pronoun 'others' indicates finite modes, and that the following distinction between proximate cause and remote cause closely fits the contours of this division.

Now, these two presuppositions are both contestable. The corollary of proposition 24 alludes, to be sure, to the duration of things produced by God, but nothing allows us to say for sure that this term takes on the signification that Spinoza will later assign it. Indeed, it rather seems that we are once again dealing with the generic sense of this term popular among the scholastics. Duration here designates temporality in general and encompasses modes in their eternal existence just as well as in their indefinite chronological continuity. Several pointers push us to adopt this hypothesis. First, it would be curious for Spinoza either to use duration in its strict sense while he had not yet defined it or to have the intention of deducing the indefinite continuity of modes without even specifying what he conceived under this term. It is more likely that he uses this word in its usual scholastic sense and that he thereby felt no need to define it. Let us, for that matter, recall that in this corollary Spinoza openly inscribes himself in the scholastic current insofar as he takes up expressions like *causa essendi* from it. Secondly, the corollary not only concerns the actual present existence of modes but can also be applied to their eternal existence. Their eternity, indeed, stems from God and not their essence. The terms existence and duration can therefore just as well refer to the eternity of modes as to their temporality. This interpretation is corroborated by the scholium of proposition 45 from Part II which refers precisely to this corollary while exclusively treating the necessary existence of things in God and explicitly dismissing any reference to duration. This proves, *a posteriori*, that the corollary of proposition 24 cannot invoke duration in the sense of indefinite continuity of existence but must instead deal with its generic meaning. With this remark, we might even be inclined to think that the corollary of proposition 24 does not establish the duration of modes in the chronological sense of the term and that the latter is only deduced from proposition 28.

One could nevertheless object that the verbs 'to begin' and 'to persevere' which appear in that corollary are charged with chronological significations. But is that so certain? The notion of beginning is suspect for Spinoza and should be handled with caution as the scholium of proposition 31 of Part V reminds us. *Incipiant* refers not only to the idea of a temporal beginning but also to the necessity of the existence of a principle producing things which are not self-caused. The verb *perseverare*, in its turn, does not systematically entail a chronological dimension. In the scholastics, and notably in Suarez, it expresses a permanence capable of taking on several modalities (eternal, aeviternal, sempiternal or temporal) according to the types of beings with which one is dealing. In the corollary, Spinoza takes up this scholastic term to designate permanence in being without assuming the nature of the temporality of modes. If we base ourselves on a consideration of the occurrences of this verb, it is obvious that Spinoza does not systematically equate perseverance in being with a duration measurable by time. Does he not declare that 'the power by which God perseveres in his being is nothing but his essence'?[23] But God cannot endure. God's perseverance in being is not of a temporal order, but an eternal one. In the same manner, if finite things persevere in being, it does not *ipso facto* mean that they endure. We must not confuse perseverance with the effort to persevere in one's being. If we follow proposition 8 from Part III, only the effort to persevere in one's being includes an indefinite duration. The force (*vis*) that makes each thing persevere in its being takes the form of an effort (*conatus*) due to the presence of external causes which determine it. Their perseverance in being is thus in part eternal since 'the force by which each one perseveres in existing follows from the

[23] CM II, 6; CWS I, 326.

eternal necessity of God's nature',[24] and in part temporal, for their effort is occasionally offset by the power of other singular things. Combined, these reasons lead us to conclude that in the corollary, Spinoza uses the concept of duration in accordance with its scholastic usage; he will not put the basics of his own conception together until proposition 28 where he will treat the causes of finite things. Earlier, his aim was limited to showing that the existence of modes, whether their nature be eternal or temporal, did not depend on their essence, but on God. Given the above, we cannot base an argument for the thesis of the duration of infinite modes in a reference to corollary 24.

The second presupposition does not stand up to scrutiny either. We have often pondered, in light of the scholium of proposition 28, over the nature of 'things immediately produced by God', and we have opposed it to or at least distinguished it from 'others', which imply intermediaries, while perhaps forgetting all too quickly that the '*et alia*' does not appear in the manuscript of the *Opera posthuma* and that the text had been modified by Gebhardt on the basis of *Nagelate Schriften*.[25] Some commentators, like Wolfson,[26] have relied on the terminology to claim that things immediately produced by God refer to infinite immediate modes and the others infinite mediate modes. In doing so, they pay no heed to indications which openly encourage us to place finite singular things in the category of those which both require intermediaries to exist and are the effects of a remote causality. Others, like Gueroult, refuse this interpretation. They consider things immediately produced by God to encompass the entirety of infinite modes and the category of others to classify finite things.[27] In absolute terms, Gueroult is right to tie infinite mediate modes to the first group and hold that they are the effects of a proximate causality, but in truth, it does not seem to be the case that Spinoza here alludes to infinite modes. Instead, he has his sights on eternal finite modes, or rather, eternal determinate[28] modes, as several references

---

[24] *Ethics* II, 45 Schol.; CWS I, 482.
[25] Cf. Gebhardt, *Opera*, II, 70 and explanatory note, 352–3.
[26] Wolfson 1962: Vol. I, 390, note 2.
[27] Gueroult 1968: 342.
[28] We must in fact note, as Pascal Sévérac does in *Spinoza: Union et désunion* (2011: 75), that Spinoza does not use the expression 'eternal finite modes', even though he acknowledges that the intellect – which is by nature eternal – can be finite or infinite in proposition 31 of Part I. Spinoza prefers to speak of the mind, as he understands it, as an eternal mode of thinking, determined by another eternal mode of thinking, notably in the scholium of proposition 40 of Part V. That likely allows him to ward off the misinterpretation according to which God's infinite intellect would be made up of finite parts.

make transparent. Contrary to a widely held idea, the sphere of extension of things immediately produced by God is not limited to infinite modes – it includes everything that follows from the absolute nature of substance and, in this respect, it includes eternal finite modes. These modes do not fall within the infinite chain of finite things, but depend on the absolute nature of God. The scholium of proposition 40 of Part V, let us recall, demonstrates that 'the mind, insofar as it understands, is an eternal mode of thinking, which is determined by another eternal mode of thinking' by relying not on proposition 28 from Part I, which brings the infinite chain of finite causes into play, but on proposition 21 of Part I, which concerns everything that follows from the absolute nature of God. Eternal finite modes are therefore the effects of a proximate cause and must be integrated into the category of things immediately produced by God. It is also evident that eternal finite modes of thought are things immediately produced by substance, since they together constitute God's infinite intellect. We cannot see how the infinite immediate mode of thought could be the effect of a proximate cause without the ideas which constitute it also being so. To produce the idea of God, is this not at the same time to engender the assortment of ideas which constitute it?

What then authorises the reduction of things immediately produced by God to only eternal finite modes at the exclusion of infinite modes? It would be logical for Spinoza to refer to eternal finite modes insofar as proposition 28 is dedicated to singular things and not to infinite modes. But beyond this simple consideration, the key to the problem resides in the function assigned to things immediately born from God: they serve as intermediaries for the production of singular things. It thus becomes clear that Spinoza cannot be thinking of infinite modes, since only a finite modification can produce a finite modification. Didn't proposition 28 just amply demonstrate this fact? Neither God in its absolute nature nor an infinite modification can produce a singular thing. Only God insofar as it is affected by a finite modification is capable of doing so. There can be no further doubt: the infamous things immediately produced by God are here well and truly eternal finite modes.

This conclusion allows us to shed new light on the Latin text of the *Opera posthuma*. Is it really legitimate to modify the text by adding '*et alia*' when we know that in reality Spinoza did not oppose one category of things to the other, but in fact considered the same things under a dual aspect? The aim of the scholium is fundamentally focused on a distinction between what in things, falling under the jurisdiction of a proximate causality, follows from the absolute nature of God, and what falls under the jurisdiction of a remote causality, involving the infinity of finite causes. This distinction is crucial for finite modes, for they are the only ones that depend both on the common order of nature and on the absolute essence of God. It is important for their salvation that they be connected to God and endeavour to the greatest possible extent to be determined intrinsically as opposed to extrinsically. For this reason, Spinoza works to mitigate against a fallacious interpretation of remote causation by strongly emphasising the necessary link between all effects and God. If the scholium is ultimately dedicated to singular things directly following from proposition 28, the return to the corollary of proposition 24 is perfectly coherent and no longer offers any ammo to the argument concerning a duration of infinite modes.

Even if we had accepted both of Prélorentzos' presuppositions, and thereby retained the strict sense of duration and considered infinite modes to be the only things immediately produced by God, the corollary of proposition 24 still could not prove that infinite modes endure, for in this corollary, Spinoza does not affirm that *every* mode endures. He merely says that the essence of every mode includes neither existence nor duration. That fact remains true even for those that do not endure.

Ultimately, if infinite modes do not meet the criteria for being allowed to endure, and if the corollary of proposition 24 from Part I is not conclusive on the subject, then duration is the exclusive property of finite modes. With a curious reversal in perspective, if there is a monopoly in the Spinozist system, it is not God who holds it, since God concedes, as it were, God's eternity, but finite modes, jealously possessive of their duration. Shall we call this a sad privilege? In a philosophy of joy, there is no room to deplore the existence of duration with its flow of images and memories; they have, like all things, a perfection proper to themselves. Memory and imagination can serve (*servir*) us or subjugate (*asservir*) us according to their use. They therefore become precious aids to the intellect and strengthen its cognitive power on the condition of being applied to objects capable of being imagined. In themselves, they constitute a wealth of which death robs us, since only the intellect remains. From this point of view, eternal salvation should not be systematically analysed in terms of gain, but also in terms of loss.

Conclusion

Paradoxically, Spinozist eternity has a history: a mere extrinsic denomination in the *Short Treatise*, it becomes a real property in the *Ethics* and should be counted among the ranks of common notions. In this way, it stops belonging exclusively to substance to be extended to infinite and finite modes. The *Ethics* therefore marks a decisive turning point in relation to *Metaphysical Thoughts*, since Spinoza breaks the divine monopoly on eternity and replaces, once and for all, the doctrine of the immortality of the soul with that of the eternity of the intellect. At the same time, the status of modes finds itself shaken up: particular *natura naturata* is no longer content to enjoy a finite duration, or even an endless duration. It now sees itself endowed with an actual present existence and an actual eternal existence. The discovery of the exact ontological nature of eternity once again highlights the fecundity and originality of Spinoza's theory of common notions, for the existence of these infamous notions is the condition of possibility for the extension of a property characteristic of substance to infinite and finite modes. The theory of common notions thus picks up where the scholastic doctrine of communicable attributes had left off and turns out to be the key to reading the final propositions of the *Ethics* which establish the eternity of the human intellect. Without this theory, the communication of this property would appear to be a sleight of hand – more of a nominal than real communication. We can therefore understand why in *Metaphysical Thoughts*, where this doctrine is not yet elaborated, or at least does not explicitly appear, Spinoza indeed refrains from attributing eternity to created things and carefully reserves it for the creator, thereby avoiding the metaphysical conundrum of a 'substantialisation' of modes or a 'modalisation' of substance, as well as the accusation of creating a lesser divinity. Recourse to common notions allows us to evade these inextricable difficulties, for those properties which ground our reasoning express that through which two or more beings agree. They reveal the existence of a certain similarity between beings without implying an identity of nature. Substance and modes can therefore share eternity without for all that being of the same nature. Their commonality does not preclude their ontological difference and is not based on a denaturation. Common notions should not be assimilated to properties that are strictly identical in every being. They exclude disagreement, but not difference.

Their presence renders futile the search for temporal categories specific to each type of being. God possesses a necessary existence, so modes enjoy a necessity of existing. Though the first exists through itself and the second through another, they come together in their necessity. While this necessity is not of a strictly identical nature, it is nevertheless common and takes the name eternity whether it is connected to substantial or modal existence. In this way, the theory of common notions consummates the relegation of *aevum*, alongside a whole series of temporal categories developed for differ-ent types of beings, to the realm of useless and dubious metaphysical curios-ities. Under the banner of universal eternity, there is absolutely no need to claim a co-eternity for attributes, a sempiternity for infinite modes and an immortality for finite affections.

The enigma concerning eternity's being shared by beings as different as substance and modes dissipates together with its array of bastard solutions in favour of the only real question raised by Spinozist thought: is eternity a universal common notion belonging to every mind, or does it turn out to be the property of certain minds only? There still, man is not a dominion within a dominion, and does not possess eternity within particular *natura naturata* in an exclusive manner, for man shares this property with every body endowed with a '*mens*'. The major problem is therefore no longer that of being eternal, but of knowing that one is eternal in order to enjoy beati-tude and ward off the fear of death. The line of demarcation between beings takes shape according to the degree of consciousness they have of this truth that is fundamental for salvation. The soul of an animal body, like that of a political body, is eternal – but do they know it? Can one really speak of their consciousness of this fact? Nothing in the Spinozist *corpus* allows us to affirm such a thing. At the human level, by contrast, the problem of a consciousness of the intellect's eternity is reducible to that concerning the perception of universal common notions by all men. It becomes one particu-lar case which finds its solution in a more general framework. Consciousness of eternity follows the fate granted to universal common notions: everyone possesses them, but not all have the same knowledge of them. In the same way that for Marx, men always make their own history, even if they are not always aware of this fact, men are, for Spinoza, always eternal, even if they are not fully aware of it. The angles of approach of what we might call 'this fact of understanding' vary in accordance with the cognitive power of men. Imagined and confused with an endless duration, universally felt in the experience of certainty, or adequately known by the sage, common eternity is, regardless, neither banal nor resemblant of a vague fusion of souls in some universal *We*. Neither personal nor impersonal, eternity expresses the particular existence of a being and reflects that being's aptitude for action.

The eternity of the intellect proves to be the condition of possibility for all adequate knowledge, including a conception *sub specie aeternitatis*, which depends on our grasping the essence of the body. When we conceive things in their truth and necessity on the basis of properties of our body, we perceive them *sub quadam specie aeternitatis*. When we conceive them on the basis of the essence of our body, we perceive them *sub specie aeternitatis*. The adjective *quadam*, however, introduces no difference of nature between the two approaches, for adequate knowledge of properties includes that of the body's essence. By developing that which is enveloped, reason better grasps the nature of properties and thereby passes from a perception *sub quadam specie* to a perception *sub specie aeternitatis*. A conception *sub specie aeternitatis* is connected to the real, true existence of things that we must distinguish both from an existence that is merely contained in the attributes of God and from actual present existence. By excluding a relation to time and place, such a conception refuses the representation of things in their chronological succession as well as their spatial juxtaposition in order to prioritise a vision that is *tota simul* and immanent. It is akin to a synoptic view that consists in embracing from within the nature of things such as this nature is necessarily contained in God. For this, such a conception mobilises not the eyes of the body, which are sensitive to what appears (*se montre*), but the eyes of the mind, sensitive to what is demonstrated (*se démontre*). For this reason, the phrase *sub specie aeternitatis* could be translated by the expression 'under an eternal gaze (*regard*)'.

The relationship between duration and eternity is ceaselessly reworked throughout the development of the system. After *Metaphysical Thoughts*, the distinction between the two properties is rooted less and less in the nature of beings, to the point that, in the *Ethics*, the definitions of eternity and duration will no longer be explicitly tied to substance and modes. From this perspective, Spinoza turns his back on every tradition according to which there is a type of temporality allocated to each kind of being and intended to measure it. At first, he preserves a vestige of this idea of chronological measure in his definition of time, but very quickly abandons that category, which remains too marked by quantitative determinations and is unfit for delivering the essence of even duration in anything other than an abstract manner. Time is to duration what measure is to quantity. It serves to determine it and allows one to imagine it more easily. Time is thereby defined as a mode of thought and more precisely as an auxiliary of the imagination.

Spinoza equally breaks from the current of Platonic thought by refusing to distinguish eternity and duration on the basis of the criterion of immutability. Even though it entails constancy, eternity is not the property of motionless things and duration that of mobile ones. On this point, Spinoza links arms with Descartes, who does not consider the duration of motionless things to be of a different nature than that of things in motion.

Neither is eternity the privilege of infinite beings and duration that of finite ones. Even if Spinoza assimilates that 'chief attribute of God' to infinite existence in Metaphysical Thoughts, he soon stops making a strict equation between finitude and duration, on the one hand, and infinitude and eternity, on the other. The symmetry is doubly broken, for not only is eternity applied to finite modes, but duration entails a form of infinity. What thereby differentiates the two concepts is the type of infinity to which they refer. What is eternal is infinite by nature, or by the strength of its cause. What is durational is indefinite, or, in other words, what is limited neither by its nature nor that of its efficient cause, and what is innumerable and does not exclude an external cause of destruction.

The three requisite criteria for having an indefinite existence should not, however, lead us to believe that duration is opposed to eternity as the contingent is to the necessary. If it is true that, in Metaphysical Thoughts, duration was tied to beings whose essence only includes possible existence, Spinoza abandons this characterisation in Letter XII, a characterisation unsuitable for a system in which everything is necessary. The two properties are distinguished by virtue of the nature of their link to a thing's essence. Eternity expresses the necessary link between essence and existence. Duration, by contrast, names a certain dissonance between essence and existence, for it does not depend on the thing's nature. It is not for all that contingent; it answers to another type of necessity, the one of the common order of nature.

This different way of relating to essence does not, however, correspond to the classical dichotomy according to which eternity is the property of essences and duration that of existences. Duration and eternity are both affections of existence and cannot be really conceived without it. They are only differentiated by a distinction of reason, in conformity with what Suarez had already claimed. This observation allows us to understand why

Spinoza did not make the enigmatic relationship between duration and eternity a central theme in his philosophy. It would have been futile to artificially separate what is necessarily tied to existence. The crux of the relationship between the two concepts lies at the heart of a doubly actual existence and cannot be detached from it. We must observe, finally, that throughout the successive analyses of these two properties of existence, reference to essence fades away little by little to make room, in the *Ethics*, for the notion of definition,[1] which allows us to include the affections of substance in the sphere of eternity thanks to the introduction of their proximate cause. Thus, the nature of modes includes existence by virtue not of their essence, but of the essence of God.

Consequently, what is eternal is that which is either self-caused or the object of a proximate causality, in other words, that which is immediately produced by God and falls under the jurisdiction of the absolute nature of God's attributes. In this respect, human intellects, insofar as, taken together, they constitute the immediate infinite mode of thought, are provided with it and are the product of a proximate causality, just like the divine intellect. The human mind, by contrast, is not wholly governed by a proximate causality, for the memory and imagination have, like anything that has to do with a body, a part that is tied to duration. They therefore fall under the jurisdiction of a remote causality. This form of causality does not entail an absence of a link with the effect but applies to things that cannot be immediately produced without contradiction. Duration, insofar as it affects singular things, stems directly neither from God nor from God's attributes, nor even from infinite modes, otherwise it would be eternity. Instead, it involves an infinite chain of finite causes, a chain that can allow for no beginning. It therefore depends on finite eternal things, immediately produced by God, things that serve as intermediaries and relays. A finite singular thing can only be determined by a finite cause. For this reason, God is only the remote cause of a finite singular thing. Split between their actual present existence and their actual eternal existence, the interplay of these two causalities arises in a sharp and intense manner for finite modes. This relationship can be conceived on the model of the one between the eternal doctrine of religion and the provisional precepts outlined by Spinoza in the *Theologico-Political Treatise*. On this basis, four possible figures of the relationship between duration and eternity take shape: coincidence, convergence, divergence and corrective gap. By all rights, this paradigm can be applied to the entirety of the system, since the method valid for Scripture

---

[1] *Ethics* I, Def. 8; CWS I, 409.

is the reflection of that which prevails in the interpretation of nature in general.

The relevance and significance of this method in domains other than Biblical exegesis therefore remains to be measured. The *Ethics* offers a privileged field of investigation allowing us to test the validity of this model. The importation of the framework provided by the comparison of provisional precepts and the eternal doctrine of religion does not seem inappropriate, for the figure of perfect coincidence between present existence and eternal existence is found under the features of the *amor erga Deum* which proves to be the exact transcription of the intellectual love of God into duration. Spinoza specifies in the scholium of proposition 20 from *Ethics* V that this feeling, the most constant of all, called *amor erga Deum*, insofar as it relates to the body, is nothing other than the intellectual love of God, eternal and immutable, when it is related to the mind. In the first case, this love is linked to the fact that we imagine God as present, and in the second, to the fact that we understand that God is eternal.[2]

Viewed from the angle of duration, joy, whether it be active or passive, is the image more or less consistent with eternal beatitude. Under the form of a passage from a lesser to a greater perfection, it converges toward beatitude, which is perfection itself.[3] The more active it is, and the more directly it procures satisfaction from the soul, the more it tends to coincide with freedom.

By contrast, in a general manner, sadness and its derivative affects incarnate the figure of divergence between present existence and eternal existence. They take us all the further away from beatitude as they subject us to the pressure of external causes unfavourable to our power. Far from being determined from the inside by a proximate, immanent causality, we are instead tossed around by external causes that prevent us from possessing real satisfaction of the soul. Nevertheless, divergence is never total, for sadness is not absolute imperfection, but the passage to a lesser perfection. It therefore still contains a piece of dormant joy that reminds us, *sub duratione* and in a distant manner, of beatitude.

The figure of corrective gap could correspond in the *Ethics* to some sad feelings that, taken in themselves, lead us away from eternal beatitude, but sometimes connect us to it in particular circumstances. Pleasure, in general, is more advantageous than pain, but there are cases where that arduous feeling can be good – when, for example, it prevents against excesses that

[2] Cf. *Ethics* V, 32 Cor.; CWS I, 611.
[3] Cf. *Ethics* V, 33 Schol.; CWS I, 611.

are in the long-term harmful for pleasant sensations.[4] In the same manner, fear might be beneficial when, in stopping us from committing an otherwise advantageous crime, it makes us listen to reason in spite of ourselves. It is this mechanism of threat that Spinoza advises being implemented[5] in the second scholium of proposition 37 in Part IV to strengthen a society that reason could not manage to rule over alone, since a feeling can only be restrained by a more powerful feeling. Fear is thus reason for unreasonable beings.

This sketch of relations between an actual present existence and an eternal existence illustrates well the fecundity of the religious paradigm in the *Theologico-Political Treatise* that should probably be exploited in a more extensive manner by establishing, term by term, correspondences between temporal and eternal affects. Spinoza explicitly authorises us to do so in the scholium of proposition 37 of Part V. It is no accident that he uses the same word 'glory' to designate the eternal affect expressing the internal impact of beatitude and the passion tied to the image of praise from other people. In both cases, he understands a joy that accompanies the idea of an internal cause. The eternal affect therefore indeed has a temporal correlate; no doubt is possible on the subject since, through his analysis of eternal glory, Spinoza explicitly refers to his definition of temporal glory elaborated in Part III. Short of giving an exhaustive overview of the correspondence, we must agree that the relationship between actual present existence and eternal existence in the *Ethics* mirrors the four forms outlined by the *Theologico-Political Treatise* and confirms the relevance of this model. Our eternity and our duration do not necessarily clash with one another; they agree and disagree in accordance with the cognitive power of each of us. For the wise, they form a duo, for the ignorant, a duel.

---

[4] Cf. *Ethics* IV, 43; CWS I, 570.
[5] *Ethics* IV, 37 Schol. 2; CWS I, 567.

Bibliography

Primary Sources

Aquinas, T. [1485] (1947), *Summa Theologica*, trans. Fathers of the English Dominican Province, Cincinnati: Benzinger Brothers.

Aristotle [350 BCE] (1984), *Topics*, trans. W. A. Pickard-Cambridge, in *Complete Works of Aristotle, Volume 1: The Revised Oxford Translation*, ed. Jonathan Barnes, Princeton: Princeton University Press.

Aristotle (1999), *The Metaphysics*, trans. Hugh Lawson-Tancred, New York: Penguin Classics.

Aristotle (2004), *The Nicomachean Ethics*, trans. J. A. K. Thomson, New York: Penguin Classics.

Aristotle (2018), *Physics*, trans. C. D. C. Reeve, Indianapolis: Hackett Publishing.

Arnaud, A. and N. Pierre [1662] (1996), *Logic or the Art of Thinking*, ed. Jill Vance Buroker, Cambridge: Cambridge University Press.

Boethius [524] (1999), *The Consolation of Philosophy*, trans. Victor Watts, New York City: Penguin Classics.

Descartes, R. [1664] (1982) *Principles of Philosophy*, trans. Valentine Rodger Miller and Reese P. Miller, Boston: Kluwer Academic Publishers.

Duns Scotus, J. (1305), *The Ordinatio of Blessed John Duns Scotus*, trans. Peter L.P. Simpson, at <https://www.aristotelophile.com/current.htm>

Heereboord, A. (1657), *Hermeneia Logica seu Explicatio Synopseos Logicae Burgersdicianae*, Leyde: Bibliothèque Nationale.

Heereboord, A. (1654), *Meletemata philosophica*, Leyde: Bibliothèque nationale.

Hume, D. [1739] (2003), *Treatise on Human Nature*, Mineola, NY: Dover Publications.

Ibn Gabirol, S. (2004), *Fons Vitae*, trans. John A. Laumakis, Milwaukee: Marquette University Press.

Leibniz, G. W. [1765] (1996), *New Essays on Human Understanding*, ed. Peter Remnant and Jonathan Bennett, Cambridge: Cambridge University Press.

Lucretius, *De Rerum Natura*, Cambridge, MA: Harvard University Press, 1982.

Maimonides, M. [1190] (2002), *The Guide for the Perplexed*, trans. M. Friedländer, Skokie: Varda Books.

Menasseh Ben Israël [1650] (2004), *The Hope of Israel*, ed. Gerard Nahon and Henri Mechoulan, Liverpool: Liverpool University Press.

Ovid (8) (2004), *Metamorphoses*, trans. David Raeburn, New York: Penguin Classics.

Plato [375 BCE] (1992), *Republic*, trans. G. M. A. Grube, Indianapolis: Hackett Publishing.

Plato (2009), *Timaeus and Critias*, trans. Robin Waterfield, Oxford: Oxford World Classics.

Plotinus [270] (2019), *Enneads*, ed. Lloyd P. Gerson, Cambridge: Cambridge University Press.

Proclus (1992), *Elements of Theology*, ed. E. R. Dodds, Oxford: Clarendon Press.

Spinoza (1925), *Opera* II, ed. Carl Gebhardt, Heidelberg: Carl Winters Universitätsbutchhandlung.

Spinoza (1955), *Oeuvres Complètes*, trans. R. Caillois, Paris: Gallimard.

Spinoza (1985), *The Collected Works of Spinoza, Volume I*, ed. Edwin Curley, Princeton: Princeton University Press.

Spinoza (2016), *The Collected Works of Spinoza, Volume II*, ed. Edwin Curley, Princeton: Princeton University Press.

Suarez [1597] (2009), *Disputationes Metaphysicae in Omnia Opera*, Hildesheim: Georg Olms.

Secondary Sources

Alexander, S. (1920), *Space, Time and Deity*, London: Allen and Unwin.

Alexander, S. (1992), *Spinoza and Time*, London: Allen and Unwin.

Alquié, F. (1967), *Servitude et liberté selon Spinoza*, Paris, C.D.U., 'Les Cours de Sorbonne'.

Alquié, F. (1961), *Nature et Vérité dans la philosophie de Spinoza*, Paris, C.D.U., 'Les Cours de Sorbonne'.

Alquié, F. (1981), *Le rationalisme de Spinoza*, Paris: PUF, Épiméthée.

Ansaldi, S. (2001), *Spinoza et le baroque. Infini, désir, multitude*, Paris: Kimé.

Balibar, É. (1985), *Spinoza et la politique*, Paris: PUF.

Balthasar, N. (1941), *L'immortalité consciente de l'âme humaine et la mortalité du corps de l'homme chez Spinoza*, Tijdschrift voor Philos., Gen, 1941-III, 123–42.

Bastide, G. (1948), 'Temps, durée et éternité dans la philosophie de Spinoza', *Études philosophiques* III, Paris, pp. 77–8.

Bennett, J. (1984), A *Study of Spinoza's Ethics*, Cambridge: Cambridge University Press.

Bertrand, M. (1983), *Spinoza et l'imaginaire*, Paris: PUF.

Beyssade, J.-M. (1990), 'Sur le mode infini médiat dans l'attribut de la pensée', colloquium dedicated to *Ethics* V, Université de Paris IV.

Boss, G. (1982a), *L'enseignement de Spinoza. Commentaire du Court Traité*, Zürich: Éditions du grand Midi.

Boss, G. (1982b), *La différence des philosophies, Hume et Spinoza*, 2 vols, Zürich: Éditions du grand Midi.

Bove, L. (1996), *La stratégie du conatus*, Paris: Vrin.

Bréhier, É. (1928), *Histoire de la philosophie* II, Paris: PUF, 1928-38-81, 'Spinoza', pp. 139–75.

Brinker, M. (1966), 'L'être déterminé et sa relation à l'éternité et au temps selon Spinoza', *Iyyun* 4, pp. 193–211.

Broad, C. D. (1946), 'Spinoza's Doctrine of Human Immortality', *Mélanges Anders-Karitz*, pp. 139–48.

Brochard, V. (1901), 'De l'éternité des âmes dans la Philosophie de Spinoza', *Revue de métaphysique et de morale* 9(6), pp. 688–99.

Brunschvicg, L. (1951), *Spinoza et ses contemporains*, Paris: PUF.

Brykman, G. (1972), *La judéité de Spinoza*, Paris: Vrin.

Casellato, S. (1942), 'La durata infinita e la dura finita nella dottrina di Spinoza', *Sophia* 1.

Chalier, C. (1993), *Pensées de l'éternité. Spinoza Rosenzweig*, Paris: Les Éditions du Cerf.

Chartier, É. (Alain) (1965), *Spinoza*, Paris: Gallimard.

Chassay, F.-É. (1850), *Conclusion des démonstrations évangéliques. Catéchisme historique des incroyants*, ed. J.-P. Migne, Paris.

Courtine J.-F. (1990), *Suarez et le système de la métaphysique*, Paris: PUF.

Cristofolini, P. (1987), *La scientia intuitiva di Spinoza*, Naples: Morano Editore.

Curley, E. M. (1969), *Spinoza's Metaphysics: An Essay in Interpretation*, Cambridge, MA: Harvard University Press.

Curley, E. (1988), 'Le corps et l'esprit du *Court Traité* à l'*Éthique*', *Archives de philosophie* 51, no. 1, pp. 5–14.

Darbon, A. (1946), *Études spinozistes*, Paris: PUF.

Delbos, V. (1926), *Le spinozisme*, Paris: Vrin.

Delbos, V. (1990), *Le problème moral dans la philosophie de Spinoza et dans l'histoire du spinozisme*, Lille: Presse de l'Université de Paris Sorbonne.

Deleuze, G. (1968), *Spinoza et le problème de l'expression*, Paris: Minuit.

Deleuze, G. (1981), *Spinoza, Philosophie pratique*, Paris: Minuit.

Di Vona, P. (1960), *Studi sull'ontologia di Spinoza*, Parte I, *L'ordinamento delle scienze filosofiche. La 'ratio'. Il concetto di ente*, Firenze: La Nuova Italia Editrice.

Di Vona, P. (1969), *Studi sull'ontologia di Spinoza*, Parte II *'Res' e. 'Ens'. La necessità. Le divisioni dell'essere*, Firenze: La Nuova Italia Editrice.

Di Vona, P. (1988), 'Il problema delle distinzioni nella filosofia di Spinoza', *Studia Spinoziana* 4.

Diodato, R. (1990), *Sub specie æternitatis. Luoghi dell'ontologia spinoziana*, Milan: CUSL.

Donagan, A. (1979), 'Spinoza's Proof of Immortality', in M. Grene (1979), *Spinoza: A Collection of Critical Essays*, South Bend, IN: University of Notre Dame Press, pp. 241–58.

Dufour-Kowalska, G. (1973), *L'essence de l'origine, l'origine selon l'*Éthique *de Spinoza*, Paris: B.A.P., Beauchesne.

Fraisse, J.-C. (1978), *L'œuvre de Spinoza*, Paris: Vrin.

Francès, M. (1937), *Spinoza dans les pays néerlandais de la seconde moitié du* xvii*esiècle*, Paris: F. Alcan.

Fullerston, G. S. (1899), 'On Spinozistic Immortality', Philadelphia, Publication of the University of Pennsylvania, *Series in Philosophy* 3.

Giancotti-Boscherini, E. (1970), *Lexicon Spinozanum*, The Hague: Martinus Nijhoff.

Giancotti-Boscherini, E. (1985), *Baruch Spinoza*, Rome: Editori Riuniti.

Gilson, É. (1979), *Index scolastico-cartésien*, Paris: Vrin.

Grene, M. (ed.) (1979), *Spinoza: A Collection of Critical Essays*, South Bend, IN: University of Notre Dame Press.

Gueroult, M. (1966), 'La lettre de Spinoza sur l'infini', *Revue de métaphysique et de morale* 4, pp. 385–411.

Gueroult, M. (1968), *Spinoza I, Dieu*, Paris: Aubier.

Gueroult, M. (1970), *Études sur Descartes, Spinoza, Malebranche et Leibniz*, New York: Georg Olms Verlag Hidelsheim.

Gueroult, M. (1974), *Spinoza II, L'âme*, Paris: Aubier.

Hallett, H. F. (1930), *Æternitas: A Spinozistic Study*, Oxford: Clarendon Press.

Hallett, H. F. (1962), *Creation, Emanation and Salvation*, The Hague: Martinus Nijhoff.

Hardin, C. L. (1978–80), 'Spinoza on Immortality and Time', in R. Shahan and J. Biro (eds), *Spinoza: New Perspectives*, Norman: University of Oklahoma Press, pp. 129–38.

Harris, E. (1973), *Salvation from Despair*, The Hague: Martinus Nijhoff.

Israël, N. (2001), *Spinoza. Le temps de la vigilance*, Paris: Payot.

Jaquet, C. (1997), 'La perfection de la durée', *Les Études philosophiques*, April–June.

Jaquet, C. (2004), *L'unité du corps et de l'esprit. Affects, actions, passions chez Spinoza*, Paris: PUF.

Jaquet, C. (2005), *Les expressions de la puissance d'agir chez Spinoza*, third part, Spinoza dans le temps, Paris: Publications de la Sorbonne.

Kneale, M. (1979), 'Eternity and Sempiternity', in M. Grene (ed.), *Spinoza: A Collection of Critical Essays*, South Bend, IN: University of Notre Dame Press, pp. 227–40.

Knecht, Y. (1968), 'Temps et modes chez Spinoza', *Dialectica* 22, nos. 3/4, pp. 214–37.

Koyré, A. (1935), 'Ethica more scolastico rabbinicoque demonstrata. A propos d'un livre récent', *Revue philosophique de la France et l'Étranger* 120, nos. 9/10, pp. 282–94.

Lachièze-Rey, P. (1950), *Les origines cartésiennes du Dieu de Spinoza*, Paris: Vrin.

Lacroix, J. (1970), *Spinoza et le problème du salut*, Paris: PUF.

Lagrée, J. (2004), *Spinoza et le débat religieux*, Rennes: Presses universitaires de Rennes.

Laux, H. (1993), *Imagination et Religion chez Spinoza*, Paris: Vrin.

Lécrivain, A., 'Spinoza et la physique cartésienne', *Cahiers Spinoza* 1 and 2.

Levinas, E. (1937), 'Spinoza philosophe médiéval', *Revue des études juives* 1 (101), pp. 114–119.

Lucas, J. P. (1927), *La vie de feu Monsieur de Spinoza*, London: George Allen and Unwin.

Macherey, P. (1978), *Hegel ou Spinoza*, Paris: Maspero.

Macherey, P. (1994–98), *Introduction à l'Éthique de Spinoza*, 5 vols, Paris: PUF.

Matheron, A. (1969), *Individu et communauté chez Spinoza*, Paris: Minuit.

Matheron, A. (1971), *Le Christ et le salut des ignorants chez Spinoza*, Paris: Aubier.

Matheron, A. (1972), 'Remarques sur l'immortalité de l'âme chez Spinoza', *Les Études philosophiques*, July–September, pp. 369–78.

Matheron, A. (1986/2011), *Anthropologie et politique au xviie siècle (Études sur Spinoza)*, Paris: Vrin. Republished as *Études sur Spinoza et les philosophies de l'âge classique*, Lyon: ENS Éditions.

Matheron, A. (2002), 'Idée de l'idée et certitude dans le *Tractatus de Intellectus Emendatione* et dans l'*Éthique*', G.R.S., *Travaux et documents* 2, pp. 93–104.

Matheron, A. (1991a), 'Physique et ontologie chez Spinoza: l'énigmatique réponse à Tschirnhaus', *Cahiers Spinoza* 6, pp. 83–109.

Matheron, A. (1991b), 'Essence, Existence and Power in *Ethics* I: The Foundations of Proposition 16', in Y. Yovel (ed.), *God and Nature: Spinoza's Metaphysics*, Leiden: Brill.

Matheron, A. (1994), 'La vie éternelle et le corps selon Spinoza', *Revue philosophique de la France et de l'étranger* 1, January–March, pp. 27–40.

Matson, W. (1969), 'Death and Destruction in Spinoza's *Ethics*', *Inquiry* 20, pp. 403–17.

Mechoulan, H. (1990), *Amsterdam au temps de Spinoza*, Paris: PUF.

Meinsma, O. (1983), *Spinoza et son cercle*, Paris: Vrin.

Messeri, M. (1990), *L'epistemologia di Spinoza. Saggio sui corpi e le menti*, Milano: Il saggiatore.

Mignini, F. (1979), 'Nuovi contributi per la datatione e l'interpretatione del *Tractatus de intellectus emendatione* di Spinoza', *La cultura* 17, pp. 87–160.

Mignini, F. (1983), *Introduzione a Spinoza*, Roma/Bari: Laterza.

Mignini, F. (1985), 'Sur la genèse du *Court Traité*: L'hypothèse d'une dictée originaire est-elle fondée ?', *Cahiers Spinoza* 5, pp. 147–65.

Mignini, F. (1994), '*Sub specie æternitatis*', *Revue philosophique de la France et de l'étranger* 1, January–March, pp. 41–54.

Millet, L. (1970), *Pour connaître la pensée de Spinoza*, Paris/Montréal: Bordas.

Misrahi, R. (1972), *Le désir et la réflexion dans la philosophie de Spinoza*, Paris/London/New York: Gordon and Breach.

Misrahi, R. (1992), *Spinoza. Un itinéraire du bonheur par la joie*, Paris: Jacques Grancher.

Moreau, J. (1971), *Spinoza et le spinozisme*, Paris: PUF, Q.S.J. no. 1422.

Moreau, P.-F. (1975), *Spinoza*, Paris: Seuil, coll. 'Écrivains de toujours'.

Moreau, P.-F. (2002), 'Métaphysique de la substance et métaphysique des forms', G.R.S, *Travaux et documents* 2, pp. 9–18.

Moreau, P.-F. (1994a), 'Métaphysique de la gloire', *Revue philosophique de la France et de l'étranger* 1, January–March, pp. 55–64.

Moreau, P.-F. (1994b), *L'expérience et l'éternité*, Paris: PUF.

Morfino, V. (2010), *Le temps de la multitude*, Paris: Éditions Amsterdam.

Morfino, V. (2012), *Le temps et l'occasion. La rencontre Spinoza-Machiavel*, Paris: Classiques Garnier.

Mugnier-Pollet (1976), L., *La philosophie politique de Spinoza*, Paris: Vrin.

Negri, A. (1982), *L'anomalie sauvage*, Paris: PUF.

Osier, J.-P. (1983), *D'Uriel da Costa à Spinoza*, Paris: Berg International.

Parkinson, G. H. R. (1954), *Spinoza's Theory of knowledge*, Oxford: The Clarendon Press.

Prélorentzos, Y. (1992), *La durée chez Spinoza*, Doctoral thesis.

Prélorentzos, Y. (1996), *Temps, durée, et éternité dans les* Principes de la philosophie de Descartes *de Spinoza*, Paris: Presses de l'université de Paris-Sorbonne.

Préposiet, J. (1967), *Spinoza et la liberté des hommes*, Paris: Gallimard.

Ramond, C. (1995), *Qualité et quantité dans la philosophie de Spinoza*, Paris: PUF.

Revah, I. S. (1958), 'Spinoza et les hérétiques de la communauté judéoportugaise d'Amsterdam', *Revue de l'histoire des religions*, vol. CLIV, 2, pp. 173–218.

Revah, I. S. (1959), *Spinoza et le docteur Juan de Prado*, Paris/The Hague: Mouton & cie, *Études Juives* I.

Ricardou, A. (1890), *De humanæ mentis æternitate apud Spinozam*, Paris.

Rice, L. C. (1969–70), 'The Continuity of "Mens" in Spinoza', *The New Scholasticism* 43(1), pp. 75–103.

Robinson, L. (1932), 'L'immortalité spinoziste', *Revue de métaphysique et de morale*, October–December.

Rodis-Lewis, G. (1986), 'Questions sur la cinquième partie de l'*Éthique*', *Revue philosophique* 2, April–June.

Rousset, B. (1968), *La perspective finale de l'*Éthique *et le problème de la cohérence du spinozisme*, Paris: Vrin.

Rousset, B. (1988), 'Le réalisme spinoziste de la durée', Colloquium dedicated to time, Dijon.

Schaub, M. (1972), 'Spinoza ou une philosophie politique galiléenne', *Histoire de la Philosophie*, under the direction of F. Châtelet, vol. 3, Paris: Hachette.

Sévérac, P. (2005), *Le devenir actif chez Spinoza*, Paris: Champion.

Sévérac, P. (2011), *Spinoza: union et désunion*, Paris: Vrin.

Shahan, R. and J. Biro (eds) (1978–80), *Spinoza: New Perspectives*, Norman: University of Oklahoma Press.

Strauss, L. (1965), *Spinoza's Critique of Religion*, New York: Schocken Books.

Suhamy, A. (2010), *La communication du bien chez Spinoza*, Paris: Classiques Garnier.

Tosel, A. (1984), *Spinoza et le crépuscule de la servitude. Essai sur le* Traité théologico-politique, Paris: Aubier-Montaigne.

Tosel, A. (1994), *Du matérialisme de Spinoza*, Paris: Kimé.

Vernière, P. (1954), *Spinoza et la pensée française avant la révolution*, Paris: PUF.

Vinciguerra, L. (2005), *Spinoza et le signe*, Paris: Vrin.

Wolfson, H. A. (1940), *Philo: Foundations of Religious Philosophy in Judaism, Christianity and Islam*, Cambridge, MA: Harvard University Press.

Wolfson, H. A. (1962), *The Philosophy of Spinoza*, 2 vols, Cambridge, MA: Harvard University Press.

Yakira, E. (1989), *Contrainte, nécessité, choix. La métaphysique de la liberté chez Spinoza et Leibniz*, Quebec City: Éditions du Grand Midi.

Yovel, Y. (1992), *Spinoza and Other Heretics*, Princeton, NJ: Princeton University Press.

Zac, S. (1959), *La morale de Spinoza*, Paris: PUF.

Zac, S. (1963), *L'idée de vie dans la philosophie de Spinoza*, Paris: PUF.

Zac, S. (1965), *Spinoza et l'interprétation de l'écriture*, Paris: PUF.

Zac, S. (1979), *Philosophie, théologie, politique dans l'œuvre de Spinoza*, Paris: Vrin.

Zac, S. (1985), *Essais spinozistes*, Paris: Vrin-Reprise.

Zourabichvili, F. (2002a), *Une physique de la pensée*, Paris: PUF.

Zourabichvili, F. (2002b), *Le conservatisme paradoxal de Spinoza*, Paris: PUF.

Reviews

Archives de philosophie, vol. 51, no. 1, January–March 1988: 'Les premiers écrits de Spinoza'.

Cahiers Spinoza, no. 1, autumn 1977, Édition Réplique, Paris.

Cahiers Spinoza, no. 2, spring 1978, Édition Réplique, Paris.

Cahiers Spinoza, no. 3, winter 1979–1980, Édition Réplique, Paris.

Cahiers Spinoza, no. 4, winter 1982–1983, Édition Réplique, Paris

Cahiers Spinoza, no. 5, winter 1984–1985, Édition Réplique, Paris.

Cahiers Spinoza, no. 6, spring 1991, Édition Réplique, Paris.

Études philosophiques (Les), Spinoza special edition, July–September, 1972.

Études philosophiques (Les), 'Spinoza', October–December, 1987.

Études philosophiques (Les), 'Durée, temps, éternité chez Spinoza', April–June, 1997.

Groupe de recherche spinoziste. Travaux et Documents, Paris: Presses de l'université de Paris-Sorbonne, 1: 'Lire et traduire Spinoza', 1989.

Groupe de recherche spinoziste. Travaux et Documents, Paris: Presses de l'université de Paris-Sorbonne, 2: 'Méthode et Métaphysique', 2002.

Revue internationale de philosophie, 31st year, nos. 119–20, 1977.

Revue philosophique de la France et l'Étranger, no. 167, 1977: 'Spinoza (1632–1677)'.

Revue philosophique de la France et l'Étranger, no. 2, April–June 1986: 'Descartes Spinoza'.

Revue philosophique de la France et l'Étranger, no. 1, January–March 1994, 'Spinoza. La cinquième partie de l'*Éthique*'.

Studia Spinozana, no. 4, 1988.

Index